Exploring Alaska's Prince William Sound
its fiords, islands, glaciers and wildlife

by Neil and Elizabeth Johannsen

Photo opposite: Steller sea lions are named for Georg Steller, who recorded their existence in 1741. Hundreds of these large marine mammals congregate in noisy colonies in Prince William Sound.
RICHARD W. MONTAGUE

Editors: Susan Hackley Johnson, Richard W. Montague
Cartography, Layout and Design: Clark Mishler and Associates
Illustrations: Bud Root
Printing: Craftsman Press, Seattle

Cover: *A graceful ketch lies at anchor in one of the numerous isolated coves in the proposed Nellie Juan Wilderness Area in western Prince William Sound.*
PHOTOGRAPH © NANCY SIMMERMAN, 1974

Alaska Travel Publications Inc.

*P.O. Box 4-2031
Anchorage, Alaska 99509*

Other books published by Alaska Travel Publications Inc.

Exploring Mount McKinley National Park *by Richard W. Montague and the Editors of Alaska Travel Publications Inc.*

Exploring Katmai National Monument *by the Editors of Alaska Travel Publications Inc.*

Photo opposite: Numerous glaciers ring Harriman Fiord in northern Prince William Sound.
MYRON WRIGHT

ACKNOWLEDGMENTS

Most of the information in this guidebook came not from books but from people. Dozens of interviews, followed by numerous manuscript reviews, have resulted in a comprehensive assemblage of information, much of which is unrecorded elsewhere.

Perhaps greatest credit should go to Pete Isleib, a long-time Cordova fisherman and ornithologist. Pete contributed extensive information on the geography and wildlife of the sound and carefully reviewed the final manuscript. The bird checklist at the back of the book is adapted from one he compiled.

Other Cordova residents also made contributions: Barbara Tilsner of the Cordova Chamber of Commerce, Glenn Mast of the Cordova Historical Society, Jack O'Brien and Tom and Stephanie Parker.

Jack Hopkins and Del Bradford are among the many employees of the Alaska Marine Highway System who supplied information on the state ferry routes across Prince William Sound.

The history chapter of the book was greatly enhanced by the help of several key people. Robert and Dorothy Clifton of Valdez are perhaps more knowledgeable than anyone about the history of their home town. Owen Meals, a Valdez pioneer, and George Flemming, lifelong resident of Flemming and Knight islands, provided fascinating personal insights into local history. Phyllis Carlson, an early-day Cordova resident and now resident of Anchorage, helped in the search for the scanty written material of the area. Karen Workman and Cecil Barnes provided information on Native history.

John Johnson and John Raynor of the U.S. Forest Service helped clarify some of the complex land-use problems that currently beset the wilderness of the sound.

Austin Post, Larry Mayo and Chet Zenone, all of the U.S. Geological Survey, and Tom Sheehy of the U.S. Forest Service provided a wealth of data on the geology of the area. Mr. Post was particularly helpful in supplying extensive, never-before-published material on Columbia Glacier.

The wildlife chapter had many contributors. John Vania and Karl Schneider of the Alaska Department of Fish and Game furnished valuable information about marine mammals. Julius Reynolds of the Cordova office of the Department of Fish and Game shared many of his personal wildlife observations. Pete Mickelson of the U.S. Forest Service in Cordova provided data for the mammal checklist at the back of the book.

Larry Haddock of the U.S. Fish and Wildlife Service devoted much of his career to systematic study of the birds and marine mammals of Prince William Sound and passed much of this information on to us. In October, 1974, the plane from which he and several companions were making bird studies was lost over the Gulf of Alaska. Larry is irreplaceable; we regret his passing.

Bob Myers is to be credited with editing the chapter on fishing. Ralph Pirtle, commercial fisheries biologist with the Alaska Department of Fish and Game in Cordova, provided data on the status of this important industry.

For the ferry guides and boating chapter, we supplemented our own knowledge with the expertise of people who have spent much time in the sound.

ACKNOWLEDGMENTS

In addition to Pete Isleib, the following people supplied information: Marla Adkins, Ted Chad, Charles Evans, Martin Goresen, John and Loyette Goodell, Scott Harrison, Norm Howse, Ketch Ketchum, Brad Phillips, Ron Quilliam, William Quirk, Ed Shepherd, Eric Singer, Richard Warren and Ted West.

Susan Hackley Johnson and Richard W. Montague of Alaska Travel Publications Inc. deserve special mention for their patience with our project.

EXPLORING ALASKA'S PRINCE WILLIAM SOUND is the result of the efforts of numerous people. We are grateful to them.

NEIL AND ELIZABETH JOHANNSEN

Photo following pages: The beauty of this island-dappled waterland is often dramatic . . . and sometimes subtle, as in this misty coastline scene.

NEIL AND ELIZABETH JOHANNSEN

To

Harold and Pauline Johannsen
Who also love the sound;
And Harold and Anne Sederquist . . .
Their encouragement makes this
their book, too.

Wilderness is not in this book,
Nor is adventure marked on a sea-chart.
They can only be found in the spirits
of those who seek them.

We hope wilderness and adventure will always
be a part of Prince William Sound.

TABLE OF CONTENTS

TABLE OF CONTENTS

TABLE OF CONTENTS

An Accessible Coastal Wilderness

A Diversity of Scenery. Only 60 miles [*96 km*] east of Anchorage, largest city in Alaska, lies a restless coastal wilderness. Known as Prince William Sound, this island-dappled waterland, containing more than 3500 miles [*5600 km*] of contorted shoreline, offers some of the most diversified scenery in Alaska. Grinding glacial ice and jarring earthquakes shape the snowy Chugach and Kenai mountains, which rise above the islands to heights greater than 13,000 feet [*4000 m*]; a few miles distant, chilly blue-green ocean waters reach depths of nearly 3000 feet [*915 m*]. In between, luxuriant green forests are saturated by more than 10 feet [*3 m*] of annual rainfall. This wildland abounds with brown bear and spawning salmon, killer whales and sea otters, majestic bald eagles and noisy nesting colonies of marine birds.

A Special Heritage. This land of fiords and countless islands has an unsettled past and faces an uncertain future. Natives, miners and fishermen have played an important role in the tumultuous history of the region. Today this area, though 15 times the size of San Francisco Bay, is relatively devoid of people; the population of shore-side communities totals about 5000. More and more visitors are reaching the sound by boat or aircraft, enjoying views of virgin forests and massive tidewater glaciers. This growing stream of visitors has spawned the need for this first comprehensive guidebook exclusively about Prince William Sound.

Although the authors hope that this book will increase visitors' knowledge of this fascinating area, it is also hoped that this new understanding will manifest itself in responsible use of the sound and in actions aimed at protecting this very special land of forest and sea.

Photo opposite: The crystalline salt waters of Prince William Sound fluctuate more than 12 feet [4 m] *daily, exposing great masses of seaweed and blue mussels.*

© NANCY SIMMERMAN, 1975

How to Use This Guidebook

A Comprehensive Visitor Guide. EXPLORING ALASKA'S PRINCE WILLIAM SOUND will add to your enjoyment of this land of fiord and forest, whether you plan a one-day fishing trip on Passage Canal, a weekend ferry outing to Valdez, or a week-long expedition to Montague Island.

The chapters group information by subject and may be read out of sequence. Topics include how to get to the sound, visitor facilities in and near the sound, history of the area, geology, wildlife, fishing, plantlife and weather. Of special interest to many Prince William Sound visitors is the mile-by-mile guide to features along the state ferry routes. In the cruising section private boaters will find valuable information on anchorages and where, for example, to throw the crab pot over the side. Maps supplement these chapters. As an aid to foreign visitors, measurements are given in the English system followed in brackets by the metric equivalent.

Many visitor services in the sound, such as some of the lodges or some of the ferry routes, only operate during the summer. Rates and schedules are subject to frequent change.

Additional Sources of Information

References and Addresses. Visitors may desire information beyond the scope of this guidebook. In addition to the references listed in Chapter 16, the following information sources are recommended.

Chamber of Commerce Offices. These offices operate specifically to aid visitors with their questions about sightseeing attractions and facilities.

Cordova Chamber of Commerce
P.O. Box 99
Cordova, Alaska 99574

Valdez Chamber of Commerce
P.O. Box 62
Valdez, Alaska 99686

Seward Chamber of Commerce
P.O. Box 756
Seward, Alaska 99664

Chugach National Forest. The U.S. Forest Service, with management control over most of the land in Prince William Sound, operates offices in Anchorage and Cordova. These offices, containing files of information open to the public, also offer brochures and maps. U.S. Forest Service resource personnel gladly share their area knowledge. Contact:

Chugach National Forest
121 West Fireweed Lane, Suite 205
Anchorage, Alaska 99503
Telephone: (907) 272-4485

Chugach National Forest
(Federal Building)
P.O. Box 280
Cordova, Alaska 99574
Telephone: (907) 424-3326

Alaska Travel Publications. Although the authors have endeavored to make this first edition of EXPLORING ALASKA'S PRINCE WILLIAM SOUND as factually accurate as possible, we recognize that errors may occur and that some information may become outdated. We encourage additions or suggestions for subsequent editions. Write to:

Guidebook Editor
Alaska Travel Publications Inc.
P.O. Box 4-2031
Anchorage, Alaska 99509

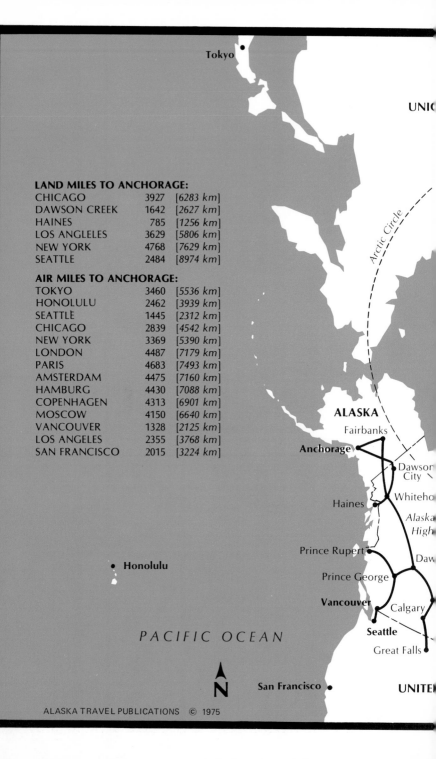

F SOVIET SOCIALIST REPUBLICS

• Moscow

Stockholm
•

Copenhagen
• • Frankfurt
Hamburg
•
Amsterdam
• • Paris

London
•

RCTIC

North
+
Pole

OCEAN

GREENLAND

eek

CANADA

onton

ATLANTIC OCEAN

TATES

Chicago
• • New York

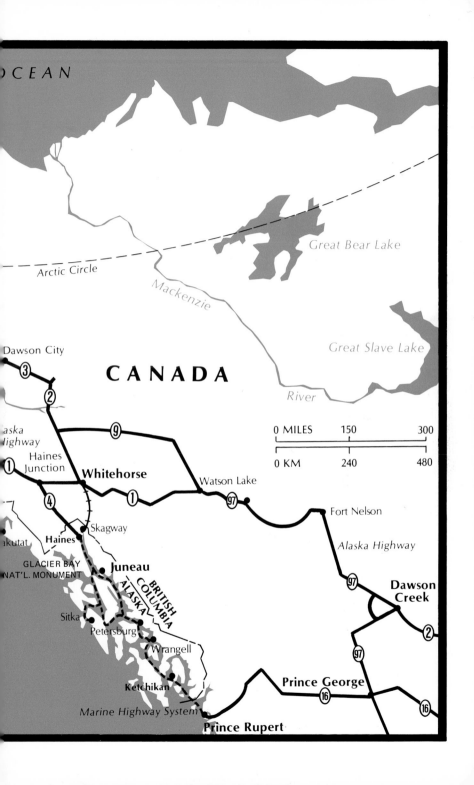

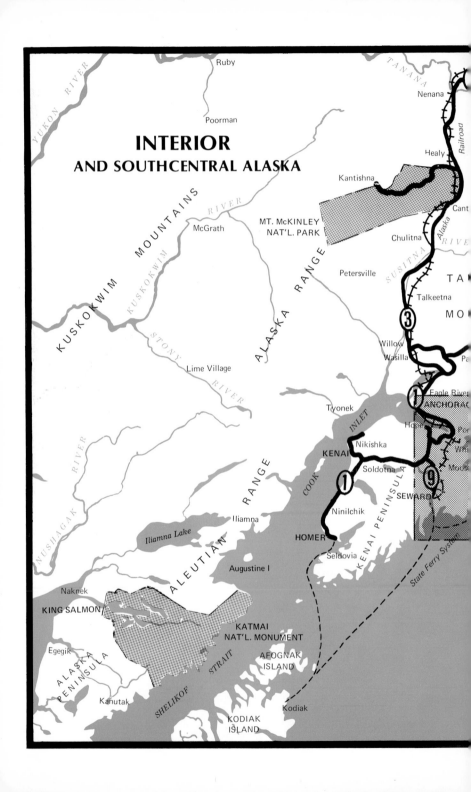

INTERIOR
AND SOUTHCENTRAL ALASKA

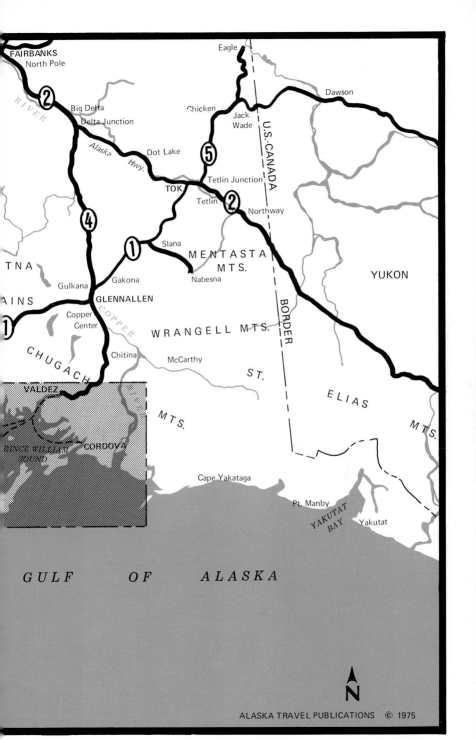

FAIRBANKS
North Pole
RIVER
②
Big Delta
Delta Junction
Alaska Hwy.
Dot Lake
Eagle
Chicken
Jack Wade
Dawson
⑤
U.S.-CANADA
Tetlin Junction
TOK
Tetlin
②
Northway
①
Slana
M E N T A S T A
M T S.
Nabesna
YUKON
TNA
Gulkana
Gakona
④
AINS
GLENNALLEN
①
Copper Center
COPPER
BORDER
W R A N G E L L   M T S.
CHUGACH
Chitina
McCarthy
S T.
E L I A S
VALDEZ
M T S.
M T S.
RINCE WILLIAM SOUND
CORDOVA
Cape Yakataga
Pt. Manby
YAKUTAT BAY
Yakutat

G U L F   O F   A L A S K A

N

ALASKA TRAVEL PUBLICATIONS © 1975

An Accessible Waterland

Easy Access by Air or Water. Prince William Sound enjoys a dual distinction: it is one of the few untrammeled regions remaining in a too-crowded world; it is also one of the most accessible wilderness areas of Alaska.

The city of Anchorage, situated about 60 miles [*97 km*] northwest of the sound, has earned a well-deserved reputation as "Air Crossroads of the World." The map on preceding pages shows air mileages between Anchorage and major cities in the Orient, Europe and North America.

A variety of transportation options are available between Anchorage and Prince William Sound. Many visitors, for example, drive the Seward Highway from Anchorage to Portage, ride in their automobiles (loaded "piggyback") on the Alaska Railroad shuttle from Portage to Whittier, then cross Prince William Sound with their automobiles by state ferry. A wide variety of package tours accommodates the visitor seeking a headache-free means of seeing parts of the sound. Numerous air carriers fly between Anchorage and Prince William Sound, ranging in size from single-engine float-equipped planes, ideally suited for landing on remote bays, to larger aircraft providing scheduled daily service to communities bordering the sound. Perhaps the best way to see Prince William Sound is by small boat. This means of access, recommended for the adventurous and self-reliant, is described in detail in the Recreational Boating chapter.

Highway Access

Limited Highway Development. Traveling by automobile is the least efficient way to see Prince William Sound. The Alaska highway system touches the sound at only one point: Valdez. The steep terrain of the area has made road-building prohibitively expensive; the sparse population and lack of development, as well as the presence of relatively unspoiled wilderness, have made highways undesirable.

Photo opposite: Foot passengers prepare to embark on the state ferry M/V Bartlett *at Whittier. Traveling by state ferry is one of the most economical and enjoyable ways to see Prince William Sound.*

NEIL AND ELIZABETH JOHANNSEN

Valdez. From Anchorage, drive north on the Glenn Highway(*Alaska Route 1*) and turn south on the Richardson Highway (*Alaska Route 4*) at Glennallen. From Fairbanks, drive south the length of the Richardson Highway. Valdez is 304 highway miles [*489 km*] from Anchorage and 364 highway miles [*586 km*] from Fairbanks. The southern section of the Richardson Highway, ending at Valdez, is highly scenic. The highway skirts easily accessible Worthington Glacier and crosses 2722 foot [*830 m*] Thompson Pass before passing through waterfall-lined Keystone Canyon. Although the Richardson Highway, a good-quality, two-lane paved road, is open year-round, deep winter snow in the Thompson Pass area can make driving hazardous. Check road conditions before using this route in winter (Anchorage residents may call 936-2828 for a taped motorist forecast; in Valdez, call Alaska State Troopers, 835-4359, for local road conditions).

Scheduled bus service is available between Anchorage and Valdez. The trip takes 8 to 9 hours. For current information on rates and schedules contact the Sheffield House in Valdez (907) 835-4391 or:

> *Anchorage Transit System*
> *1040 East First Avenue*
> *Anchorage, Alaska 99501*
> *Telephone: (907) 279-3958*

Whittier. From Anchorage, drive east on the Seward Highway to Mile 46, about 1 mile [*1.6 km*] before the turn-off to Portage Glacier. Roadside signs indicate areas where foot passengers and automobiles board the Whittier Railroad Shuttle. Contact The Alaska Railroad office in Anchorage for rates and schedules:

> *The Alaska Railroad*
> *(1st and C Streets)*
> *Pouch 7-2111*
> *Anchorage, Alaska 99510*
> *Telephone: (907) 265-2685 or 265-2688*

Seward. The 127 mile [*205 km*] Seward Highway leads from Anchorage, around the end of Turnagain Arm, and through vistas of snow-capped mountains, lakes and forests. This good-quality, paved, two-lane road is kept open year-round. The city of Seward, although about 35 miles [*56 km*] west of Prince William Sound, is one of the major access points to the sound and offers many visitor facilities.

Mt. McKinley Bus Lines provides scheduled bus service between Anchorage and Seward. The trip takes 3 to 4 hours. For rates and schedules, contact:

> *Mt. McKinley Bus Lines*
> *741 "C" Street*
> *Anchorage, Alaska 99501*
> *Telephone: (907) 279-1133*

Aircraft Access

A Rapid Means of Transportation. One of the best ways to see Prince William Sound is by air. Numerous air taxi operators in Anchorage fly from Lake Hood Seaplane Base and Merrill Field, reaching the sound through low-lying Portage Pass. It is also possible to fly from Anchorage via Alaska Airlines jets that make daily scheduled stops at Cordova both northbound and southbound on flights between Anchorage and Seattle.

For a real glimpse into the scenic highlights of Prince William Sound, fly with one of the locally based air taxi operators. These bush pilots know every bay and glacier and where to see everything from brown bears to salmon. They fly to a variety of destinations, ranging from the wide sand beaches of outer Montague Island to the calving tidewater terminus of Columbia Glacier.

Allow leeway when planning a trip by aircraft, as flights may be delayed or cancelled due to weather.

The following air services specialize in flying Prince William Sound.

Cordova. Two veteran charter operators, both based at Eyak Lake, serve this fishing community. Parkair boasts an impressive array of ski or float-equipped aircraft, all available for charter. Parkair offers reasonably-priced flightseeing trips to nearly every part of the sound. Frequent flights also go to Yakutat, Cape Yakutaga and Icy Bay (all east of the sound) and to the Interior of Alaska. During salmon fishing season, regular flights are scheduled to fishing grounds on the Copper River Delta and throughout Prince William Sound. Contact:

Parkair
P.O. Box. 506
Cordova, Alaska 99574
Telephone: (907) 424-3208

Chitina Air Service is an offshoot of a merger between Alaska Airlines and Cordova Airlines. The two sons of Merle "Mudhole" Smith, famous bush pilot and owner of Cordova Airlines, formed Chitina Air Service to make regular flights to many small communities in the Interior and around Prince William Sound. Chitina Air Service has daily scheduled flights between Cordova and Valdez and also offers scheduled flights to Cape Yakutaga, to Icy Bay (east of the sound), and to Boswell Bay on Hinchin-brook Island. Flight arrangements may be made through travel agents or Alaska Airlines offices, or by directly contacting:

Chitina Air Service
Box 118
Cordova, Alaska 99574
Telephone: (907) 424-3534

Valdez. A number of aircraft operators (Parkair, Chitina, Polar, Alaska Airlines and Alaska Aeronautical) make frequent flights to Valdez, but only one aircraft operator is actually based in the town. Kennedy Air Service offers some worthwhile flights for visitors. One of the best is an hour-long Columbia Glacier tour. Kennedy Air Service also offers a 3 to 4 hour flightseeing tour over Columbia Glacier, Cordova and the lower Copper River Canyon. Contact:

Kennedy Air Service
Box 485
Valdez, Alaska 99686
Telephone: (907) 835-4304

Seward. Harbor Air Service, based at the Seward airport, also handles charter work in Prince William Sound. Harbor Air Service operates a series of cabins for goat hunters along the coast between Seward and Prince William Sound, landing with a floatplane on small lakes in this vicinity. This air service also offers short scenic flights over the Harding Ice Field on the Kenai Peninsula west of Seward. Contact:

Harbor Air Service
Box 1417
Seward, Alaska 99664
Telephone: (907) 224-5720 or 224-5725

Anchorage. Three airlines provide scheduled flights between Anchorage and Prince William Sound communities.

Alaska Airlines jets make daily scheduled stops at Valdez and at Cordova Airport, a few miles east of town. For reservations and information, contact a travel agent or any Alaska Airlines ticket office. In Anchorage, telephone (907) 274-6666; in Cordova, telephone the city ticket office on Main Street (907) 424-3280.

Polar Airways, based at Merrill Field, has a number of aircraft available for charter, and operates several scheduled flights daily between Anchorage and Valdez. Flying time between the two cities is one hour. Polar Airways also offers a 2.5 hour Columbia Glacier flightseeing tour. Contact:

Polar Airways
2600 East Fifth Avenue
Anchorage, Alaska 99501
Telephone: (907) 279-5555

Alaska Aeronautical Industries Inc., based at Anchorage International Airport, offers several daily flights to Cordova and Valdez. For information, contact:

Alaska Aeronautical Industries Inc.
P.O. Box 6067 (International Airport)
Anchorage, Alaska 99502
Telephone: (907) 279-6554

A number of air taxi operators provide flightseeing tours from Lake Hood Seaplane Base to Prince William Sound. Float-equipped Cessna 185's or Cessna 206's are generally used. Although many visitors fly to the sound to take advantage of the superb sportfishing, the destination of most sightseers is awesome Columbia Glacier. The Columbia Glacier air tour, lasting from 2.5 to 3.5 hours, includes bird's-eye views of Alyeska, Portage Pass, the numerous fiords and islands of Prince William Sound (where passengers often glimpse seals, whales and bald eagles), and, of course, huge Columbia Glacier. On some flightseeing tours, aircraft land on protected waters near Glacier Island or Heather Island, within sight of the active face of this glacier. The following charter services are among those that provide flights to Prince William Sound and Columbia Glacier.

Alaska Bush Carriers
4801 Aircraft Drive (Lake Hood)
Anchorage, Alaska 99502
Telephone: (907) 272-5155

Alyeska Air Service
P.O. Box 6164 (Merrill Field)
Anchorage, Alaska 99510
Telephone: (907) 277-5002
(In Girdwood, telephone: 783-6712)

Big Red's Flying Service, Inc.
P.O. Box 6281 (Anchorage International Airport)
Anchorage, Alaska 99502
Telephone: (907) 277-8032

Ketchum Air Service, Inc.
2708 Aspen Drive (Lake Hood)
Anchorage, Alaska 99502
Telephone: (907) 279-5511

Rust's Flying Service
Box 6301 (Lake Hood)
Anchorage, Alaska 99502
Telephone: (907) 272-2926

Access by State Ferry: The Alaska Marine Highway System

Two Ferries. Two state ferries operate on Prince William Sound. The M/V *E.L. Bartlett* travels between Whittier, Valdez and Cordova. The M/V *Tustemena* voyages between Seward, Valdez and Cordova. Offering one of the easiest and least expensive ways to see Prince William Sound, these large, well-appointed ships annually transport thousands of visitors.

The M/V BARTLETT, *193 feet* [59 m] *long, has traveled between Whittier and Valdez since 1969. Make reservations early for this popular trip.*
NEIL AND ELIZABETH JOHANNSEN

The *Bartlett*. Named for E. L. "Bob" Bartlett, Alaska's first United States Senator, this ship is manned by an enthusiastic and friendly crew, who, with the help of unequalled scenery and wildlife, have made the Whittier-Valdez ferry trip the most popular in Alaska. Built in 1969 at a total cost of about $3.25 million, the *Bartlett* travels at a service speed of 14.5 knots, is 193 feet [*58.8 m*] long and carries 170 passengers and 38 standard-sized automobiles. Although the vessel possesses no staterooms, passengers may relax either in one of the two lounges or in the solarium. The dining room specializes in fresh Prince William Sound seafood.

The state ferry M/V TUSTEMENA, *296 feet* [90 m] *long, travels through Resurrection Bay en route between Valdez and Seward. The ship also makes scheduled trips to Kodiak, Homer, Seldovia and Port Lions.*

NEIL AND ELIZABETH JOHANNSEN

The *Tustemena*. This vessel, larger than the *Bartlett,* was named for Tustemena Glacier and Lake on the Kenai Peninsula. It is 296 feet [*90.2 m*] long and has a capacity of 200 passengers and 47 standard-sized automobiles. The ship possesses 25 two-berth staterooms and two four-berth staterooms, a dining room, cocktail lounge, solarium and observation lounge. The *"Tusty"* began service in 1964 and in 1969 was lengthened by being cut in two and having 56 feet [*17 m*] added to the midsection. Total construction for the ship was about $5 million.

Reservations. Make reservations as far in advance as possible through any office of the Alaska Marine Highway System. Local offices are:

Alaska State Ferry System
Alaska Railroad Building, First Avenue
Box 2344
Anchorage, Alaska 99501
Telephone: (907) 272-7116 or 272-4482

Alaska State Ferry System
Box 40
Cordova, Alaska 99574
Telephone: (907) 424-7333 or 424-7334

Alaska State Ferry System
P.O. Box 66
Seward, Alaska 99664
Telephone: (907) 224-5485

Alaska State Ferry System
P.O. Box 181
Valdez, Alaska 99686
Telephone: (907) 835-4436

Include the following information when making reservation requests: names and number of persons in the party, including ages of all under 12 years; length, width, and height of vehicle and over-all connected length, including hitch if with trailer. Be accurate, as wrong information may void reservations.

Motel accommodations are limited in Cordova and Whittier and particularly "tight" in Valdez because of pipeline construction activity. Ferry passengers planning to overnight in these communities should have advance reservations. Passengers must depart the *Bartlett* upon arrival in port, as there are no overnight accommodations on that vessel.

The ferry routes are described in detail in later chapters.

Access by Railroad

A Relaxing Alternative. Passengers taking a vehicle on the *Bartlett* between Whittier and Valdez must ship their vehicles by rail from Portage as no road connects Whittier with the highway system. Vehicles are transported by flatbed railroad cars.

Many visitors traveling to Whittier park their cars at Portage and ride as coach passengers on The Alaska Railroad. A more relaxing alternative is to take the train from Anchorage and ride the entire way. The train travels the 50 mile [*80 km*] stretch between Anchorage and Portage at a leisurely 25 to

30 miles per hour [*40 to 65 km/hr*], allowing ample opportunities to observe the vistas of Turnagain Arm and Chugach State Park without distractions from the busy Seward Highway. The train makes a stop at Portage to hook on the flatbed railroad cars that carry the automobiles, then proceeds to Whittier, permitting passengers a few hours before the arrival of the state ferry for exploration of this small community. After the train arrives in Whittier, it makes several shuttle trips between Whittier and Portage, coinciding with the ferry schedule, before returning to Anchorage in early evening. The train ride between Anchorage and Portage takes 1.5 hours while the 12.4 mile [*19.9 km*] long Portage — Whittier trip lasts 35 minutes. For vehicle size limitations, rates and schedules, contact:

> *The Alaska Railroad*
> *Pouch 7-2111*
> *(1st and C Streets)*
> *Anchorage, Alaska 99510*
> *Telephone: (907) 265-2688, 265-2685, or 265-2683*

Tours and Package Arrangements

Worry-free Travel. For convenience and worry-free viewing of the scenic highlights of Prince William Sound, try a package tour. The often difficult to obtain motel reservations are already made, and knowledgeable guides heighten your appreciation of the area. A full spectrum of services includes everything from primitive wilderness camps (see Facilities chapter) to the best in luxurious motorcoaches and first-class accommodations. Make arrangements through a travel agent or by directly contacting one of the organizations listed below.

Glacier Queen. A luxurious alternative to the state ferry *Bartlett*, the 61 foot [*19 m*] cruise boat, the *Glacier Queen*, makes scheduled round trips between Whittier and Valdez during summer months, stopping en route at Columbia Glacier. The trip, which takes 5.5 hours one way, is enhanced by the captain's lively narrative. Much of the Whittier-Valdez ferry log, described in detail in a later chapter, is applicable to the *Glacier Queen* trip. Passengers may purchase hot meals and alcoholic beverages. Make reservations through any Westours office or through a travel agent.

Trader Ed's Cruises. The comfortable sightseeing boat used for these cruises has a capacity of 30 passengers. The large windows on the vessel permit easy viewing of the glaciers, islands, whales, seals, crab and shrimp pots and bird nesting colonies seen during the two-hour cruises. The boat departs from Whittier twice daily during the summer season, coinciding with the arrival of railroad shuttles from Portage. The boat cruises 25 mile [*40 km*] long Passage Canal and the Whittier vicinity. Make arrangements through any Anchorage travel agent.

Binoculars and cameras are trained on a massive icefall from the face of Columbia Glacier. Flightseeing tours, cruise boats and state ferries all make Columbia Glacier the focal point of their trips.

NEIL AND ELIZABETH JOHANNSEN

Westours. This international travel organization offers a memorable tour. Travel by motorcoach the Glenn and Richardson highways, overnight in Valdez, then sail to Whittier on the 61 foot [*18.6 m*] *Glacier Queen*, stopping en route at Columbia Glacier. The reverse trip is also possible. Make reservations through a travel agent or any Westours office. In Anchorage, contact:

> *Westours*
> *527 West Third Avenue*
> *Anchorage, Alaska 99501*
> *Telephone: (907) 277-5581*

American Sightseeing. Leave Anchorage by motorcoach for Whittier, board the state ferry *Bartlett* and sail to Valdez via Columbia Glacier. Overnight in Valdez, then return to Anchorage by motorcoach via the Richardson and Glenn highways. Make reservations well in advance through a travel agency or:

American Sightseeing
(Captain Cook Hotel, Fifth and K Streets)
P. O. Box 1699
Anchorage, Alaska 99510
Telephone: (907) 279-2471

Alaska Glacier Tours. This Anchorage-based travel agency features several package tours. For example, travel by motorcoach from Anchorage to Seward, overnight in Seward, sail on the state ferry *Tustemena* past wilderness islands of southwestern Prince William Sound, stop at Columbia Glacier, then overnight in Valdez. The following day return by motorcoach to Anchorage via the Richardson and Glenn highways. This trip is also possible in reverse order. Another popular trip involves sailing on the state ferry *Bartlett* between Whittier and Valdez, then returning to Anchorage by motorcoach via the Richardson and Glenn highways. For rates and information, contact:

Alaska Glacier Tours
720 West Fifth Avenue
Anchorage, Alaska 99501
Telephone: (907) 274-4721

Charter Boats

The Fish House. Fourteen to fifteen charter boats work through the Fish House, located next to the small-boat harbor in Seward. Boat sizes range from 21 to 80 feet [*6 to 24 m*], and capacity varies from 4 to 46 passengers. Several of the larger boats provide charter trips to Prince William Sound. During the busy summer season, make reservations at least a month in advance. The Fish House maintains a marine and citizen band radio service during the summer season, and sells ice, fishing and hunting licenses and an impressive array of fishing and boating gear. For rates, information and reservations, contact:

The Fish House
Box 1345
Seward, Alaska 99664
Telephone: (907) 224-3674

Whittier Boat Rentals. Located on the fuel dock at the Whittier small-boat harbor, Whittier Boat Rentals rents small boats with outboard engines. Visitors may also rent fishing equipment such as crab rings, shrimp pots and saltwater fishing poles and reels. Bait, ice and incidental boating supplies are also sold. Contact:

Whittier Boat Rentals
P.O. Box 683
Whittier, Alaska 99502
Telephone: (907) 472-2332

John Underwood Boat Charters. This firm owns and operates a 32 foot [*10 m*] sportfishing and sightseeing boat. The boat, based at Whittier and licensed to carry up to six passengers, charters for a minimum of $200 per day (subject to change). In addition to fishing and sightseeing charters, the owner is also a licensed guide; he offers transportation to hunts for bear, mountain goat and Sitka black-tailed deer.

Valdez. Several charter boat firms, featuring fishing trips and sightseeing trips to Columbia Glacier, are based in Valdez; inquire locally for details.

Where to Stay

Plan Ahead. The Prince William Sound area offers a variety of visitor facilities and accommodations. Area restaurants, with a diversity of menus and prices, specialize in seafood taken from the waters of the sound. Air taxi services and charter fishing boats (described in the Gateways chapter) provide transportation to good fishing grounds and backcountry camping. Visitors traveling by car, camper or motorhome to the larger communities will find grocery stores, service stations and laundromats and will be able to purchase fishing supplies, propane and ice.

Accommodations range from rustic campgrounds to first class hotels. For visitors who seek accommodations off the beaten "visitor track," backcountry lodges or public cabins in outlying areas maintained by the U.S. Forest Service offer wilderness retreats in splendid settings. During the height of the visitor season, July through August, hotels and motels are frequently booked solid. In addition, communication with backcountry lodges may take weeks or even months. Make your plans and reservations as far in advance as possible.

Hotels and Motels

Valdez. Construction of the Trans-Alaska Pipeline and Valdez Pipeline Terminal has put severe strains on accommodations in Valdez. If you plan to stay in a motel in Valdez, make reservations as far in advance as possible.

The Sheffield House, located next to the small-boat harbor and largest motel in Valdez, has 100 units, with additional units planned. Adjoining the Sheffield House are large dining and banquet facilities and a cocktail

Photo opposite: Prince William Sound Inn, a herring saltery now converted into a rustic lodge, is only one of the many kinds of accommodations to be found in the region.
© NANCY SIMMERMAN, 1975

lounge. Guests may buy or rent fishing tackle, purchase diesel fuel and gasoline from the adjacent dock, charter fishing boats and purchase souvenirs in the gift shop. Make reservations through any of the other Sheffield hotels (Whitehorse Travelodge, Kodiak Travelodge, Juneau Baranof, Anchorage Red Ram, Anchorage Travelodge, Barrow Top of the World, or Kotzebue Nul-lukvik) or through:

Sheffield Enterprises
Plaza 201, East Third Avenue
Anchorage, Alaska 99501
Telephone: (907) 274-6631

or by directly contacting:

Sheffield House
P.O. Box 568
Valdez, Alaska 99686
Telephone: (907) 835-4391

Other motels in Valdez, all located in the central part of town, cater primarily to pipeline personnel. They may, however, have rooms available.

Lamplighter Motel (10 rooms)
Valdez, Alaska 99686

Totem Inn (24 rooms, adjacent restaurant,
cocktail lounge, gift shop)
P.O. Box 663
Valdez, Alaska 99686
Telephone: (907) 835-4443

Valdez Motel (55 units, adjacent restaurant,
cocktail lounge)
P.O. Box 443
Valdez, Alaska 99686
Telephone: (907) 835-4444

Valdez Village Motel (20 housekeeping cottages)
P.O. Box 365
Valdez, Alaska 99686
Telephone: (907) 835-4445

Whittier. Motel accommodations in Whittier are limited to the Sportsman's Inn, which has 45 units, adjacent restaurant, cocktail lounge, liquor store and grocery store. Contact:

Sportsman's Inn
P.O. Box 698
Whittier, Alaska 99501
Telephone: (907) 472-2352

Seward. Of all the communities serving Prince William Sound, Seward is perhaps the best equipped to handle visitors. It is relatively close to Anchorage by highway (127 miles [*205 km*]), and campgrounds are fairly numerous in the vicinity. Two motels in Seward contain about 11 units each. Each unit offers television and complimentary coffee. Contact:

> *Merle's Marina Motel*
> *(Seward Highway near small-boat harbor)*
> *P.O. Box 1134*
> *Seward, Alaska 99664*
> *Telephone: (907) 224-5518*

> *Murphy's Motel*
> *(near downtown)*
> *P.O. Box 736*
> *Seward, Alaska 99664*
> *Telephone: (907) 224-5650*

The New Seward Hotel, located near downtown, has 36 units. The gift shop in the lobby boasts a fine collection of authentic native art and handicrafts, including such items as handcrafted baskets and ivory carvings. Contact:

> *New Seward Hotel*
> *217 Fifth Avenue*
> *Seward, Alaska 99664*
> *Telephone: (907) 224-5517*

Cordova. Four motels and hotels serve this fishing community. The newest and largest is the Reluctant Fisherman, located next to the small-boat harbor. This 48-unit motel contains a fine restaurant, cocktail lounge and coffee shop. Contact:

> *Reluctant Fisherman*
> *P.O. Box 399*
> *Cordova, Alaska 99574*
> *Telephone: (907) 424-3206*

The 16-unit Prince William Motel is located in the business district, adjacent to a bowling alley, restaurant, coffee shop, cocktail lounge and liquor store. Contact:

> *Prince William Motel*
> *P.O. Box 438*
> *Cordova, Alaska 99664*
> *Telephone: (907) 424-3201*

Two picturesque, rustic hotels, built in 1908, are located on Cordova's main street. Contact:

Alaskan Hotel (15 rooms)
P.O. Box 19
Cordova, Alaska 99574
Telephone: (907) 424-3288

Cordova House (25 rooms)
P.O. Box 700
Cordova, Alaska 99574
Telephone: (907) 424-3324

Camping

Few Developed Campgrounds. Developed campgrounds (those containing at least picnic tables, fireplaces and pit toilets) are located near Whittier, Valdez, Cordova and Seward. Campsites are allotted on a first-come, first-served basis. Holding tank dump stations are located in Valdez, Cordova and Seward; ice, propane and groceries may also be bought in these communities. Camping is permitted on public lands throughout the sound.

Campground Locations

Cordova. Temporary parking for self-contained vehicles is located across the street from the small-boat harbor. The U.S. Forest Service maintains 10-unit Cabin Lake Campground at Mile 13 on the Copper River Highway near the airport. Drive 2.5 miles [*4 km*] north on Cabin Lake Road. Campers should bring their own drinking water from Cordova, or, if obtaining it from nearby streams, boil it before using.

Seward. Motorhomes and campers may utilize gravel parking areas near the small-boat harbor for a fee of $1.00 per night. Shower facilities are available for a small fee in the harbormaster's office. Just outside of Seward on the Seward Highway, a Tesoro gas station operates a small campground with water and waste hook-ups. Fee is $3.50 per night. The City of Seward maintains the 25-unit Forest Acres Campground, charging $1.00 per night. Near Kenai Lake, the U.S. Forest Service maintains campgrounds at Primrose Landing (10 units), Ptarmigan Creek (16 units) and Trail River (72 units).

Valdez. Self-contained recreational vehicles may park in open areas near the state ferry dock. The City of Valdez maintains Valdez Glacier Campground (100 units). To reach this campground, drive about 4 miles [*6 km*] from Valdez on the Richardson Highway, turn left at the Valdez Airport sign, and drive about 1 mile [*1.6 km*] past the airport. The fee is

$2.00 per night. In addition to this large campground, small state-operated waysides are found at Mile 9 and Mile 23 on the Richardson Highway.

Whittier. No maintained campgrounds are located in Whittier. Self-contained recreational vehicles, however, may park in gravel areas near the town. The nearest campgrounds to Whittier are located in Portage Valley. These campgrounds are accessible from Whittier by traveling on the Alaska Railroad shuttle to Portage, then driving several miles on the Portage Glacier Access Road. The campgrounds contain a total of 55 campsites.

Backcountry Camping

Suggested Camping Practices. Though camping in backcountry areas currently requires no fees or permits, visitors should be aware of certain recommendations and regulations.

1. Pack out refuse. Plastics and metals, in particular, take years to decompose and mar the wilderness beauty of the sound.
2. If you must build a campfire, build it on mineral soil, free of vegetation or tree roots, as thick organic duff may smolder for months and spring into flame during dry periods. Drown the fire cold before you leave.
3. Inform a friend or relative of travel plans and expected time of return. Allow extra travel time, as inclement weather may delay return.

Special Camping Equipment. Campers should prepare for cool temperatures, rain and occasional strong winds. Warm clothing, raincoat, rainpants, waterproof hat and boots are essential. Backcountry campsites may often be found only in open damp boggy areas. Such sites require adequate groundcloths or, preferably, a tent with built-in waterproof floor. Tents, of course, should be rainproof and wind-sturdy. Camping veterans have found that sleeping bags insulated with polyester fiberfill instead of down are more suitable for use in wet environments. Polyester fiberfill dries quickly and maintains its insulating loft even when damp. Campers should carry a portable stove, as firewood is often damp or unavailable. Waterproof match containers or wax-dipped matches are recommended.

Backcountry Lodges

Prince William Sound Inn. For a picturesque and memorable sampling of oldtime "Alaskana," stay at this former herring saltery, now renovated into a rustic lodge. The old buildings, in which herring was processed from 1928 to 1959, are located on protected Thumb Bay on Knight Island, reputed to be the most beautiful island in the sound with its craggy mountain peaks and convoluted bays.

Guests stay in the "gibber" dormitory ("gibbers" were women who cleaned herring), an old-fashioned building now furnished with modern conveniences, where 28 bunks are divided between three dormers and five private rooms. Family-style meals are served in the old dining hall, decorated with local antiques such as a player piano, rolltop desk and old safe. Skiffs with outboard motors are available for rent; the area offers fishing for pink salmon, halibut and red "snapper." Access is via charter boat or charter aircraft (see Gateways chapter). Rates include both room and board. For reservations, contact:

Port Oceanic
Knight Island
Via Cordova, Alaska 99574

or

World Wide Travel
431 G Street
Anchorage, Alaska 99501
Telephone: (907) 277-9571

Alaska Outdoor Services. This organization operates a hunting lodge at the site of the Native village of Nuchek on Hinchinbrook Island. Facilities include a 2500 square foot [*762 sq m*] pre-fab cedar lodge, tent camps, floatplane and 42 foot [*13 m*] boat (available for charter). Guided hunts are offered for black bear, brown bear or mountain goat. Guided photography "hunts" may also be booked. Write:

Alaska Outdoor Services
P.O. Box 878
Cordova, Alaska 99574

LaBounty's Montague Island Resort. Offering brown bear hunting, this rustic lodge is located at McLeod Harbor, Montague Island, one of the most remote and untouched corners of Prince William Sound. Guests stay in cabins equipped for light housekeeping. Visitors may hunt, fish, dig clams, beachcomb, pick berries or cross-country ski. The lodge is accessible by aircraft or boat. For information, contact:

Clarence LaBounty
Montague Island Resort
Star Route
Seward, Alaska 99664

Photo opposite: Wilderness camps and schools offer a pleasant escape from the pressures of civilization. Guests may learn kayaking, camping and other wilderness skills.
NEIL AND ELIZABETH JOHANNSEN

Wilderness Camps

National Outdoor Leadership School. During summer months state ferry passengers and other recreationists may see groups kayaking the coves and fiords of the sound. These people are enrolled in the National Outdoor Leadership School (NOLS), headquartered in Lander, Wyoming. Founded in 1965 with the goal of educating wilderness users in techniques of practical conservation, NOLS courses are given throughout the world. The 35-day Prince William Sound course, which has been held each summer since 1971, is one of the most demanding. Small expeditions learn basic seamanship, saltwater fishing, cooking, camping, map reading and wilderness traveling skills. The groups are equipped to take brief trips into mountains where fundamentals of mountaineering are taught. The last few days of the course are devoted to survival training; in small groups, the students kayak their own way back to Whittier, living off land and sea.

All equipment, except some personal items, is provided or may be rented. Contact:

> *Prince William Sound Course*
> *National Outdoor Leadership School*
> *Box AA*
> *Lander, Wyoming 82520*

Bear Brothers Whole Wilderness Experience. Visitors who do not wish to undergo the ambitious NOLS program may find Bear Brothers to be better suited to their needs. Headed by two former NOLS instructors, Bear Brothers establishes temporary wilderness camps in selected areas of Prince William Sound. From these camps guests may kayak the innumerable shallow coves and islands characteristic of the sound. All outdoor equipment, including outer clothing, backpacks, fishing gear and kayaks, is provided. Contact:

> *Bear Brothers Whole Wilderness Experience*
> *P.O. Box 4-2969*
> *Anchorage, Alaska 99509*

Wilderness Trek Guide Service. Wilderness Trek arranges and leads a variety of outdoor activities throughout the sound, including canoe trips, photo safaris, backpacking and mountaineering expeditions, fishing trips and winter ski tours. Guests may stay at Prince William Sound Inn on Knight Island or at base camps throughout the Prince William Sound area. Wilderness Trek specializes in custom tours to fit any group. Contact:

> *Wilderness Trek Guide Service*
> *740 North Flower Street*
> *Anchorage, Alaska 99504*
> *Telephone: (907) 274-1767*

U.S. Forest Service Recreation Cabins

A Great Bargain. Small cabins may be rented from the U.S. Forest Service for $5.00 per party per day. These modest shelters are located in outlying areas on a lake, salt water, or along a trail system. For details on how to reach these cabins, consult the Gateways chapter.

Facilities. These simple accommodations are equipped with either a wood or oil stove for cooking and heating, tables, bunks and outdoor toilets. None of the cabins is wired for electricity. Small skiffs are available at some cabins. Water, obtained from nearby lakes or streams, should be boiled before drinking. Users must provide bedding, cooking utensils and oil for the stoves (5 gallons of either automotive diesel or good grade stove oil will last about 48 hours in summer). You may wish to take a portable camp stove for cooking and a small axe or camp saw so that you may leave a supply of cut firewood before departing. The nearest Forest Service office will provide complimentary plastic litter bags, as all garbage must be removed, except for burnable refuse that may be disposed of in wood stoves. Leave the cabin the way you would like to find it.

Take warm clothing, insect repellent and raingear. If a cabin is accessible only by aircraft, carry additional rations in the event weather prevents the plane from returning on schedule.

Reservations. Contact the Anchorage or Cordova office of the Chugach National Forest (open Monday through Friday from 7:45 a.m. to 4:30 p.m.) to obtain an application for a cabin permit. The permit is issued on a first-come first-served basis to anyone 18 years of age or older. Permits are limited to a maximum of seven nights. Make reservations early, as cabins are often filled on weekends, particularly during summer months and during peak hunting and fishing times.

Information sheets on these cabins are available from offices of the Chugach National Forest. Numbers in the following list (which includes only those cabins situated in Prince William Sound) refer to locations on the Chugach National Forest map, also available from these offices.

Reservations Handled through the Anchorage Office. The Anchorage office works primarily with cabin reservations on the Kenai Peninsula. However, they do handle reservations for two cabins in northwest Prince William Sound. For reservations, contact:

Chugach National Forest
121 West Fireweed Lane, Suite 205
Anchorage, Alaska 99503
Telephone: (907) 274-6061

Shrode Lake (A-13). This 16′ x 16′ A-frame cabin sleeps eight and has an oil stove. It is reached via a 30 mile [*48 km*] boat trip from Whittier or by a

The public may rent small cabins built and operated by the U.S. Forest Service. Nearly all these cabins are located in remote regions of Prince William Sound and the Copper River Delta. This pre-fab structure, which has bunks for four people, is located at Galena Bay.
U.S. FOREST SERVICE

one hour flight from Seward or Anchorage. In late summer, Shrode Lake offers fishing for dolly varden char and silver salmon. A skiff with oars is furnished. Because this area receives heavy snowfall, the cabin may not be open until early summer.

Pigot Bay (A-12). This 16' x 16' A-frame cabin has bunks for eight and an oil stove. Twenty miles [*32 km*] from Whittier, it is accessible by boat or via a one hour flight from Seward or Anchorage. The area affords good fishing for crab, halibut and salmon. In past years, both logging and gold mining have taken place near Pigot Bay.

Reservations Handled through the Cordova Office. Contact:

> *Chugach National Forest*
> *Federal Building*
> *P.O. Box 280*
> *Cordova, Alaska 99574*
> *Telephone: (907) 424-3326*

Sawmill Bay (C-1). Located on a small bay of Valdez Arm, 17 miles [*27 km*] from Valdez, this cabin may be reached by floatplane or boat. The 12′ x 14′ cabin has four bunks and an oil stove. There is good fishing for silver and pink salmon, dungeness crab and halibut. Butter clams are fairly common in the area.

Galena Bay (C-2). This 12′ x 14′ cabin, located about 4 miles [*6.4 km*] from the head of Galena Bay, is about 17 miles [*27 km*] from Valdez. The cabin contains an oil stove and bunks for four people. Saltwater fishing for pink and silver salmon is found in the area.

Simpson Bay (C-3). This 12′ x 14′ cabin has bunks for four and an oil stove. It is 15 miles [*24 km*] by boat from Cordova or 8 miles [*13 km*] by airplane. From the cabin, hike the 2.5 mile [*4 km*] Milton Lake Trail, maintained by the Forest Service, and fish for silver salmon or cutthroat trout.

Double Bay (C-4). This cabin, located on Hinchinbrook Island, is 22 miles [*35 km*] from Cordova by boat or 13 miles [*21 km*] by aircraft. The cabin has bunks for four and an oil stove. Sitka black-tailed deer and brown bear

Shrode Lake Cabin, also built and operated by the U.S. Forest Service, is located on a trout-filled lake that is often covered with snow and ice until July. The A-frame cabin, which sleeps eight, is accessible by floatplane or boat.

NEIL AND ELIZABETH JOHANNSEN

inhabit the island. Fishing for pink salmon and trout is fairly good. This is an excellent area to watch sea otters and harbor seals.

Canoe Passage (C-5). Located on Hawkins Island, this 12′ x 14′ cabin has an oil stove and bunks for four. It is accessible by floatplane or boat. The distance from Cordova by water is 22 miles [*35 km*] and by air, 13 miles [*21 km*]. Hunt for black-tailed deer or fish for cutthroat trout and dolly varden. Hike a 4.2 mile [*6.8 km*] trail from the cabin to the south shore of Hawkins Island.

Pete Dahl Slough Cut-off (C-6). This 12′ x 14′ cabin, located on the Copper River Flats, is 16 air miles [*26 km*] from Cordova. A skiff may reach the cabin in 6 miles [*9.7 km*] from the Alaganik Slough boat ramp near the Copper River Highway. The cabin has an oil stove and bunks for four. This is an excellent place to observe or hunt waterfowl.

Eyak River (C-7). This 12′ x 14′ cabin, equipped with an oil stove and bunks for four and located on the Copper River Flats, is accessible via a 3 mile [*4.8 km*] trail from the Copper River Highway or a 3 mile [*4.8 km*] skiff trip on the Eyak River from the Eyak River boat landing. Wildlife includes moose, black and brown bear and waterfowl. Anglers find cutthroat trout and dolly varden char in addition to some good silver salmon fishing in season.

Tiedeman Slough (C-8). Also situated on the Copper River Flats, this cabin is 12′ x 14′, has an oil stove and bunks for four. By floatplane it is 14 air miles [*23 km*] from Cordova, or 7 miles [*11 km*] by skiff from the Alaganik Slough boat ramp. Take binoculars along for waterfowl observation.

McKinley Trail Cabin (C-9). This is the only Forest Service cabin accessible by automobile. It is 12′ x 16′ and has a wood stove and bunks for six. Drive to Mile 22.5 on the Copper River Highway, where the cabin is located at the beginning of a beautiful 2.5 mile [*4 km*] long trail that winds through rainforest vegetation to McKinley Lake. Wildlife seen in the area includes moose, black and brown bear and waterfowl. Trout and grayling are in nearby lakes.

Martin Lake (C-10). This scenic area, 42 miles [*68 km*] southeast of Cordova, is accessible only by floatplane. The 12′ x 14′ cabin has an oil stove and bunks for four. Hunters find mountain goats, black and brown bear, moose and waterfowl. Trout and salmon fishing is good in the lake and outlet stream. A boat with oars is provided.

Indian Creek (C-11). This cabin, located 4 miles [*6.4 km*] inside the north shore of Galena Bay, is 19 miles [*31 km*] from Valdez. The cabin is 14′ x 14′ and has an oil stove and bunks for four. Good saltwater fishing is found in the area.

Hook Point (C-12). This 16′ x 16′ cabin, situated 2.5 miles [*4 km*] west of Hook Point on the Gulf of Alaska side of Hinchinbrook Island, 25 air miles [*40 km*] from Cordova, can only be reached by wheel plane at low tide. The A-frame is furnished with an oil stove and bunks for seven. Land mammals on Hinchinbrook Island include brown bear and Sitka black-tailed deer. Good ocean beachcombing is found nearby. Sea otters are common in this area. Black-legged kittiwakes, a type of gull, have a nesting colony in this vicinity.

Beach River (C-13). Ocean beachcombing for Japanese glass floats, driftwood, and assorted flotsam and jetsam is found here. Located near Patton Bay on the Gulf of Alaska side of Montague Island, 69 miles [*111 km*] from Cordova, and accessible only by wheel plane at low tide, this 12' x 20' cabin has an oil stove and bunks for six. Brown bear and black-tailed deer live on the island. Anglers may fish for dolly varden char from late July to mid-September.

Patton Bay (C-14). This cabin, 2 miles [*3.2 km*] northeast of Nellie Martin River in Patton Bay on the Gulf of Alaska side of Montague Island, 78 miles [*126 km*] from Cordova, is accessible only by wheel plane at low tide. The 14' x 32' cabin has an oil stove and bunks for six. Brown bear and deer are found in the vicinity. Good beachcombing is found on the vast sand shores of the area. Catch silver, red or pink salmon and dolly varden char in Nellie Martin River from late July to mid-September. This bay rose 15 feet [*4.6 m*] in the 1964 Good Friday earthquake.

A Lively Past

From Kayaks to Tankers. Fur, fish, gold, copper . . . and a steep, fiord-rid-
dled land beautiful almost beyond comprehension have beckoned women
and men to Prince William Sound.

Humans first arrived thousands of years ago from the west, finding in the
verdant forests and bountiful seas a place more abundant in food than their
more austere former homes.

Europeans first set foot on Alaskan soil in 1741, when Vitus Bering's men,
sailing under the Russian flag, went ashore on Kayak Island for fresh water,
just southeast of Prince William Sound. Over the next few decades, a
plethora of sailing ships, flying the flags of half a dozen major world powers,
plied waters of the sound. The ships, vainly seeking the elusive Northwest
Passage, instead found unexpected wealth in the form of sea otters, whose
pelts were sold for great sums on the Oriental market.

At the beginning of the twentieth century another wave of men, first lured
north by the whisper of Klondike gold, stayed to gouge glittering metal from
thousands of mining claims throughout the sound.

Capitalizing on a fashion trend during the 1920s, a few individualists tried
to make their fortunes by raising blue foxes on isolated "farms" on many of
the tiny islands.

Weather-silvered boards, worm-eaten docks and rotting fish nets are
remains from another epoch; during the first half of this century dozens of
canneries processed the harvest of seemingly limitless millions of salmon.

Although most efforts of these pioneers have long since been camou-
flaged by moss and thick alder bushes, dramatic episodes continue. Possibly
the most significant chapter in the history of the sound is currently being
written, as the old mining community of Valdez readies itself for the "black
gold" that will pour through the Trans-Alaska Pipeline to waiting tankers.

*Photo opposite: Oldtimer George Flemming personifies the colorful
history of Prince William Sound. Born on Flemming Island, he has
witnessed the boom and bust of fox farming, gold and copper mining,
canneries and towns.*

NEIL AND ELIZABETH JOHANNSEN

The First Human Inhabitants

Chugach Eskimos. Alaskan Natives discovered Prince William Sound thousands of years ago. The Chugach Eskimos, who today call themselves Aleuts (although many authorities have pointed out the similarities between the language of the Chugach Eskimos and the Upik dialect of the upper Alaska Peninsula), came from the west. Perhaps these people struggled across windswept Portage Pass, or perhaps they paddled their large open boats, called umiaks, around the tip of the Kenai Peninsula and through the angry waters of the Gulf of Alaska.

In Prince William Sound, the most southerly home of the Eskimos, this ethnic group found a majestic land of abundance. They hunted whales, otters, seals and sea lions from fragile-looking but seaworthy baidarkas and built weirs to catch salmon, which choked the streams throughout the summer. Eskimos in the eastern part of the sound also pursued mountain goats, especially in winter when snow drove goats close to shore.

If hunting or fishing was not productive, a gourmet's array of food was available for the gathering. Clams, mussels and kelp could be harvested at low tide. In summer, a dozen varieties of edible berries, some of which the women preserved for winter use, carpeted the forests and alpine tundra. The luxuriant plantlife also provided the Eskimos with cow parsnip, sorrel, nettles and a variety of medicinal herbs.

The Chugach Eskimos, numbering perhaps some 500 people dispersed into eight tribes throughout the sound, periodically warred with each other, capturing slaves and booty. Permanent village sites, located on shore with easy access to food and drinking water, were selected primarily with an eye for defensive position. The Natives sought sites with a good view of potential enemies approaching by land or sea, as well as a quick escape route.

The Chugach Eskimos dressed dramatically. Both men and women adorned themselves with nosepins, labrets (decorations, usually of bone, inserted in the lips), beaded headbands and tattoos. Rainsuits were usually made of bear gut or seal gut, but men often used whole bearskins for protection from the weather, with the bears' heads covering their heads. Few Natives wore anything to protect their feet, even in the cold of midwinter.

Shamanism and superstition dominated their lives. They practiced mummification of their dead, hiding the carefully prepared bodies of upper caste individuals together with their belongings in sea caves throughout the

Photo opposite: The Chugach Eskimos, a proud, warlike people, have inhabited the sound for thousands of years. An artist traveling with Captain James Cook on his voyage of exploration in 1778 sketched this somewhat fanciful likeness of a Native woman who visited the H.M.S. RESOLUTION while it was anchored in Snug Corner Cove.

ENGRAVING AFTER WEBBER BY BASIRE

sound. Natives today maintain their tradition of avoiding and respecting these burial caves. More recently arrived inhabitants of the sound, however, have extensively pilfered and looted these important archeological sites, so that today few of these caves remain undisturbed.

In 1933, archeologist Frederica de Laguna and her assistants made systematic excavations at the prehistoric village of Palugvik on the southwest shore of Hawkins Island near Cordova. The diggings showed evidence of the great age and gradually evolving culture of the Chugach Eskimo. The Palugvik site was declared a national historic landmark in 1963. A plaque describing the site is displayed in the Cordova Centennial Museum.

Eyak Indians. The Chugach Eskimos maintained a constant vigil toward a wholly different cultural group to the east, the Eyak Indians. Occupying the area between the present town of Cordova and Martin River, these Indians probably migrated from the Interior of Alaska via the Copper River. The Eyak Indians and the Chugach Eskimos maintained an uneasy relationship, which occasionally erupted into violent territorial disputes. Most of the time, however, the two groups traded peaceably.

Unlike the Eskimos, the Eyaks seldom hunted sea mammals. They were, instead, primarily land hunters, pursuing mountain goats and brown and black bears. Every July, the abundant waterfowl of the Copper River Delta molted, making easy marks for clubs and sharp arrows. The main food of the Eyak Indians, however, was salmon. They used spears and dip baskets, stationing themselves at places such as Mountain Slough on the Copper River Delta and Point Whitshed a few miles south of Cordova.

The Eyak Indians never numbered more than several hundred and at various times Chugach and Tlingit tribes completely overran their lands, decimating the Eyak population. The final blow to the Eyak culture, however, came around the beginning of the twentieth century. Cordova cannery and railroad operations resulted in assimilating the Indians into a different way of life. The route of the Copper River and Northwestern Railway crossed over the village of Alaganik, literally annihilating it. Today, only a few Natives speak the almost extinct Eyak language.

Tlingit Indians. This highly complex Indian culture, the largest Native group in Southeastern Alaska, founded its northernmost permanent settlement at Yakutat. From this glacier-bound outpost Tlingit warriors made sporadic forays to the north. During the last part of the eighteenth century they temporarily gained control of much Eyak and Chugach territory, thwarting a previous southward expansion of the Chugach Eskimos by driving them from Controller Bay and Kayak Island. In 1793 and again in 1805, Tlingit war parties invaded Prince William Sound but were soundly routed by the Chugach Eskimos with the help of Russian sea otter hunters.

The first European to enter Prince William Sound was Captain James Cook, Royal Navy, who anchored in Snug Corner Cove for eight days in 1778. He named the sound after Prince William Henry, the Duke of Clarence and third son of King George III, who became King William IV of England upon his father's death in 1830.
WATERCOLOR DRAWING BY WEBBER
FROM WEBBER ALBUM, DIXSON LIBRARY

Sailing Ships from West and South

Vitus Bering. In 1741, Vitus Bering (1680-1741), a Dane, led a Russian expedition that became the first of European origin to set foot on Alaskan soil. Bering's ship, the *Saint Peter*, anchored on the lee side of Kayak Island in the Gulf of Alaska south of the present town of Cordova. The famous German naturalist Georg Wilhelm Steller (1709-1746), who accompanied this expedition, sketched and named many plants and animals in the area, and found an Eskimo camp whose occupants had temporarily fled. These first European visitors stayed on shore only a few hours. While returning to Russia, the *Saint Peter* was driven ashore on Bering Island where Bering and many members of the crew died of scurvy during the long winter. A few survivors, including Steller, finally succeeded in reaching the Russian mainland in a boat salvaged from wreckage of the *Saint Peter*.

On the Bering expedition Alexei Chirikov commanded a sister ship, the *Saint Paul,* which early in the voyage was separated from the *Saint Peter.* Both the *Saint Paul,* which eventually returned to Russia intact, and the survivors from the *Saint Peter* sold sea otter pelts for fabulous sums to Chinese nobles, touching off a mad stampede of Russian fur hunters to this newly discovered corner of North America.

Captain Cook. The next visitor was the English navigator Captain James Cook (1728-1779), Royal Navy, who on his third voyage of exploration sailed the H.M.S. *Resolution* into the Gulf of Alaska and explored Prince William Sound and Cook Inlet. The goal of the expedition was to explore the northwest coast of North America and to discover, if possible, the Northwest Passage, a sea route across the continent. In May of 1778 Cook became the first European to sail into the sound. Cook named the embayment Sandwich Sound after the First Lord of the Admiralty, the Fourth Earl of Sandwich. Between the time of Cook's naming and the publishing of his journals, the name was changed to Prince William Sound. This name refers to William Henry (1765-1837), the Duke of Clarence and third son of King George III, who became King William IV of England upon his father's death in 1830.

Cook's crew included William Bligh, better known for his involvement with the mutiny on the H.M.S. *Bounty* in 1789, and midshipman George Vancouver, who commanded an expedition to the area a few years later and named Bligh Island after his former shipmate. Captain Cook stayed in the sound for eight days, making repairs and getting fresh water in Snug Corner Cove, then sailed to Unalaska in the Aleutian Chain. There he met Russian fur traders and told them of the great numbers of sea otters the expedition had observed in Prince William Sound.

Explorers from Many Countries. Following these initial voyages of exploration, many nations focused attention northward. Spanish explorer Salvador Fidalgo, searching for the Northwest Passage, sailed through much of eastern Prince William Sound. He gave many of the embayments the Spanish names that survive to this day.

French, Portuguese, American and British ships also made brief appearances in the sound. One Englishman, John Meares (1756?-1809), commanding the *Nootka,* stayed longer than he wanted, when in the winter of 1786-1787 he was shipwrecked near the Native village of Tatitlek. Though lacking in food, he and his crew stayed alive in a rather unorthodox fashion by partaking of their ample supply of alcohol. The group, however, was severely decimated by scurvy by the time another Englishman, George Dixon (1755-1800) of the *Queen Charlotte,* rescued them the following spring. A century later, geologists named a large glacier at the head of Unakwik Inlet in honor of Meares.

Captain George Vancouver. This English explorer (1757-1798), commanding the H.M.S. *Discovery* and *Chatham,* repaired his ships at Port Chalmers on Montague Island in late May and early June of 1794. His two lieutenants, Whidbey and Johnstone, using smaller vessels, respectively made careful surveys of western and eastern Prince William Sound. In spite of rainy, windy weather, these men mapped such areas as Portage Pass, Port Wells, Port Bainbridge, Columbia Glacier and Hawkins Island. Johnstone and his men spent several days at Fort Constantine, a Russian sea otter hunting settlement at Port Etches on Hinchinbrook Island. The Englishmen were effusively welcomed by the lonely Russians who manned the post. In return for a breakfast of hair seal (with the hair still attached) and bird eggs, Johnstone gave the Russians chocolate, bread and rum. The survey work of the expedition was so thorough that it formed the basis for sailing charts for years after Alaska became a possession of the United States in 1867.

Russian Explorers and Sea Otter Hunters. Throughout the period of European discovery voyages, the Russians exerted the strongest and most permanent influence on the area. In 1783, five years after Captain Cook became the first European to enter Prince William Sound, three Russian vessels under the command of Potap Zaikov, in search of sea otters, reached the sound from their base at Unalaska in the Aleutian Islands. The ships first anchored near Kayak Island, from where Nagaiev, canoe maker of the expedition, explored the mainland and reported the discovery of the Copper River, which he ascended for many miles. The Zaikov party named the sound "Guba Chugatskay" (Chugach Gulf), "Chugach" being derived from the name that the Natives gave themselves. Zaikov hoped to trade with the Eskimos, but the population would not submit to the same abuse with which the Russians had treated the docile Aleuts.

Eskimo tradition gives another version of these first encounters with the Russians. Legend relates that some Russians landed on Green Island, north of Montague Island. A few hunters from the nearby Native village of Nuchek on Hinchinbrook Island happened to see them, and returned to their village to tell of the strange creatures they had seen: smoke came out of their mouths and their legs ended in hooves (boots). The Natives threw away the proffered flour, hardtack and snuff, because they did not know how to use them and thought they were being poisoned.

Grigorii Shelekhov (1747-1796), founder of the first Russian establishment at Kodiak, sent sea otter hunting parties to the sound between 1785 and 1792. By this time, however, the Russians faced competition, as numerous other nations were dispatching expeditions to harvest sea otter pelts and to seek the elusive Northwest Passage.

In 1793, Shelekhov strengthened Russia's position in Prince William Sound by building the first permanent European outpost, Fort Constantine, at Port Etches on Hinchinbrook Island. Here the Russians maintained an uneasy relationship with the Natives. The Eskimos praised Zaikov, commander of the post, but complained of Polutov, a mate who had stolen their sea otter skins, shot several people and carried off some women. As a result, the Natives killed Polutov and his companions one dark fall night when they had gone to chop firewood, but spared Zaikov.

Aleksandr Baranov (1747-1819), later leader of the Russian-American colony at Kodiak, gradually gained political strength over the Prince William Sound area, aided by his marriage to Anna, a proud Native princess from the village of Chenega in western Prince William Sound. The beautiful and tragic Anna is described in Hector Chevigny's book, *Lord of Alaska,* the story of Baranov and his company.

An interesting historical footnote is the fact that while Baranov was chief manager at Kodiak he sent an English shipwright, James Shields, to Resurrection Bay, near the present location of Seward, southwest of the sound, to build the *Phoenix* — the first ship of European design launched on the west Pacific coast.

Over the years, the Russians succeeded in breaking the proud spirit of many of these Natives, forcing them to hunt sea otters and imprisoning them in dark, underground cells for slight infractions.

A Quiet Period. Life in Prince William Sound settled into a quiet routine for the next hundred years following the initial flurry of voyages of exploration. By the time the Russian-American Company at Nuchek turned its operations over to the Alaska Commercial Company in 1867, sea otters were scarce, and Prince William Sound was home only to Natives and a handful of traders.

Gold!

Valdez Trail to the Klondike. In 1897, tales of fabulous wealth in the Klondike filtered south. Eager stampeders sought the shortest route north. Pamphlets composed mostly of unfounded information advertised an "All-American Route" to the Klondike that would circumvent unsympathetic Canadian customs officers. Hastily formed companies filled ships of the Pacific Steam Whaling Company and sailed from West Coast ports to Valdez in 1897 and 1898.

The new arrivals who faced the grueling overland winter trip from Valdez were ignorant of the dangers of traveling in this vast primitive land. They soon learned, however. Setting out from Valdez, they dragged their sleds of belongings some 6 miles [10 km] to the terminus of Valdez Glacier. This forbidding river of ice reached 1 mile [1.6 km] into the sky, and stretched 20 miles [32 km] northward into the Chugach Mountains. The dogged goldseekers found that the glacier rose in a series of icefalls so steep that block and tackle were necessary to hoist the cumbersome outfits.

At first the men and women who landed at Valdez possessed a youthful sense of adventure, but the nearly insurmountable glacier chipped away at their strength and enthusiasm. The stampeders suffered snow blindness and sunburn, while fog and noisy icefalls frightened all but the most intrepid. Otherwise stalwart men claimed they were haunted by a troll-like demon who lived in the glacier's crevasses.

With the advent of spring, the Valdez Glacier Trail became all but impassable. A rainy May caused avalanches, and one heavy slide buried more than two dozen people. Rescuers heard the victims' cries for help from under the snow but were able to save only two. The most tenacious individuals finally reached the other side of the glacier to build rafts to float the Klutina River (appropriately named, Klutina means "glacier river" in the Ahtena Indian dialect). Unfortunately, the first few miles of the river were deceptively gentle, but the river then deteriorated into a seething mass of white water laced with snags. Of the 3500 adventurers who started, only some 200 successfully navigated these waters, and of this group, only a few ever completed the long miles to the Klondike.

The unsuccessful stampeders who returned to Valdez found themselves marooned in that town for the winter. Hungry men jammed twenty to a 12 by 15 foot [*4 by 5 m*] cabin, and many died of scurvy, misdiagnosed as gangrene.

Transporting supplies over Valdez Glacier in the winter of 1897-1898 was a dangerous and tedious ordeal.

Local Mining

Gold and Copper. These painful beginnings signified a new era for all of Alaska. The fabulous gold veins of Dawson City in the Klondike gave out in a few years, but people still drifted north, seeking gold and adventure. Valdez matured from a bawdy tent city into a permanent settlement, hosting miners who awaited good weather to travel the Richardson Trail to Interior Alaska. Many, not wishing to remain idle, prospected the gullies and peaks around Valdez. Mineral Creek, a few miles from town, with its many hundreds of gold claims established at the dawn of the century, reflects the aspirations of these early Prince William Sound visitors. Many of these prospectors became permanent residents, gradually mining the widespread mineral deposits of the region.

An imaginary dividing line runs through the center of Port Valdez, then trends in a southwesterly direction through Valdez Arm and Culross Island in western Prince William Sound. To the north of this line prospectors found gold, and to the south they staked numerous copper claims. Eventually the number of gold and copper claims ran into the many thousands, and elaborate mining operations sprang up on coves and cliffs throughout Prince William Sound.

Cliff Mine. This gold mine, located just east of Shoup Bay in Port Valdez, was the most productive gold mine in the sound. "Red" Ellis, who founded the mine in 1906, gained his nickname because he refused to cut his long red hair from the time he staked his claim until the mine started operating a few years later. The mine shaft ran under the floor of Port Valdez. When the mine finally closed during World War II, almost one million dollars worth of gold had been gouged from the rock. The 1964 Good Friday earthquake and ensuing tidal wave destroyed the old mine buildings.

Port Wells. The glacially carved cliffs bordering this large fiord in northwestern Prince William Sound have yielded much gold. The largest mine in this region was Granite Mine, located just north of Hobo Bay on the west side of Port Wells. It operated sporadically from before World War I until the early 1960s. A cluster of gold claims on the east shore of Port Wells spawned the short-lived mining camp of Golden, which existed from about 1904 to 1916.

The Big Four and Ramsey-Rutherford Mines. These gold mines in the mountains behind Valdez were productive for many years. Bob Reeve, Alaska's "glacier pilot" and founder of Reeve Aleutian Airways, earned his reputation as a bush pilot in the 1930s by making hair-raising landings on crevasse-ridden glaciers near these mines.

Gold fever was the epidemic of the day from about 1898 to about 1918. Thousands of gold and copper mining claims once pocketed the hillsides of Prince William Sound.

KEN HINCHEY — ALAGCO COLLECTION
COOK INLET HISTORICAL SOCIETY

The town of Ellamar evolved around a productive copper mine. Since the main mine shaft went under the bay, miners built a huge cofferdam to hold back the water. The town has been largely abandoned for several decades.

KEN HINCHEY — ALAGCO COLLECTION
COOK INLET HISTORICAL SOCIETY

Midas Mine. In a quest for copper, the Granby Consolidated Mining, Smelting, and Power Company (Ltd.) developed the fabulous Midas Mine, discovered by "Red" Ellis in 1901 near Port Valdez. In 1915 the company completed a 5.25 mile [*8.4 km*] long double aerial tramway with 22 miles [*35 km*] of cable and 77 tram towers, at that time the longest tram in Alaska. The mine was highly profitable. Today a visitor standing in Old Valdez with a pair of binoculars may be able to see remains of the tram towers in Solomon Gulch to the right of Sugarloaf Mountain.

Ellamar. This almost deserted mining town, nestled beneath precipitous Copper Mountain on the eastern edge of Prince William Sound, owed its existence to copper. The town began with the formation of the Ellamar Mining Company in 1898. The main body of chalcopyrite (copper) ore extended offshore, so miners dug their tunnels with a 400 foot [*120 m*] cofferdam holding back the water.

Dozens of smaller copper mines riddled the coastal indentations of nearby Port Fidalgo and Galena Bay. Today a visitor to the area may see traces of these old mine tailings and rusty mining equipment on some of the beaches.

Latouche. This island, located in southwest Prince William Sound, was the largest producer of copper in the sound. The Beatson Mine began operations about 1903, and by World War I the town of Latouche, with a reported population of about 3000, boasted a hospital, movie theatre, bowling alleys, stores, warehouses and a three-story bunkhouse. The mine closed in 1928. Today a collection of dangerously unstable buildings marks the townsite.

Knight Island. Prior to a sudden decline in copper prices in 1907, this island, with its steep rocky peaks and deeply indented fiords, received its share of copper prospectors, particularly at Drier Bay, site of several large mines and a tramway. Miners also dug a network of tunnels at Rua Cove.

Kennecott Mines. Although one of the richest copper mines in the world was 193 miles [*311 km*] by railroad inland from Cordova, its development profoundly affected the history of the sound for several decades. Katherine Wilson captured the mood of early mining days when she described the 1900 discovery of copper at this mine in her work, *Copper Tints.**

Photo opposite: Much of Ellamar still stands. Located on the eastern edge of the sound, its ruins are visible from many miles offshore.
GIL MULL

In the late afternoon Tarantula Jack and his partner halted their pack horses. It had been a long day's tramp and the foothills of the Wrangell Range offered nothing in the way of shelter for man or beast. Naked and glacier-scarred, the mountains rose at their approach in towering unwelcome and retreated darkly into their high-up ice caves. It was while the prospectors were loosening their pack-straps to get at the shrunken food bag for the animals, that the eye of Tarantula Jack was caught by a patch of green apparently overgrowing a slide well up the face of the mountain. "Looks like that might be grass up there," he observed to his companion, and as he staked out the hungry horses and gave them as much as he dared of the feed, he kept glancing now and then at that vivid patch of color so promising of fresh forage. When the flapjacks and coffee had been disposed of and pipes lighted up, Tarantula rose to his feet. "Think I'll take a turn up the mountain and prospect that vegetation," he announced. He was gone some time.

"Grass?" his partner ventured.

Tarantula Jack spat explosively, "Grass nothing," he fumed in disgust. "That there green is malachite and chalcocite-copper ore, or I never saw Arizona . . . and a whole blamed mountain of it!"

And so was discovered the Bonanza Mine.

The partners staked out claims . . . a dozen or so they located in their names, Jack Smith and Clarence Warner, and to cover as much ground as possible, in those of a trail party with whom they had traveled inland as far as the Chitina.

Months later at Valdez they notified the others of their find. The latter were but mildly interested, a copper property not being like a placer [surface gold mine], a poor man's mine. However, a dozen of the "Sourdoughs" recorded their claims. But when, the following year, they were offered what to them was the fabulous price of $25,000 apiece . . . and [with] what alacrity! [They] sold their interests to a "green young college feller" from New York.

----

*Courtesy of the Cordova Times and the Cordova Historical Society, 1967.

That "green young college feller," Stephen Birch, quietly developed his copper properties in the face of much ridicule from more experienced miners. With the help of the Guggenheim and Morgan interests, financial magnates of the East Coast, he formed the Kennecott Copper Corporation in 1906. By 1919 the mine had become the richest known concentration of copper in the world.

Photo opposite: The ghost town of Latouche, located in southwestern Prince William Sound, was once inhabited by several thousand people. The Beatson Copper Mine, owned by Kennecott Mining Company, operated here from 1903 to 1930 and was the largest and most productive copper mine in the Prince William Sound region.
NEIL AND ELIZABETH JOHANNSEN

*Michael J. Heney sank his personal fortune into building a railroad
from Cordova to the Alaskan Interior. This 1906 photograph shows
workers beginning construction of the railroad from Cordova. Spike
Island is in the distance.*

KEN HINCHEY — ALAGCO COLLECTION
COOK INLET HISTORICAL SOCIETY

*The "Million Dollar Bridge," considered impossible to build, spanned
the Copper River between Miles and Childs glaciers. The Copper
River and Northwestern Railway eventually linked the Kennecott
copper mines with the saltwater port of Cordova.*

KEN HINCHEY — ALAGCO COLLECTION
COOK INLET HISTORICAL SOCIETY

Railroad Building

Railroad from Valdez. Miners in the Interior needed a way to get their ore to market. In early 1898, a government reconnaissance party under the direction of B. F. Millard sought a feasible railroad route from tidewater to the town of Eagle on the Yukon River. This party made two initial surveys, one up the Copper River and the other from Valdez through Keystone Canyon. They determined that the railroad should be built from Valdez, due to the great engineering difficulties involved with the Copper River route. Construction of the new railroad from Valdez started in 1905, supervised by Millard and financed by money from the East Coast.

Michael J. Heney. During that year a newspaper reporter interviewed industrial magnate Daniel Guggenheim in New York about his interests in Alaska. Guggenheim enthusiastically mentioned his plans for the railway project from Valdez. Michael J. Heney, who had been contracting constructor for the White Pass and Yukon Railway, one of the greatest engineering feats of the era, happened to hear about the interview.

The following winter Heney landed at Valdez with a few companions and headed up the Valdez railroad right-of-way and over the mountains. A few weeks later Heney dashed to New York, told Guggenheim that he was making a mistake, and showed him a survey of the Copper River route that he had just made. Guggenheim temporarily halted the Valdez project and sent an engineer to resurvey Heney's proposed alternate route. The engineer suggested starting the railway from the oil boom town of Katalla, east of the Copper River Delta, also located near the recently discovered Bering River coal beds. A million dollars was earmarked for the project. Meanwhile Heney stubbornly insisted that Cordova was the only safe year-round port in the vicinity and began his own railroad from that direction in 1906, sinking his personal fortune into the project. The first big winter storm of the year swept the artificial breakwater and wharf of Katalla from the unprotected coast.

The New York interests abandoned the Katalla project, reimbursed Heney, and awarded him a contract for building the railway. Rex Beach's novel, *The Iron Trail,* recounts the story of Heney's perseverance.

Copper River and Northwestern Railway. Prior to World War I, the federal government restricted coal mining and other mineral development in Alaska in response to coal interests on the East Coast who did not want mineral resources of Alaska developed. Without access to coal, Katalla became overnight a ghost town, and plans were abandoned for building a railroad to the Alaskan Interior. The Copper River and Northwestern Railway, however, was built according to Heney's original proposal from Cordova to the Kennecott copper mines. A spur was also built to Chitina.

The fabulously rich ore bodies of the Kennecott mines were worked until the late 1930s, with Cordova thriving as the ocean shipping port for the copper ore. By 1938 most high-grade ore had been removed, making the mines unprofitable. The railway shut down soon afterwards. Today portions of the old railway bed have been converted to highway, and engineering monuments, such as the Million Dollar Bridge across the Copper River near Miles Glacier, recall a busier era.

Fox Farming

First Attempts. Many prospectors who originally traveled north in quest of glittering metal soon found a new source of income that permitted them to maintain lifestyles of solitude and independence.

In Alaska, fox farming had its beginnings in the 1890s on the Pribilof Islands. Believing that fox farming might be successful in Prince William Sound, Fred Liljegren, a Swede, in 1894 planted blue foxes, a species originally imported from Greenland, on tiny Seal Island, east of Knight Island. The following year he expanded by moving a few miles north to larger Storey Island. Numbers of local residents followed Liljegren's example and established fox farms, but most of these early attempts failed because of a poor market for the furs.

Fox Farms Become Widespread. Beginning in 1913, however, the fashion-conscious of New York and Paris suddenly decided that blue fox furs were stylish. By the 1920s, nearly every available island in the sound was being used as a fox farm. Pelts rose from a price of $12.50 each in 1903 to $250.00 in 1921. In 1922 the Prince William Sound fox farms shipped $100,000 worth of skins from the distribution center of Valdez.

To establish oneself as a fox farmer required a considerable investment of time and money. A breeding pair of foxes could cost up to $400.00. A prospective farmer had to build a cabin, feed houses, perhaps a dock and other improvements, and even then it was at least two years before he could sell the first pelt.

A good fox island, leased from the U.S. Forest Service for a nominal sum, filled several requirements. As the foxes ran in a largely wild state, the island had to be far enough from other land to prevent the animals from swimming away. The foxes also needed denning grounds in well-drained soil under trees, rocky ledges or other naturally sheltered areas. The farmer had to have an adequate harbor for boat access. Further, there had to be a dependable food supply; the foxes ate spawning salmon from streams, fish heads and intestines discarded by local canneries, or even an occasional whale washed up on the beach.

The fox farmer usually fed his animals from 8 foot [2.4 m] square log feed houses built at intervals along the shore. The foxes became familiar with these feed houses, and during the trapping season in December, when the foxes were about 10 months old, the entryway to the feedhouse was rearranged to enable the animal to enter but not leave.

Many fox farmers led a dual existence, prospecting for gold or copper in the summer and retiring to their fox islands in the winter. During Prohibition, some farmers supplemented their income by manufacturing bootleg liquor, sidestepping federal officials suspicious of the large shipments of grain ostensibly ordered to feed hungry foxes. The Cordova Centennial Museum displays a large old copper still of this era.

By 1926 inferior pelts flooded the world market, the whims of fashion changed, and the fox farmers had to find a new way to make a living.

Canneries and Salteries

Herring, Salmon and Fish Traps. Only a few canneries existed in Prince William Sound prior to the 1920s. A salmon cannery is reported to have operated on Wingham Island (southeast of Cordova) as early as 1889. The Orca cannery, just north of Cordova, began processing salmon in 1893. By the turn of the century, fishermen were harvesting red salmon of the Copper River and boating their catches to Eyak Lake, then hauling them by mule-drawn tram to floating canneries at Odiak Slough on Orca Inlet.

By World War I, canneries and salteries, a few of which even imported Chinese workers from San Francisco for the summer, were in operation all

Seemingly limitless quantities of salmon prompted the construction of dozens of canneries in the 1920s. Here red salmon are being unloaded at Eyak, near Cordova.

over Prince William Sound. Some places, such as the saltery at Port Oceanic on Knight Island, rendered herring into oil, meal and fertilizer. Many female workers, called "gibbers" (after a type of tiny fish-cleaning knife) were imported each season from the Pacific Northwest to clean herring. During most of the year these salteries were staffed by an all-male crew. A significant percentage of the gibbers did supplemental work, usually at night, and were able to return south with a handsome stake.

Canneries processed salmon taken by pursing and seining boats and by fish traps, which caught tens of thousands of fish en route to spawning grounds. One Prince William Sound fish trap caught a million salmon a season. Some fish traps were attached to pilings along the shore, while in deep water, floating traps were secured by huge long-line anchors.

The use of fish traps soon became controversial. Many fishermen felt the traps depleted the salmon runs, since no provisions were made to insure the perpetuity of populations of spawning salmon. The traps provided a substantial income for "Lower Forty-Eight" cannery owners. Consequently, "fish pirates" (local fishermen) by the dozens regularly robbed the traps. Watchmen stationed at the traps were dealt with by bribery or violence. The pirates then audaciously sold their "catch" to the cannery owners, who, while desperately needing the fish, were often powerless to stop the "fish pirates" because local courts were reluctant to convict local fishermen. In his autobiography, *North to Danger,* Virgil Burford, who lived in Cordova most of his life, recounts many of these confrontations. With the advent of statehood in 1959, fish traps became illegal in the sound. By the 1960s, runs of salmon had become much smaller, resulting in the closing of many canneries in the sound.

Scientific Expeditions

Harriman Expedition. A few people journeyed to Prince William Sound for reasons other than wealth. One such group was the Harriman Alaska Expedition, composed of a large group of scientists, who, in 1899, under the sponsorship of railroad financier Edward Henry Harriman (1848-1909) chartered the steamship *George W. Elder.* For about a month, the expedition intensively studied the glaciers, flora and fauna of the sound. They named Columbia Glacier for Columbia University in New York. They also named the glaciers of College Fiord — those on the west for women's colleges and those on the east for men's colleges. While exploring College Fiord, the Harriman party discovered a new fiord, which they named Harriman Fiord, in honor of the expedition's leader. Their scholarly, voluminous reports rank among the most important records ever compiled about Prince William Sound.

Photo opposite: Rotting fish nets at Port Nellie Juan Cannery symbolize the slowdown of salmon fishing, once a thriving industry in Prince William Sound.

NEIL AND ELIZABETH JOHANNSEN

Government Expeditions. With the influx of prospectors in 1898, the research work of the U.S. Coast and Geodetic Survey and the U.S. Geological Survey assumed added importance. Grant, Higgins and Shrader were among the first geologists to survey and map Prince William Sound, naming many geographic points for local miners or fox farmers.

Captain Abercrombie and Captain Glenn of the U.S. Army also made extensive reconnaissances of Prince William Sound. Abercrombie and his men, working from their base at Fort Liscum (then called Fort Valdez), near the mining town of Valdez, provided assistance in the form of food, shelter and rescue work for the hordes of "98ers" attempting to reach the Klondike.

Observing the difficulties that these first prospectors had in trying to cross Valdez Glacier, Abercrombie pioneered a route to the Interior via the Lowe River and Thompson Pass. This route later became known as the Richardson Trail. Today, the Richardson Highway closely parallels the route of the original trail.

Looking Ahead

Land Ownership. Nearly all land within the sound lies in Chugach National Forest. Other types of land ownership in the sound, in addition to the private land contained in the communities of Valdez, Cordova and Whittier, include Native village and corporation lands, patented mining claims, federal lighthouse withdrawals, state lands and a scattering of small private home, industrial and fish cannery sites.

Chugach National Forest. Named for the Chugach Eskimo, Chugach National Forest, oldest and second largest of the National Forests, was set aside in 1892 by President Benjamin Harrison and enlarged in 1907. It encompasses nearly 7400 square miles [20,000 sq km] and includes most of Prince William Sound, the eastern half of the Kenai Peninsula, the Copper River Delta and Afognak Island.

The U.S. Forest Service coordinates use of such natural resources as timber, minerals, fisheries, wildlife and recreation. Such coordination can be complex and controversial. For example, if too much timber were cut, recreation values might suffer, and likewise, if logging ceased, local mills could close, costing jobs and forest products. Planning in Chugach National Forest revolves around zoning based on major vegetative ecosystems and human needs. In addition, special management zones have been set aside to protect unique values such as wilderness, scenery and wildlife. Harriman Fiord and Columbia Glacier are under study for possible management as Scenic Areas, which means that they would be managed in a near natural state. The Nellie Juan area of western Prince William Sound is being studied for classification as a Wilderness Area. The Forest Service cooperates with the Alaska Department of Fish and Game in maintaining most of the Copper River Delta as a Game Management Area.

A few areas of the sound are managed for timber production. Logging operations are located on Montague Island and in the Port Wells area. Timber from Montague Island is rafted to Seward, where about half is exported to Japan after primary manufacture as cants, and the remainder is used locally for lumber. Logs from the Port Wells area are towed to Whittier and then shipped by rail to Anchorage, where most of the lumber is used for construction. Species cut are Sitka spruce, western hemlock and mountain hemlock. Since the sound is near the northern and western limits of these species' range and because growing seasons are relatively short, management plans take into account the 110 years needed for a new forest to regenerate and reach commercial size.

The Native Claims Act. The Alaska Native Land Claims Settlement Act of 1971 is having a profound impact on the sound. Under the Act, the Native villages of Tatitlek and Chenega are each entitled to select more than 69,000 acres [*27,900 hectares*] from Chugach National Forest. The selections must be made within the general vicinity of the villages. These Native lands should be respected as private property by visitors to the sound.

Trucks carrying lengths of 48 inch [122 cm] *diameter pipe for construction of the Trans-Alaska Pipeline lumber toward the top of Thompson Pass near Valdez.*
ALYESKA PIPELINE SERVICE COMPANY

The Trans-Alaska Oil Pipeline. In early 1974, construction began on the Trans-Alaska Pipeline, the most expensive privately funded construction project in history. Resulting from a major oil discovery in 1968 on Alaska's North Slope, the 48 inch [*122 cm*] diameter pipeline, stretching 798 miles [*1284 km*], will deliver the "black gold" from the North Slope to Port Valdez.

Oil line construction was delayed several years to meet requirements for a detailed environmental impact statement and because of court injunctions placed by concerned fishermen and conservation groups. To prevent oil spillage along the pipeline, the Alyeska Pipeline Service Company plans construction of an Oil Movement Control Center at Valdez. Here a computer system will receive continuous input from flow, pressure, and seismic sensors along the route. Should a problem occur, such as an earthquake of a certain intensity, the oil line could be shut down, limiting the chance for major spills.

From the huge tank farm on the south shore of Port Valdez, tankers weighing up to 150,000 deadweight tons and up to 800 to 1000 feet [*270 to 300 m*] long will deliver crude oil to markets in the western United States. Some local fishermen are concerned about the tankers' impact on commercial fishing. Plans are being made to reduce pollution in the waters of Port Valdez through use of a tanker ballast water treatment center at the Valdez terminal. Ballast water from arriving tankers will be processed to remove residual oil; the treated water, discharged into Port Valdez, must meet state and federal water quality requirements. The Coast Guard estimates, however, that thousands of gallons of oil may be lost in waters of Port Valdez each year.

The Coast Guard is installing numerous radar and radio navigation stations along the route to minimize the possibility of accidents, particularly in such constricted areas as Valdez Narrows and Hinchinbrook Entrance. Sophisticated navigational gear will be used to regulate marine traffic in the tanker lanes. Despite such measures, however, crab, halibut and shrimp fishermen may find their livelihood hampered by tankers striking and severing long-line gear.

A Restless Land

Sudden or Slow. Incessantly, powerful geologic forces work to reshape the topography of Prince William Sound. Movements deep within the earth's crust thrust mountain masses upward. Such movements may be sudden and violent, as demonstrated by the 1964 Good Friday earthquake, or almost imperceptible, as the land is carved into sawtoothed mountains and U-shaped valleys by flowing water and scouring glacial ice. Although less extensive today than thousands of years ago, when glacial ice covered most of Prince William Sound, glaciers are still the most visible sculpturing agent of the sound.

Valdez and Orca Formations. Situated near the "Rim of Fire" that girdles much of the Pacific Ocean, Prince William Sound is linked to the highly active volcanic belt that stretches from the Alaska Panhandle through Southcentral Alaska to the Aleutian Chain. The rugged mountain masses of the sound are witness to the extensive tectonic activity of this region.

The highly contorted sedimentary and volcanic rocks of the sound are of comparatively recent origin. Geologists have identified two major formations: the Valdez group, in the northern and western parts of the sound, which is a predominantly slate and granitic sequence of probable Jurassic or Cretaceous age (135 to 180 million years old), and the Orca group in southern and eastern Prince William Sound, which is a sequence of folded siltstone, argillite, graywackes and mixed metamorphic and volcanic rocks of early Tertiary age (less than 63 million years old). Outcrops of both formations may be found in several locations. Among the more prominent are the granitic cliffs of Esther Passage near Port Wells and Granite Bay near the head of Wells Bay. Pillow lava, formed by molten rock flowing into water, is visible along the edges of Knight Island and on the south coast of Glacier Island.

Photo opposite: Granite Bay in northern Prince William Sound is flanked by precipitous rock cliffs. Glaciers carved the rugged peaks and valleys of the sound thousands of years ago.
WILL TROYER

Submergence and Uplift. Shorelines record the periodic process of uplift and submergence. In areas of subsidence, salt water encroaches on the land, killing plant root systems and transforming beachfront trees into a gray ghost forest. Where the land has risen, new beachlines are created below the former water levels. Such changes are caused by movements of the earth's crust along "faults," zones of weakness. Slippage of the earth's crust along these lines may be gradual over a period of centuries, or violent and extremely sudden, as in the case of earthquakes. Valdez, on the northeastern corner of the sound, has experienced more than 70 major earthquakes since records began to be kept in 1898. Each earthquake measured 5.0 or greater on the Richter scale.

1964 Good Friday Earthquake

A Cataclysmic Upheaval. The mountain-shaping forces of Prince William Sound came to a sudden, dramatic climax in the late afternoon of March 27, 1964. Deep in bedrock below Miner's Lake a few miles west of Columbia Glacier, layers of twisting and straining rock abruptly gave way with a force that spread devastation over a 500 mile [*800 km*] wide area. Shock waves — crackling, billowing and shuddering their way through the earth at thousands of miles per hour — capriciously wreaked havoc throughout Southcentral Alaska. In Anchorage, 100 miles [*160 km*] from the epicenter, many buildings were flattened, while adjacent structures amazingly withstood the tremors without so much as a crack. An unstable layer of blue clay underlying part of the city caused a portion of the Turnagain residential area to slide toward upper Cook Inlet.

The ocean bottom plunged and shook violently. Ensuing submarine landslides set millions of tons of water in motion. Localized seismic sea waves and great tsunamis inundated most of the shorelines and communities of Prince William Sound, destroyed much of the city of Kodiak and even flooded Crescent City, California, thousands of miles to the south.

In a matter of minutes, 115 people lost their lives. Damages were estimated at more than $750,000,000.

The Good Friday earthquake was the most violent ever recorded on the North American continent. Registering between 8.4 and 8.6 on the Richter scale, the earth tremors lasted three to five minutes. Shock waves produced immediate, cataclysmic changes. In the northwestern sound, land subsided an average of 2.5 feet [*0.8 m*], while in the eastern sound, land rose an average of 6 feet [*1.8 m*]. At the south end of Montague Island, land rose as much as 38 feet [*12 m*], producing extensive new beachlines.

Most damage and loss of life from the earthquake occurred in Prince William Sound. Although earth tremors were in themselves disastrous, huge seismic sea waves caused most of the horror and destruction.

At Patton Bay, Montague Island, was one of the few visible fault lines resulting from the 1964 Good Friday earthquake.
U.S. GEOLOGICAL SURVEY

Valdez. Many townspeople were standing on the Valdez city dock watching the *Chena*, a 400 foot [*122 m*] freighter, discharge cargo, when at 5:36 in the afternoon the earthquake struck. As violent rolling motions increased, the city dock slipped into the deep waters of Port Valdez and bystanders vanished in seconds. Generated by an underwater landslide beneath the dock, huge waves sloshed back and forth in Port Valdez, first tossing the *Chena* inland, then washing it back out into open water. The earthquake took a toll of 31 lives in Valdez.

A few miles west of Valdez, near Shoup Glacier, massive sea waves from an undersea landslide, similar to the one beneath the Valdez city dock, swept 170 feet [*52 m*] above the tideline and destroyed the abandoned buildings of the Cliff Mine. After the earthquake geologists confirmed that Valdez was situated on highly unstable glacial sediments, which could avalanche again into Port Valdez during a severe earthquake. Residents resolved to rebuild their town at a new location on bedrock several miles to the west. Modern Valdez now occupies this site.

Whittier. Following long minutes of violent, teeth-jarring earth movements, residents of Whittier saw three successive sea waves strike their town. The

Seismic sea waves tossed the freighter CHENA *inland and then back out to sea when the 1964 Good Friday earthquake devastated the town of Valdez. The ship survived the disaster almost unscathed. A few weeks later, the vessel was able to anchor amid the debris of badly-damaged Whittier.*
U.S. ARMY PHOTO

second wave, caused by an undersea slide, was the highest and most destructive. Eyewitnesses described it as a pillaring wall of water, 30 to 50 feet [*9 to 15 m*] high, which welled up in the center of Passage Canal, as if caused by a mighty underwater explosion, and then rolled shoreward. A few miles from Whittier the wave crested at 104 feet [*32 m*] on the northwestern shore and reached 82 feet [*25 m*] at the north end of Passage Canal about 2 miles [*3 km*] from Whittier. Thirteen people died, ten of whom were visiting the home of a worker at the Columbia Lumber Company. Hardly a trace of the lumber mill remained after the sea wave hit.

Cordova. Cordova, on the eastern side of the sound, suffered comparatively little sea wave damage, though lands were uplifted more than 6 feet [*1.8 m*]. Extensive redredging of the harbor and rebuilding of cannery docks were required after the quake. The airport runway, 13 miles [*20 km*] from Cordova, was split by earth cracks. At Point Whitshed, a few miles south of Cordova, one man was drowned by sea waves.

These trees, 100 feet [30 m] above tidewater, were toppled by a seismic sea wave resulting from the 1964 Good Friday earthquake. The wave, created by an undersea landslide in Port Valdez near Shoup Glacier, deposited silt and sand 220 feet [73 m] above salt water.

U.S. GEOLOGICAL SURVEY

Seward. This port community, located a few miles southwest of Prince William Sound and facing the Gulf of Alaska, suffered extensive damage. Part of the waterfront shuddered into Resurrection Bay. Seismic sea waves engulfed the town. The result was 13 dead amid a tangle of railroad cars, burning oil storage tanks and debris. Two weeks after the earthquake an enterprising local fisherman towed back to town one of the railroad tank cars that had been swept miles out into the bay. Another freight car still rests hundreds of yards inland next to the Seward Highway.

Chenega. The worst single disaster of the Good Friday earthquake took place in southwest Prince William Sound at the native village of Chenega. A sea wave sucked away all the buildings except for the school and one house. Twenty-three of the some eighty inhabitants of this village, thirteen of them children, were swept away by water. The survivors abandoned the village and moved to Tatitlek on the eastern edge of the sound.

Glaciers and Fiords

Shaper of the Land. Glaciers occur in most major drainages in Prince William Sound. More than any other single geologic force, these "rivers of ice" have sculpted the region's peaks, fiords and islands.

World temperatures began to grow colder about one million years ago. With gradually colder annual temperatures, winter snowpacks did not completely melt during the following warm seasons. Over a period of years, accumulations of snow were compressed by successive snowfalls that slowly recrystallized into glacial ice. Such compressed ice, though a crystalline solid, flows downhill in response to the forces of gravity. Glacial ice casts a brilliant aqua reflection, absorbing other colors.

Flowing rivers of ice, reaching down from mountain peaks, joined to form extensive piedmont glaciers, which covered Prince William Sound with a blanket of ice several thousand feet thick. These Ice Age glaciers created the basic topography of the sound as it exists today. Armed with debris from landslides, freeze-thaw frost action, and, most important, a great volume of rocks carried along on the bottom of the ice mass, glaciers scoured and grooved the sides of mountains and floors of valleys, or completely covered smaller mountains, thereby creating the precipitous landforms of peaks and fiords and multitude of gently rounded islands that today are so characteristic of the scenery of the sound.

When temperatures in Alaska began to moderate, ice sheets covering large parts of Alaska and Canada retreated. Many of the extensive terminal moraines deposited by the retreating glaciers are now hidden beneath the waters of the sound.

Today, two glacial areas are of special interest to the visitor: College Fiord – Harriman Fiord and Columbia Glacier.

Harriman Fiord - College Fiord

"Glacier Bay of the North." Dozens of glaciers dominate the iceberg-choked fiords of northwestern Prince William Sound. Expanses of barren rock show that plantlife has not yet had sufficient time to gain a foothold in this recently ice-mantled landscape. This northwestern region contains an excellent natural laboratory in which to study the effects of retreating and advancing glaciers. This region also contains the highest mountain in the Prince William Sound area, Mt. Marcus Baker, 13,176 feet [*4016 m*].

Photo opposite: Harvard Glacier, at the head of College Fiord, is one of dozens of glaciers in the College Fiord — Harriman Fiord region. These glaciers were named for American colleges and universities by the Harriman Alaska Expedition of 1899.
LARRY MAYO, U.S. GEOLOGICAL SURVEY

Harriman Fiord. The Harriman Alaska Expedition of 1899, which made extensive studies of the major glaciers of the sound, discovered and named glacier-rich Harriman Fiord for E. H. Harriman (1848-1909), founder of the Great Northern Railroad and sponsor of the expedition. Previous explorers had assumed that land lay behind the tidewater terminus of Barry Glacier, but the Harriman Expedition followed the face of the glacier into a heretofore unknown and highly scenic body of water encircled by at least eleven major glaciers.

College Fiord. Harvard and Yale glaciers dominate this iceberg-choked arm of Prince William Sound. Ferry passengers traveling across Port Wells may see the blue shimmer of Harvard Glacier 30 miles [*48 km*] to the north. This glacier, about 24 miles [*39 km*] long, is one of two in the sound that in recent years has increased slightly in size due to local tidal influences (the other is Meares Glacier at the head of Unakwik Inlet).

Small hanging glaciers line both sides of College Fiord. Sierra Club founder John Muir, a member of the Harriman Expedition, likened this aggregation to the glaciers of his beloved Glacier Bay, and wrote of College Fiord:

> *. . . the cascading glaciers . . . named for Wellesley, Vassar, Bryn Mawr, Smith and Radcliffe colleges are the finest and wildest of their kind, looking, as they come bounding down a smooth mountainside through the midst of lush flowery gardens and goat pastures, like tremendous, dancing cataracts in the prime of flood.*

The expedition named the glaciers on the west side of College Fiord for American women's colleges, while the glaciers on the east side and at the head of the arm received the names of men's colleges.

Columbia Glacier

An Immense River of Ice. This impressive and active glacier, named by the Harriman Expedition for Columbia University in New York City, is the largest in Prince William Sound and one of the largest tidewater glaciers in Alaska. About 41 miles [*66 km*] long, Columbia Glacier covers approximately 440 square miles [*708 sq km*]. During recent studies, the scientists of the U.S. Geological Survey discovered ice depths as great as 4200 feet [*1300 m*], 2500 feet [*750 m*] of which are below sea level. Viewed from Columbia Bay, only 10 to 12 miles [*16 to 19 km*] of the glacier are visible. Peaks of the Chugach Mountains on the left (as seen from the bay) rise to heights of 9000 feet [*2700 m*], while at the head of the glacier, peaks reach even greater heights, culminating in Mt. Witherspoon, 12,012 feet [*3661 m*], Mt. Valhalla, 12,135 feet [*3700 m*], Mt. Gilbert Lewis, 12,200 feet [*3720 m*], and Mt. Willard Gibbs, 12,225 feet [*3726 m*].

Uncertain State of Equilibrium. Columbia Glacier has three main branches. The northern branch, with its source in the highest peaks of the Chugach Mountains, is very active and produces great volumes of ice, while the two more southern branches are less extensive and in recent years have receded, creating a virtual state of equilibrium at the glacier terminus in Columbia Bay. The position of the terminus apparently has not undergone significant change since it was first sighted in 1794 by Captain George Vancouver of the British Royal Navy. This is in contrast to other glaciers in the sound, most of which have shrunk considerably since scientific observations began.

Columbia Glacier has been subject, however, to small fluctuations. The last such advance peaked only a few decades ago when the terminus overrode the northern end of Heather Island. Some geologists believe that the equilibrium of the glacier may have been drastically altered in 1973 by the sudden emptying of a glacially dammed lake on the northwest side. The disturbance may set off a monumental retreat of ice over the next few decades. Most scientists maintain, however, that the glacier is quite vigorous and "healthy."

Glaciologists of the U.S. Geological Survey have measured the flow rate at the center of the glacier by tracing the movement of medial moraine debris on the glacier surface. Their research shows the rate of flow averages 10 feet [3 m] per day. This figure is matched by few other glaciers in Alaska.

Aquamarine Cliff of Ice. The width of the terminus on the west side of Heather Island is about 2.5 miles [4 km]. The glacier's front continues to the east of Heather Island for nearly 2 miles [3 km] across the shallow waters of the eastern arm of Columbia Bay. The tidal terminus in the western arm of Columbia Bay, which rises in spots as high as 300 feet [100 m] above the water, discharges the greatest volumes of ice. Water depths at the face range from approximately 12 to 40 feet [4 to 14 m], according to recent studies in which a remote-controlled skiff was used to take soundings.

Contrary to popular opinion, recent research has also shown that there is no underwater ice shelf in front of Columbia Glacier. Where measured, the ice cliff has been shown to be nearly vertical in profile and similar to the visible portion of the ice cliff above water.

Icebergs. Giant pieces of ice that regularly topple from the face of the glacier are an ever-fascinating spectacle. Onlookers may sometimes predict the location of the next big icefall into Columbia Bay by watching for an outward-leaning spur of ice with small trickles of ice falling from behind the spur.

Photo following page: Columbia Glacier, one of the largest tidewater glaciers in Alaska, has its origins in the high snowfields of the Chugach Mountains. This 41 mile [66 km] long "river of ice" moves downslope as rapidly as 10 feet [3 m] a day, ending at an ice cliff in Columbia Bay that is over 4 miles [7 km] wide.

AUSTIN POST, U.S. GEOLOGICAL SURVEY

The icebergs that Columbia Glacier discharges into Columbia Bay are too small to last more than a few weeks in salt water, and most fall apart and melt in a few hours or days. The actual age of these icebergs, often covered with rock debris carried down from mountain peaks, is difficult to determine. Glaciologists estimate that icebergs calved from the tidal terminus today may have fallen as snow on the upper reaches of the glacier about the time of Christ.

Gold and Sightseers. Various motives have attracted persons to Columbia Glacier. Following the discovery of gold near the glacier in 1911, miners hauled heavy equipment and supplies over an arduous 8 mile [*13 km*] trail that led from the shore of Port Valdez past Shoup Glacier and then over a 4400 foot [*1340 m*] pass to reach Gold King Camp, situated on the upper flanks of the glacier. The Ruff and Tuff Gold Mine, worked during the 1930s, was located on a nunatak (mountain "island" in a "river" of ice) in the middle of the glacier! The mine could only be reached by courageous bush pilots who landed near the mine on smooth areas of snow-covered ice. Alaska bush pilot Bob Reeve, owner of the Ruff and Tuff Gold Mine and founder of Reeve Aleutian Airways, gained his initial fame by making such landings. Using a ski-equipped plane, he took off from the mud flats near Valdez and landed on glacial ice.

In the first decades of this century ships of the Alaska Steamship Company, while en route to Valdez, made detours to Columbia Bay to allow passengers to see the glacier at close hand. Today, many visitors traveling on Alaska state ferries, cruise vessels or charter aircraft rate Columbia Glacier as the highlight of their trip to Prince William Sound.

Take Raingear

Wet but Variable Weather. The weather of Prince William Sound is characterized by extensive cloud cover and heavy precipitation, interspersed with periods of clear skies. The most favorable weather generally occurs during June and July. Periods of heavy rain, accompanied by strong, gusty winds, begin in August and last through fall. From December to April deep snows blanket the lands of the sound. Wise travelers will be prepared for abrupt changes in weather; sunshine may quickly turn to overcast and rain.

Temperature. Because of the moderating influences of the Gulf of Alaska, air temperatures in the sound do not reach extremes commonly found in Interior Alaska. Most water areas remain ice-free year-round. Average summer temperatures range from 40° to 60° F [4.4° to 15.6° C]. July and August are the warmest months. Evenings are cooler. The highest surface temperature in the sound ever recorded was 87° F [30.6° C] at Valdez; the lowest was –33° F [–36.1° C] at Cordova. Winter weather in the sound tends to be cold and stormy, with daytime temperatures averaging 25° F [–3.9° C] at sea level. Periods of sub-zero temperatures are uncommon and usually of short duration.

Precipitation. Rainfall (or in winter months, snow) can be expected throughout the year. Precipitation increases near the coastal mountains, but rain generally falls throughout the sound during the summer months approximately one-third of the time. Some years clear skies occur only about three to five days a month. Total annual precipitation ranges from 60 inches [152 cm] at Valdez to 180 inches [457 cm] at Whittier. Annual winter snowfalls at Whittier, the community with the wettest weather, often exceed 25 feet [7.6 m] per year.

Photo opposite: Prince William Sound receives up to 180 inches [557 cm] of precipitation a year. The rainy summers are made more pleasant by wearing proper clothing.

Wind. Two specialized forms of wind are found in Prince William Sound: winds occurring over large areas between high and low pressure areas and strong localized gusts known as williwaws. The rugged mountain ranges ringing the sound form a natural barrier between the weather system of the Gulf of Alaska, with its relatively stable temperatures, and that of Interior Alaska, where temperatures fluctuate more than 150° F [83° C] between summer and winter. Mountain peaks and ridges shield some parts of the sound from these winds, while in other areas they are diverted and channeled through mountain passes and fiords. When winds are "funneled" through such areas, velocities increase significantly. During winter months, for example, heavy cool air often spills from high pressure areas in Interior Alaska to low pressure areas of the sound, through such passes as Port Wells, Portage Pass, Copper River Valley or Port Valdez, creating high-velocity winds and extremely rough seas. Winds have attained sufficient force to blow empty railroad freight cars off the tracks in Bear Valley, between Portage and Whittier.

Small-boat and aircraft operators should be constantly alert to the danger of another form of windstorm: the williwaw. These localized winds, difficult to predict, can reach velocities of more than 100 miles per hour [160 km/h], quickly transforming a seemingly well-protected cove into a raging sea. Williwaws occur when a mass of air becomes "dammed up" on the windward side of a mountain, then suddenly spills over the lee side of the mountain, producing a high-velocity, down-slope wind.

Most over-water areas of the sound experience calm air about 30 percent of the time. Wind speeds in protected areas average 5 miles per hour [8 km/h] in contrast to 15 miles per hour [24 km/h] over open waters of the Gulf of Alaska.

Surface Water Temperatures. Though Prince William Sound is the most northerly ice-free embayment on the Pacific Northwest Coast, only wetsuit-equipped swimmers should venture into sound waters. Regardless of the season, if a human being is immersed in this cold water, hypothermia (loss of body heat) may occur and may result in death in minutes. Occasionally a sun-warmed cove is suitable for wading. Water temperatures vary from a high average temperature of 55° F [12.8° C] in August to a low average of 37° F [2.8° C] in February. Many of the smaller bays and coves freeze over in winter.

Personal Clothing and Equipment. The season and expected weather determine the type of clothing to wear in the sound. During summer months, when overcast and rainy weather may be expected, wear warm wool clothing and appropriate underwear. High-quality waterproof raingear, including hat and boots, is essential.

Except for passengers on cruise vessels or state-operated ferries, a long raincoat is not recommended, as it may hamper walking through

Frequent winter snowstorms alternate with beautiful blue-sky days. Snow has been reported in drifts 100 feet [33 m] deep. This scene is at Double Bay, Hinchinbrook Island.

CHARLES D. EVANS

undergrowth or snag on boat fixtures. A three-quarter length rainjacket, worn with rainpants, makes the best ensemble. Avoid pants with cuffs, as they hold sand, gravel, twigs and rain and may catch on boat fittings. Waterproof boots with nonslip soles are best. Boat decks, rocks, logs or piers may be coated with moss or with a film of gasoline or oil and may be as slippery as an ice-skating rink.

Ferry passengers should dress casually and comfortably. Be prepared for rain and cool temperatures but also remember to bring along sun lotion and sunglasses, as days may be sunny and bright.

A key consideration when visiting the sound is to keep both dry and warm. Wet clothing drains necessary body warmth. Always carry extra dry clothes. Fishermen, who are active in the sound summer and winter, habitually wear wool or cotton sweatshirts in layers that can be easily put on or taken off. Sou'wester hats are salty looking and practical.

In the winter visitors to the sound should be outfitted for harsh and demanding weather conditions. Snow, freezing rain and gale winds require top quality warm and waterproof clothing. Woolen clothing, warm gloves with waterproof shells and raingear are the minimum requirements. Down gear is not recommended for use in the sound. Down is exceedingly hydroscopic, absorbing and retaining moisture. A wet down jacket has virtually no insulating properties and is very difficult to dry under outdoor conditions. Woolen garments are highly recommended, as even wet wool keeps the wearer warm. Jackets and sweaters made with synthetic down-like material, such as *Polarguard* or *Fiberfill II,* are also suitable, as these synthetic materials do not absorb water and can be wrung dry should they become rain or spray soaked.

Abundance and Diversity

Diverse Wildlife Populations. The mainland and offshore islands of Prince William Sound support a variety of birds and land animals, while bays, coves, passages and open water areas contain numerous species of aquatic mammals and sea life. Species rare or locally extinct in many other parts of the world, such as bald eagles, several species of toothed and baleen whales and sea otters, are common in the sound. Binoculars, patience and sharp eyes may reward visitors with views of more than 200 species of birds, 40 species of mammals and countless species of fish. Some of the more common or typical species are described in the following pages. A complete checklist of birds and mammals is contained in the Appendix.

Land Mammals

Brown Bear *(Ursus arctos).* Brown bears inhabit the southern and eastern sound but are rarely seen by casual visitors. Often called the "brownie," this large bear is typically dark brown to blonde in color and is identified by its dish-shaped face and prominent hump between the shoulders. It is closely related to the smaller grizzly bear of Interior Alaska. Brown bears may weigh more than 1000 pounds [*450 kg*] and are dangerous, especially when accompanied by cubs or when suddenly surprised.

Feeding on both flesh and plants, the brown bear of Alaska is the largest omnivore in the world. In late summer, brown bears congregate along salmon streams, feeding on dead or spawned-out salmon. After gorging on fish and wild berries, building up a thick layer of fat, brown bears enter their winter dormancy in November or December and emerge from this hibernation-like state in April or May.

Populations of brown bears in the sound are confined to Hinchinbrook and Montague islands, and on the mainland from Port Fidalgo eastward, though a few brown bears are found on Hawkins Island and in the western part of the sound. According to historical records, early prospectors avoided Montague Island "due to the population of fierce bears."

Photo opposite: Brown bears, largest omnivores in the world, inhabit Montague and Hinchinbrook islands as well as the eastern edge of the sound. This brown bear munches his spawned-out salmon headfirst at a stream close to Valdez.

ELMER WHITE

Black Bear *(Ursus americanus)*. Ranging over much of the forested area of the sound, this bear is often seen foraging for food along tidal areas. Smaller than the brown bear, this usually shy mammal weighs about 200 pounds [*90 kg*] at maturity. The comparatively rare blue-gray color phase known as the glacier bear occurs primarily in the Yakutat Bay area to the southeast of the sound.

Except for sows with cubs and in locations of food abundance, black bears are normally solitary. Food consists of newly-sprouted vegetation, salmon, wild berries and occasional carrion. In late summer, black bears congregate along salmon spawning streams, gorging themselves on fish to accumulate fat for their winter dormancy. Black bears are common on most of the mainland and occur on some islands but are notably absent from Hinchinbrook and Montague islands, where brown bears are common. Boaters and ferry passengers may see black bears foraging on open slopes and along tidal flats.

Mountain goats lead a precarious existence on the windswept, often snow-covered mainland cliffs of Prince William Sound and the Gulf of Alaska.
NEIL AND ELIZABETH JOHANNSEN

Mountain Goat *(Oreamnos americanus)*. Mountain goats are slightly larger than deer, though stockier, and have short black horns and thick, white woolly coats. Found on alpine and sub-alpine slopes, they are frequently seen on slopes and sheer cliffs between Valdez Arm and Cordova as well as in Port Bainbridge in the southwest sound. These animals feed on alpine grasses, shrubs and mountain hemlock.

Famed English navigator Captain James Cook, R.N., who explored portions of the sound in 1778, collected from the Natives mountain goat skins, which he mistakenly recorded in his journals as being from "white bears."

In late winter and early spring, starving Sitka black-tailed deer, such as these on Hinchinbrook Island, feed on kelp at tideline. Due to the low nutrient value of kelp, however, the deer may starve to death with full stomachs.
CHARLES D. EVANS

Sitka Black-Tailed Deer *(Odocoileus hemionus sitkensis)*. These deer are found primarily on larger islands forested by spruce and hemlock. The coat of this species ranges from reddish-brown in summer to dark gray in winter. Only the male, or buck, grows antlers. Fawns weigh about 7 pounds [*3 kg*] at birth. At maturity does may weigh 100 pounds [*45 kg*] and bucks 150 pounds [*68 kg*].

This species feeds on shrubs and grasses. During winter, deep snows and extreme temperatures force these deer to retreat to the shoreline, where they feed on kelp. Due to the low caloric value of kelp, deer may starve to death even with full stomachs. Over most of their range, Sitka black-tailed deer are numerous and form an important food source for residents of the sound.

Neither Sitka black-tailed deer, nor their larger cousins, the moose, are native to the sound. Between 1916 and 1923, Sitka black-tailed deer from Alexander Archipelago in the Alaska Panhandle were introduced to the sound. The now thriving population of moose on the Copper River Delta stems from transplants made between 1948 and 1958.

Sea otters, once thought extinct, are today one of the most commonly seen marine mammals in Prince William Sound. They occur primarily in shallow southern waters of the sound, particularly on shoals at the north end of Montague Island.
DENNIS BROMLEY

Marine Mammals

Sea Otter *(Enhydra lutris).* The luxurious thick fur of the sea otter almost led to the destruction of this large member of the weasel family in the nineteenth and early twentieth centuries. Russian, and later, American, hunters attracted by the high price sea otter pelts commanded on the Oriental market, hunted this mammal to virtual extinction. Fortunately, localized populations survived, and though recovery from the early slaughter has been slow, today there are more than 100,000 sea otters in Alaska, largely due to strict protection laws. Sea otters, as well as all other marine mammals, are now protected under the recently enacted federal Marine Mammals Act.

Adult sea otters weigh 40 to 80 pounds [*18 to 36 kg*], though exceptional animals may weigh as much as 100 pounds [*45 kg*]. The pelage of the sea otter, ranging from light chocolate brown to black, consists of dense fine underfur intermixed with longer, coarser guard hairs. Older otters, with somewhat silvery heads and long whitish whiskers, are locally known as "old men of the sea."

Sea otters generally feed in shallow water, typically less than 100 feet [*30 m*] deep, diving for sea urchins, crabs, fish and mollusks. They characteristically dive forward head first in a plunging arc with feet and tail descending last. On the surface, otters often swim on their backs and are frequently seen pounding a rock held in one paw against a sea urchin held in the other, trying to crack open the shell.

Today an estimated 4000 to 5000 sea otters inhabit the sound, gradually spreading northward from a small colony at the north end of Montague Island that survived the nineteenth-century slaughter. The largest concentrations occur in shallow waters of Montague Strait and around Hinchinbrook Island. The Alaska Department of Fish and Game has transplanted otters from this group to points along the West Coast from Southeastern Alaska to Northern California. In the last few years otters have become numerous near Knight, Latouche, Bainbridge and Elrington islands. Hundreds of otters inhabit the waters of eastern Prince William Sound. Few otters have yet been seen in northern Prince William Sound with the exception of a maverick group in Harriman Fiord that apparently subsists on blue mussels.

Harbor Seal *(Phoca vitulina)*. The harbor seal, also called the spotted or hair seal, is, in addition to the sea otter, the most frequently seen marine mammal in the sound. Look for an animal about 5 to 6 feet [*1.5 to 1.8 m*] long and weighing about 200 pounds [*90 kg*], resting on floating ice, stretched out on a rock, or floating with its head above water watching for intruders. Color varies from black to cream, but generally the animal's back and sides are blue-gray with black spots, blotches and irregular whitish rings, while the undersides are a lighter color. Unlike the sea otter, with which it is often confused, the harbor seal simply sinks out of sight when diving, while the sea otter plunges in a curving arc.

Harbor seals are particularly common near tidewater glaciers. Ferry passengers may see hundreds of these marine mammals resting on icebergs near Columbia Glacier.

M. WOODBRIDGE WILLIAMS
NATIONAL PARK SERVICE TASK FORCE

Harbor seals are cosmopolitan, ranging over the fringes of the North Pacific and North Atlantic. Although found in coastal waters, this species travels up river systems, following runs of anadromous fish, such as salmon and smelt. Ungainly and slow out of water, this seal is a swift aquanaut, capable of catching fish and diving to depths of more than 300 feet [*91 m*]. Only five to six minutes are usually spent beneath the surface, though seals can remain underwater as long as 20 minutes.

The female harbor seal gives birth to one pup between June and mid July. Pups, born on remote reefs, rocks or sandy beaches, weigh approximately 28 pounds [*13 kg*] at birth and double in weight within the first month. Pups are able to swim almost immediately after birth.

Harbor seals are frequently seen near tidewater glaciers. Ferry passengers are almost certain to see seals resting on floating icebergs in Columbia Bay. Other good spots for seal watching are in College Fiord, Harriman Fiord, Blackstone Bay, Icy Bay and Cochrane Bay. A dozen or so seals are often seen on Esther Rock; watch also near Channel, Little Green and Seal islands.

Steller Sea Lion *(Eumetopias jubata).* Although less frequently seen than the smaller harbor seal, the Steller sea lion is nonetheless an abundant and important member of the wildlife of Prince William Sound. Also called the great northern sea lion, males reach 1500 to 2000 pounds [*680 to 907 kg*] and grow to lengths of 12 to 13 feet [*3.7 to 3.9 m*]; females are smaller, weighing up to 600 pounds [*272 kg*] and growing to 9 feet [*2.7 m*] in length.

In the water it is difficult to distinguish between Steller sea lions, sea otters and harbor seals. In general, the sea lion has a more massive head and points its nose skyward and, unlike the seal and sea otter, has small external ears. The species was first described by the German naturalist Georg Steller (1709-1746), who accompanied Vitus Bering on his voyage of discovery in 1741 (see History chapter). Coastal Natives intensively hunted sea lions for subsistence prior to 1900. Few people, however, have hunted these animals in recent decades, and populations have grown to near maximum levels.

Food, for which these animals dive to depths of more than 50 feet [*15 m*], consists largely of rockfish, herring and occasional salmon.

Land uplift and subsidence caused by the 1964 Good Friday earthquake altered many areas where sea lions traditionally had congregated. Fish Island, near Wooded Islands off the outer coast of Montague Island, for example, was used by about 4000 sea lions before the earthquake, but the island currently supports only half that number due to the island's being uplifted. (A children's book, *Rookery Island,* by Gary Daetz, describes this colony in detail.) Seal Rocks, south of Hinchinbrook Entrance, is now used

Steller sea lion bulls, which may exceed 1500 pounds [750 kg] *in size, jealously guard their harems of females.*
RICHARD W. MONTAGUE

by more than 1500 sea lions, while prior to the earthquake the count was approximately 300. Sea lions also congregate on the south side of Glacier Island, Eleanor Island, Point Elrington, Danger Island, Knowles Head and The Needle. During late fall and early spring, sea lions follow herring into Prince William Sound. At such times these animals are numerous in Orca Bay, Port Fidalgo and Knight Island Passage.

Dall Porpoise *(Phocoenoldes dalli).* This small, fast and friendly member of the whale family is frequently seen by visitors to the sound. Dall porpoises generally travel in groups of two to twelve and often break from the water in a series of showy splashes, frequently following alongside the bow of a boat. Ferry and cruise vessel passengers often see these porpoises in Port Wells and Valdez Arm.

An adult Dall porpoise measures 5 to 7 feet [*1.5 to 2.1 m*], weighs about 200 pounds [*91 kg*] and has white side patches on an otherwise black body. A triangular dorsal fin gives a "little killer whale" appearance. Dall porpoises, found throughout much of the open water of the sound, also inhabit coastal waters of the North Pacific from California to Japan.

A smaller and shyer relative, the Pacific harbor porpoise *(Phocoena vomerina),* brownish in color, is common near edges of bays, inlets, fiords and at the mouths of rivers.

During a spring snowstorm, a killer whale fights its way against a tidal current in Bainbridge Passage. The killer whale, one of the most intelligent members of the animal kingdom, possesses a voracious appetite.

LARRY HADDOCK, U.S. FISH AND WILDLIFE SERVICE

Pacific Killer Whale *(Orcinus orca).* The Pacific killer whale is common throughout the sound, especially in Whale Bay, Orca Inlet and southern Knight Island Passage. Visitors can distinguish this 20 to 30 foot [*6 to 9 m*] black mammal by its contrasting white head and side patches, white belly and sail-like dorsal fin. This fin, up to 7 feet [*2.1 m*] tall, is easily spotted when the whale rolls on the surface for air.

The killer whale, one of the most intelligent members of the animal kingdom, generally hunts in packs of three to fifty, but packs of as many as 100 of these whales have been observed in the sound. Killer whales in a pack simultaneously may attack prey. The whale's mouth is large enough to swallow whole seals or small porpoises. Approach of a killer whale pack will often panic other marine mammals, including other large whales, but no documented case exists of a killer whale's attacking a human being.

Humpback Whale *(Megaptera novaeangliae).* The humpback whale, weighing about 30 tons [*33 metric tons*] and reaching 30 to 40 feet [*12 to 15 m*] in length, is the largest mammal seen by most visitors to the sound. It has a dark gray or black back, white belly and long pectoral (side) fins. When this whale rolls on the surface, it spouts a column of water 20 feet [*6 m*] high, then dives, lifting its huge, white-edged tail flukes from the water. Occasionally, these massive mammals will "breach," leaping completely

A humpback whale breaches, or jumps clear of, the water. These baleen whales, which often reach 50 feet [17 m] in length, are identified by their white-edged side fins and tail.

out of the water. The humpback whale is a baleen whale; instead of teeth the humpback has coarse brush-like strips (baleen) that hang from the roof of its mouth and strain small aquatic creatures, such as shrimp and zoo-plankton, from the water. Small fish are also consumed, totalling a daily food intake of several hundred pounds.

Humpback whales are more "musical" than other whales. They have an eerie, incredibly varied repertoire of siren-like sounds. Kayakers sitting quietly on the waters of the sound have reported hearing them miles away.

After gorging themselves in the food-rich northern seas, humpback whales winter in warm southern waters near the equator, where they lose up to one-third of their body weight. They are often seen off the Hawaiian Islands swimming en route to and from the North Pacific. During the summer, look for them in open areas of the sound, such as Port Fidalgo, Port Wells, Perry Passage, Knight Island Passage, Blying Sound and Hinchinbrook Entrance.

Other Whales. Although the humpback is the most commonly seen baleen whale, visitors often see the smaller minke (piked) whale as well as the very large sei (rorqual) and finback whales. Along the outer Montague Island coast, gray whales are often seen in April and May during their northward migration from Baja California to the Bering Sea and Arctic Ocean. The beluga or white whale occurs in Cook Inlet but has not been observed in the sound.

WHALE IDENTIFICATION CHART
Species recorded in Prince William Sound and adjacent Gulf of Alaska

Surfacing and Blowing	Beginning Dive	Diving

BLUE

Surfaces and blows 8 to 15 times.

Bluish-gray; up to 100 feet (30 m) long; dorsal fin on one-third of back near tail; very rare.

Makes series of 12 to 15 second dives, then a 10 to 20 minute deep dive; sometimes shows flukes.

FIN (FINBACK)

Top of head breaks surface first. Blows 4 to 7 times.

Gray to black; up to 70 feet (21 m) long; fin slightly backcurved, shows after whale spouts; fairly common.

Rarely shows flukes; dives for 6 to 10 minutes.

SPERM

Spouts at forward angle

Blue-gray to black; up to 60 feet (18 m) long; dorsal fin irregular in shape; seen in Gulf of Alaska during spring migration.

Dives may last 90 minutes.

SEI (Rorqual)

Rises to surface so that head and dorsal fin are visible at same time. Blows 1 to 2 times.

Gray to black; skin has galvanized appearance; up to 55 feet (17 m) long. Often swims slightly submerged leaving "tracks" or swirls on water surface; fairly common.

Back not arched during diving. Dives for 1 to 2 minutes.

WHALE IDENTIFICATION CHART
Species recorded in Prince William Sound and adjacent Gulf of Alaska

Surfacing and Blowing	Beginning Dive	Diving

GRAY

Low bushy spout

Light, mottled gray; up to 45 feet (14 m) long; dorsal fin is low hump followed by series of smaller humps on dorsal ridge of tail. Seen in Gulf of Alaska during spring migration to Bering Sea.

Usually shows flukes when diving.

HUMPBACK

Low bushy spout.

Blue-gray to black; up to 50 feet (15 m) long; pectoral fins and flukes have hind edges that are irregularly shaped and white in color.

Skin has many knoblike protuberances, barnacles and whale lice; pectoral fins one-third length of body. Most common large whale in the sound.

Shows white-edged tail flukes on deep dive.

WHALE IDENTIFICATION CHART
Species recorded in Prince William Sound and adjacent Gulf of Alaska

Surfacing and Blowing	Beginning Dive	Diving

MINKE

| Spout is almost invisible | Dark gray to black; up to 30 feet (9 m) long; dorsal is slightly backcurved and is well forward on body; it is regularly seen as whale rolls; pectoral fins have white band. Often comes close to boats and is fairly common. | Flukes seldom raised when diving. |

KILLER

Dark gray to black with light gray patch just in back of dorsal fin; 22 to 30 feet (7 to 9 m) long; dorsal fin is vertical, triangular and up to 6 feet (2 m) tall. Fairly common; often travels in groups.

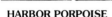

HARBOR PORPOISE

Dark brown with lighter undersides; up to 6 feet (2 m) long; common in shallower waters.

DALL PORPOISE

Black with white side patches; up to 6 feet (2 m) long. Very fast swimmer, often creating a "rooster tail." Seen in more open waters.

(For a complete checklist of marine mammals, see Appendix I)

Birds

A Major Flyway and Nesting Area. Geographic location makes the sound a major flyway for millions of birds that annually migrate to and from nesting areas in Alaska. The nearly impenetrable mountain ranges to the east of the sound restrict the flyways of many waterfowl and shorebirds to the coastline. Coastal waters, marshes, tidal flats and inland lakes harbor large concentrations of bird life. The delta of the Copper River is one of the most important nesting and staging areas in North America.

Some of the more frequently seen birds, particularly marine species, are described below. A checklist of all birds known to occur in the sound is contained in the Appendix.

Black-Legged Kittiwake *(Rissa tridactyla).* This member of the gull family is one of the most commonly seen birds in the sound. Look for its white to buff-gray color, conspicuous black "dipped in ink" wingtips and legs, and pale yellow bill. Young kittiwakes have more gray on the wings, a dark band on the back of the neck and a black band on the tail. Around nesting grounds listen for a raucous call, like "kaka-week," or "kitti-waak."

Kittiwakes nest in colonies and build their nests on sea cliffs. Two eggs are generally laid and hatched in late June. Young kittiwakes fledge by late August, when the entire colony population leaves for the open sea.

Kittiwakes are well distributed throughout the Northern Hemisphere. The same species found in the sound is also found in the Aleutian Islands (where colonies of a million birds or more often occur), Japan and the Mediterranean. Kittiwakes winter from the Aleutians south to Baja California and are common near shore only during breeding season.

Ferries and cruise vessels, when approaching or leaving Whittier, often pause near the kittiwake colony in Passage Canal. This colony, containing more than 5000 birds, is the third largest in the sound. A colony on the sea stacks in Boswell Bay, Hinchinbrook Island, containing more than 10,000 birds, is the largest in the sound.

Glaucous-Winged Gull *(Larus glaucescens).* The best known and most widely seen "seagull" in the sound, the glaucous-winged gull, is larger than the kittiwake and lacks the latter's black wingtips and legs. The gull has gray spotted wingtips, pink feet and a yellow bill. Immature gulls are gray-brown. The glaucous-winged gull makes a variety of sounds varying from a kak-kak-kak to the classic seagull sound of a high-pitched keer-keer.

Glaucous-winged gulls frequent open coasts, bays, piers and waterfronts of the sound. They are often seen soaring on air currents created by large boats. Nests are made of seaweed and grass on rocky headlands or offshore

Photo opposite: Black-legged kittiwakes, a species of gull, nest in large colonies throughout the sound. They spend most of their lives on the open ocean, coming ashore only to breed. One often-visited kittiwake nesting colony is along Passage Canal near Whittier.

NEIL AND ELIZABETH JOHANNSEN

islands, where this species lays two or three olive-brown spotted eggs. A few gulls nest along the ferry route in Passage Canal and on the Dutch Group Islands. Near Yale Glacier at the head of College Fiord is a colony used by about 4000 birds. The largest colony in the sound, containing about 20,000 gulls, is located near Cordova at the east end of Hinchinbrook Island and Egg Island. Smaller nesting colonies are scattered throughout the sound.

Arctic Tern *(Sterna paradisaea).* Streamlined and graceful, the arctic tern is more maneuverable than the glaucous-winged gull. Look for a 15 inch [*38 cm*] long bird with a white belly, gray wingtips, black cap and bright red bill. The tail is white and conspicuously forked. This tern is often seen flying over open bays, lakes and marshes throughout the sound with its bill pointed down, looking for small fish. The tern cries a loud "kee-yah" and dives at intruders. Nesting sites are usually simple depressions near salt water in beach gravels, sands or marshes where two olive, spotted eggs are laid.

One of the world's greatest travelers, the arctic tern nests in arctic and subarctic areas of North America and migrates 12,000 miles [*19,000 km*] to the tip of South America to "summer" again in the Southern Hemisphere. Although common throughout the sound, arctic terns are particularly numerous near the Dutch Group Islands, near Eaglek Bay, on the west side of Knight Island, and on the southeast coast of Green Island. Two easily accessible areas for viewing terns are the tidal flats near Portage at the head of Turnagain Arm and tidal flats just east of central Valdez.

Each year the arctic tern travels many thousands of miles from the tip of South America to breed along the shorelines of Alaska.
AL JOHNSON

Pelagic Cormorant *(Phalacrocorax pelagicus).* When in flight, this large, blackish, slender-billed bird appears to have a tail and neck of similar length and conspicuous white flank patches. At close range, a dull red patch is visible at the base of the bill. Although the cormorant perches upright, when swimming it has a low profile with an erect head and snake-like silhouette. Cormorants often fly in a wedge formation and on this account are frequently mistaken for wild geese. The cormorant, a diving bird, lives on a diet of fish and is found in bays and fiords. The bird remains in the sound throughout the year. Cormorants are found in large numbers on the southwest coast of Montague Island, on the west end of Hinchinbrook Island, and on the western point of Elrington Island.

Although the pelagic cormorant is the most common, three other species, the double-crested, the red-faced and Brandt's cormorant, also inhabit the sound.

Pigeon Guillemot *(Cepphus columba).* A member of the auk family, northern counterpart of the penguin family, the pigeon guillemot is a 12 inch [*30 cm*] long, black pigeon-like bird with large white shoulder patches, red feet and pointed bill. In flight, its small triangular wings beat so fast that they look almost blurred to the human eye. In the water, the pigeon guillemot appears as a coal-black bird with conspicuous white wing patches. When approached, this expert diver is under the surface in a split second.

Pigeon guillemots typically nest in crevices in sea cliffs, where the female lays one or two greenish or white spotted eggs. This species can be observed throughout the sound wherever rocky cliff faces, its preferred nesting habitat, rise directly from the water's edge. Guillemots usually nest in scattered pairs.

Surf Scoter *(Melanitta perspicallata).* The surf scoter is a large sea duck with a heavy blackish body. The male, sometimes called a skunkhead duck due to white patches on its crown and on the back of its neck, may be recognized by the orange, black and white markings on its large bill. Two other species of scoters, the black and white-winged scoters, are also common in the sound.

An expert diver, the surf scoter, when approached, will often dive rather than take flight. When this bird does choose to fly, watch its labored running along the surface to achieve air speed. Scoters nest on freshwater lakes in Interior Alaska. Large numbers of immature scoters and nonbreeding adults, however, spend the summer along the coast of the sound, at times in flocks of several hundred birds. Although scoters occur throughout the sound, they are particularly common in Montague Strait and in Middle Ground Shoal, just north of Hinchinbrook and Hawkins islands.

Bald Eagle *(Haliaeetus leucophalus).* The heraldic symbol of the United States of America, though an endangered species elsewhere in the continental United States, is considered common in Southeast and Southcentral Alaska. The sound has a breeding population of more than 900 pairs of bald eagles, and the region is used annually by large numbers of migrant, wandering and visitant eagles. The total bald eagle population of the sound is estimated between 7000 and 8000 birds.

An adult bald eagle is identified by its large size, yellow bill and distinctive white head and tail. Younger bald eagles lack the white feathers and appear dusky brown with a dark bill. Eagles take five years to reach maturity.

Eagles prefer fish, commonly feeding on dead and spawned-out salmon. The birds may be seen by the hundreds near salmon-spawning streams in the sound. They also snag smaller fish, such as herring or trout, from the surface of bays and lakes.

Eagle nests are usually a permanent and bulky platform of sticks situated in tall old-growth trees, typically close to the water's edge. The same nest is used year after year, and eagles add more material each season the nest is used. Sometimes this accumulation of limbs, twigs, moss and grass reaches 7 feet [*2.1 m*] in depth and 8 feet [*2.4 m*] in diameter. Nests of these birds can be seen along shorelines throughout the sound. Ferry and cruise boat passengers should look for eagles and eagle nests near Eaglek Bay and on nearby offshore islands. Look for a large bird perched on a dead tree top overlooking the water, or soaring overhead with large, outstretched "squared-off" wings. Eagles occasionally make a harsh, high-pitched creaking, crackly "kleek-kik-ik" sound.

Now protected by federal law, bald eagles were at one time under bounty. From 1917 to 1952, the Alaska Territorial Government paid a bounty on bald eagles, based on the presumption that these birds preyed on fox farms and depleted valuable salmon resources. Fox farming lost importance as an industry and biologists proved that eagles primarily ate spawned-out salmon, but by the time federal law nullified the bounty in 1952, over 129,000 eagles had been killed for a bounty ranging up to $2.00.

Steller's Jay *(Cyanocitta stelleri).* One of the most common birds of the rainforests of the sound, Steller's jay is most numerous on the forested islands and somewhat less common on the mainland. About 12 inches [*30 cm*] long, blue-black with a deep blue tail, it is the only crested jay on the west coast of North America.

Steller's jay is often seen or heard by hikers in forested areas. Its call is a loud "kwesh-kwesh-kwesh" or "shook-shook-shook." Diet is variable,

A somewhat damp bald eagle searches Orca Inlet near Cordova for a fish dinner. Thousands of these magnificent birds inhabit the shoreline trees of Prince William Sound.

M. WOODBRIDGE WILLIAMS
NATIONAL PARK SERVICE TASK FORCE

ranging from insects and carrion to food left out in camp. A bowl-shaped nest made from twigs is built in a spruce or hemlock tree, where three to five greenish spotted eggs are laid.

Jays are related to ravens, crows and magpies, species that are also common in the sound. Steller's jay was first described for the scientific world by Georg Steller, the German naturalist who in 1741 accompanied Vitus Bering on his voyage of discovery to Alaska. The sighting of this bird on Kayak Island led Steller to conclude he had reached the North American continent, as the bird appeared similar to a blue jay *(Cyanocitta cristata)* that Steller recalled having seen in a book about birds of the Carolina colonies on the Atlantic seacoast.

Northwestern Crow *(Corvus caurinus).* Flocks of this black, beachcombing bird are often seen along the waterfronts and harbors of Valdez and Cordova, where this species joins other birds, notably gulls, in foraging for cannery scraps.

The northwestern crow drops mussels and other shellfish onto rocks to break the shell, thus exposing the meat. Listen for this scavenger's hoarse, low-pitched "caw-caw." The northwestern crow is often confused with the larger raven, also a common resident of the sound.

Marbled Murrelet *(Brachyramphus marmoratum).* This small, nondescript chunky bird is one of the most common birds on sound waters. Look for a 9 inch [*23 cm*] long bird, sooty-brown above with heavily barred mottled underparts; its breast and throat turn white in winter. Though abundant and often seen, the nesting habits of this species are almost a total mystery. Local bird experts occasionally see these birds flying into the forests and mountains at dusk, but no nest of a marbled murrelet has ever been found in Alaska. (A nest of this murrelet was found in 1974 in a tree in a California redwood forest.)

Tidepool Life

Intertidal Zone. Some of the most diverse wildlife forms in the sound are those of the intertidal zone. Consult a tidebook for low-water periods, find a rocky exposed beach and prepare for a fascinating session with a special kind of Alaskan wildlife. Tidepool animals adapt to a wide variety of environments. These creatures are found in areas of extreme high or low water, on beaches pounded by heavy surf, in protected bays or estuaries, and even in polluted harbors where all but the hardiest species retreat.

Rocky Shores. Most rocky, but protected beaches are populated with colorful starfish *(Pisaster),* scampering hermit crabs *(Pagarus),* clinging shells of blue mussels *(Mytilus),* barnacles *(Balanus),* hat-shelled limpets *(Acmaia)* and periwinkles *(Littorina).* The starfish's regenerative powers permit it to grow a new arm should it lose one to an enemy or predator. The abundant blue mussel, found in clusters, is eaten by a variety of furred and feathered predators. The hermit crab makes its home in the vacant shell of a deceased periwinkle.

Mud and Sand Flats. The mud and sand flats of the sound lack protection from waves as well as attachment areas on rock for starfish and other species described above. This environment, however, has evolved specialized creatures well able to cope with the seemingly harsh conditions. Many species burrow below the action of the waves or drying power of the sun. Clam diggers are aware of the tasty bivalves, such as razor, butter and littleneck clams, that live in beach sands (see Fishing chapter). Also uncovered by clam diggers are several species of marine worms *(Polychaeta)* that have been leaving tracks across marine sands for more than 550 million years.

Reptiles and Amphibians

Western Toad. Prolonged cold temperatures and deep snow inhibit the growth and distribution of cold-blooded reptiles and amphibians. Snakes and lizards are nonexistent in Alaska. Virtually the only amphibian in the sound is the western toad *(Bufo boreas)*, which is common on the Copper River Delta and ranges northwestward to the sound.

Insects and Other Small Animals

Insects. Biting flies, such as gnats, "no see-ums," and white sox and mosquitoes, are very common, particularly during July and early August. *Lepidoptera* have not been extensively catalogued, though a few butterflies, mostly coppers and sulfurs, and a few nondescript moths have been noted.

Iceworms. Although bearing little resemblance to the giant carnival creature that makes its annual march down Cordova's main street each February, the iceworm really exists. Numerous species, belonging to the genus *Mesenchytraeus,* may be found on glaciers and on snowfields during spring and summer. The small, slim, segmented worms, black in color and usually less than one inch [2.5 cm] long, thrive at temperatures just above freezing. Occasionally carpeting the surfaces of glaciers in countless numbers, the worms emerge at dawn, dusk or on overcast days. When sunlight strikes them they burrow back down into the ice.

Industry and Recreation

An Abundant Harvest. Prince William Sound abounds with dozens of species of fish. In summer millions of salmon crowd streams and intertidal zones. Halibut, trout, rockfish, herring, crab and shrimp thrive in bays and fiords. Bald eagles, gulls, seals, sea otters, sea lions and large whales are all dependent upon these species of fish.

People also partake of this marine harvest. Traditionally, commercial fishing provides the most important economic mainstay of the region. From the standpoint of recreation, sportfishing is also significant. Sport licenses and regulations are available from most sporting goods stores. Bag limits are relatively liberal, but one should practice good conservation. Keep no more fish than you can use.

Salmon Life Cycle

A Seasonal Silver Hoard. Five of the six species of Pacific salmon occur in the sound. From June to September, runs of four of these species, numbering many thousands of fish, ascend local streams, fighting over spawning territory, laying countless eggs, and then dying. Eggs hatch during the following months into tiny sac-fry, called alevins, which remain until spring in streams or gravel bottoms. Some species of young salmon migrate directly to the open ocean while others may remain a year in fresh water. After maturing in salt water for one to three years, salmon return to their parent streams, where they in turn spawn and then die. In spawning streams salmon are preyed upon by brown and black bears, bald eagles, seagulls and people. Avoid harassment of spawning salmon, as this is detrimental to their survival.

Photo opposite: Pink salmon are piled into the hold of a cannery tender. Millions of these fish are taken each summer by local commercial fishermen.
JIM REARDEN

A fisherman pitches pink salmon out of the hold of his boat into the scale-hung brailing net of a cannery tender. Fish are then dumped into bins of the tender and taken to a cannery for processing.
JIM REARDEN

Commercial Salmon Fishing

An Important Resource. Alaskan Natives have for centuries utilized protein-rich salmon as a diet staple. The fish, taken in stream weirs and with dipnets, were preserved by being cut into strips and dried in the sun. In more recent times, salmon have been canned for the world market. Until statehood, commercial fishermen used nets and fish traps, but today they rely primarily on drift gill nets, set nets, purse seines and trolling. Various ways of taking salmon commercially are described below.

Gill Nets. Gill nets are rectangular in shape and may be as long as 150 fathoms [*900 feet or 275 m*]. Nets are usually made of very fine nylon so that salmon will unknowingly swim into the mesh and entangle themselves.

Both drift and set nets are used in the sound. Drift gill nets, as the name implies, are allowed to drift with the tide, intercepting fish traveling some distance offshore. This type of net is fished from boats ranging from 28 to 35 feet [*8.5 to 10.7 m*] in length that are outfitted with hydraulic or mechanical reels used to pay out, retrieve and store the nets. Drift gill nets are used in the Port Wells/Esther Island area, upper Unakwik Inlet, and Eshamy (Nellie Juan Light to Granite Bay). The fishing season extends from mid June to mid July except in the Eshamy area, where it is generally open until August.

A purse seiner closes the "purse" around a school of pink salmon. Fishing is one of the most important industries in Prince William Sound.

CHARLES D. EVANS

Set gill nets differ from drift nets in that one end is anchored to shore; the nets intercept fish traveling along the shoreline. This form of net is tended from small skiffs. In the sound such nets are used mainly in the Eshamy area between Nellie Juan Light and Granite Bay. The fishing season extends from early July to late August.

Purse Seines. Purse seines, large nets used to encircle schools of salmon, are tended by a seine skiff and the larger 30 to 58 foot [*9.1 to 18 m*] salmon seiner. Once a school of salmon has been encircled, a draw string is pulled tight, forming a "purse." The net is then pulled aboard the boat with the aid of a boom and power block. Purse seiners also set their nets from a point or cape of land and attempt to catch passing fish. After holding the net in the form of a hook or curving arc for 15 to 20 minutes, fishermen close the drawstring and pull in the net.

Tenders. Commercial fishermen sell their catches to salmon tenders, which transport the salmon to canneries. Most tenders are equipped with refrigerated brine systems, which preserve the fish at 29° F [*-1.67° C*] for as long as 10 days. Tenders also supply fishermen with food, fuel and supplies and record harvest information. Data provided on species, catch, catch area, harvest methods and fish weight are used by biologists to manage the fishery.

Most areas of the sound are opened for seining during years that large runs of pink and chum salmon are predicted. Seine fishing seasons are usually during July and early August.

Species of Salmon

Pink Salmon *(Oncorhynchus gorbuscha)*. Pinks are the most common species of salmon in the sound and weigh 2 to 6 pounds [*0.9 to 2.7 kg*]. Pink salmon may be identified by small scales and large oval spots on back and tail. Locally referred to as humpbacks or humpies, because of the contorted shape the males assume during spawning, these fish have a two-year life span, spawning in intertidal zones and in stream systems near salt water. Eggs are laid during late summer and autumn. Predation by other fish, disease and weather factors, such as flooding, prolonged winter cold spells and stream silting, reduces oxygen available to developing salmon, lowering the survival rate. The 1964 Good Friday earthquake hurt pink salmon populations when many streams and intertidal spawning areas were destroyed or altered. The U.S. Forest Service, in conjunction with the Alaska Department of Fish and Game, has worked to restore many of these spawning areas.

Commercial fishermen catch pink salmon with purse seines throughout the sound. Sport anglers fish for pink salmon in the latter part of the summer at major streams throughout the sound, using a variety of lures. Small spinners and spoons with flashy red and silver colors are considered most effective. An important sportfishery is found near Valdez in Jack, Galena and Sawmill bays.

Chum Salmon *(Oncorhynchus keta)*. Chum salmon, locally called dog salmon, are the second most widely distributed species of salmon in the sound. These fish usually weigh 8 to 10 pounds [*3.6 to 4.5 kg*]. They have no spots, and the tips of all fins except the dorsal are usually tinged with black. They spawn in or near the mouths of streams and rivers, normally following a four year cycle.

Commercial fishermen, using purse seines, and sport anglers, using spoon lures, catch chum salmon near the mouth of almost every major stream. Coghill River near Port Wells is the most important commercial chum salmon stream in the sound, although the 1964 Good Friday earthquake altered and reduced the acreage of these spawning grounds.

Photo opposite: Pink salmon, usually weighing five to six pounds [2 to 3 kg], *spawn near the mouths of streams leading to salt water. Pauline Johannsen prepares to clean this fat specimen.*
NEIL AND ELIZABETH JOHANNSEN

Spawned-out chum salmon crowd a stream near Valdez.
NEIL AND ELIZABETH JOHANNSEN

Sockeye Salmon *(Oncorhynchus nerka).* This species is also known as the red salmon due to the brilliant coloration it acquires after entering fresh water from the ocean. Because of the scarcity of accessible lake systems in which this species prefers to spawn, sockeyes are found in relatively few locations in the sound.

In the ocean, mature sockeyes are green and silver. They weigh 2 to 9 pounds [*0.9 to 4 kg*], averaging 6 to 8 pounds [*2.7 to 3.6 kg*]. Their color gradually changes to red when they enter fresh water in early summer, and they develop a humped back and prominent hooked jaw.

Coghill Lake, Eshamy Lake and Miner's Lake (near Unakwik Inlet) support commercially important sockeye populations. Ferry passengers traveling between Whittier and Valdez see numerous fishing boats near Esther Island between approximately mid June and mid July. Fishermen on these boats, using both purse seines and drift gill nets, are catching salmon en route to Coghill River and Coghill Lake.

Because red salmon feed primarily on plankton, sport anglers seldom catch them in salt water. Just after entry into fresh water, however, these fish put up an exciting and persistent fight. The meat of red salmon loses its tasty appeal after the fish turns red.

In addition to the commercial fishing areas listed above, sport anglers may take advantage of the small red salmon runs that occur in Cochrane Bay, Long Bay in Culross Passage, Esther Passage, eastern Columbia Bay and Jackpot Bay.

King Salmon *(Oncorhynchus tshawscha).* The king is the largest of all salmon. Variously called the chinook, spring, black-mouth, tyee and blue-back, this fish usually weighs 10 to 50 pounds *[4.5 to 22.7 kg]*, although individual king salmon weighing up to 120 pounds *[54 kg]* have been taken. Although king salmon do not spawn in streams of the sound, a limited sportfishery exists for "feeder kings" that follow schools of herring into Prince William Sound between October and June. These fish are also called "white kings" because of their light-colored meat.

King salmon have been taken in Port Wells, Port Nellie Juan, the Cordova area and Port Valdez. Kings are caught by trolling or by beach casting with artificial lures or with herring.

Coho Salmon *(Oncorhynchus kisutch).* More commonly known by local residents as silver salmon, this fish can weigh up to 21 pounds *[9.5 kg]*, although weights of 10 pounds *[4.5 kg]* are more common.

Silvers enter freshwater streams from August through November, laying eggs in clean gravel riffles of lake systems, or long, low-gradient streams with pools or slough areas. Juveniles spend at least one year in fresh water

The communities of Valdez and Seward host silver salmon derbies each August. Sport anglers find silvers to be great fighters and delicious eating.
NEIL AND ELIZABETH JOHANNSEN

before migrating to sea. Silver salmon streams are found on Montague, Hinchinbrook, and Hawkins islands, as well as in the drainages of Gravina and Coghill rivers, Shrode Lake, Eshamy Creek and Lake, and in streams near Simpson Bay and Port Valdez. Salmon runs in the Copper River and Bering River (located just east of the sound) are among the largest on the Pacific Coast. Many of these tens of thousands of mature coho move into salt waters of southwestern Prince William Sound during July and early August, just before migrating up the Copper and Bering rivers.

Sport anglers prize silver salmon for their fighting spirit and tasty flesh. Silver salmon are taken using herring, lures or salmon eggs. Valdez and Seward sponsor silver salmon derbies in August, giving substantial cash prizes for the largest fish caught.

Halibut and Rockfish

Halibut *(Hippoglossus stenolepis).* One of the most spectacular fish in the sound is the Pacific halibut, a species of flounder. Females of this bottom-feeding species may reach weights of 500 pounds [*227 kg*] and lengths of 8 feet [*2.4 m*] in 15 years. Males, however, seldom exceed 100 pounds [*45 kg*]. Adult halibut are characterized by their tremendous size and flat shape. The top or eyed side is brownish or olive in color with overlying pale blotches while the belly is white or light gray.

The halibut is a prolific, deepwater spawner; two million eggs have been counted in some large females. The hatched larvae may drift for hundreds of miles. When the larvae are less than 1 inch [*2.5 cm*] long, the blind-side or bottom-side eye begins migrating to top-side. When the young halibut reach a length of 4 to 6 inches [*10 to 15 cm*], they settle to the bottom.

Commercial fishermen catch halibut with longline gear composed of ground line of one-quarter inch [*6 mm*] nylon with hooks spaced at 18 foot [*6 m*] intervals along its length. The ground line is anchored at each end and marked with flagged orange marker buoys. Hooks may be baited with squid, herring or salmon heads.

Halibut occur in most areas of the sound. Sport anglers catch these fish by jigging a heavy line baited with a large lure or herring. Make sure a large halibut is dead before attempting to land it; a flopping fish of this size may inflict damage to both people and property and may even sink a small boat.

Rockfish *(Sebastes spp.).* Many species of rockfish inhabit the depths of the sound. These stout, thick-bodied fish have large heads, large eyes and heavy scales. The forward dorsal fin may inflict painful wounds if this fish is

Photo opposite: These large halibut were caught near Knight Island. With its delicately flavored meat, this large species deserves its reputation as a "money fish."

NEIL AND ELIZABETH JOHANNSEN

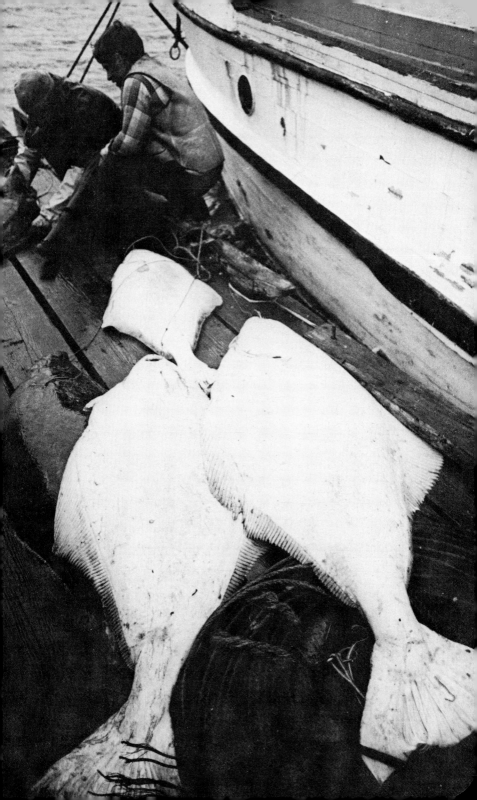

carelessly handled. Rockfish are among the few species of fish that bear living young. Millions of larvae, born in spring, represent an important food source for larger fish.

One frequently caught species is the black rockfish or "sea bass" *(Sebastes melanops),* typically found near rocky headlands where heavy swells stir up tiny food plants and animals. Commercial demand for this fish is limited. Sport anglers, however, often catch these firm-fleshed fish by jigging a spoon or herring near rocky exposed areas at a depth of about 100 feet [*30 m*].

The red rockfish or "snapper" *(Sebastes ruberrimus)* is found at depths of 1200 feet [*365 m*] or more. This brilliantly colored fish, weighing up to 20 pounds [*9 kg*], has become commercially important in recent years. It is often inadvertently caught on halibut skates; although it does not command as high a price as halibut, fresh red snapper is considered by many local residents to be the tastiest fish in the sound. Two popular fishing spots are located in Passage Canal near Billings Glacier and at the south end of Esther Passage.

Trout and Char

Dolly Varden Char *(Salvelinus malma).* This fish, resembling somewhat its cousin, the brook trout, grows to pan size in fresh water. Dolly varden that migrate to sea, however, may reach 22 inches [*56 cm*] and weigh 10 pounds [*4.5 kg*]. Dolly varden are silvery with faint light oval spots along the sides and have greenish backs.

Sea-run "dollies" may be found near most creek and river mouths. Smaller members of the species inhabit numerous freshwater streams and lakes of the region. Although dolly varden have little commercial importance, many sport anglers fill their creel with this fighting fish.

The name dolly varden derives from a character in Charles Dickens's novel *Barnaby Rudge.* The fictional Dolly Varden favored brightly colored dresses. A polka-dotted material named after this young lady was popular with settlers of the American West. In time the name was transferred to this brightly colored fish. Dolly varden char are also known by the less flattering name of bull trout.

Cutthroat Trout *(Salmo clarkii).* Cutthroat trout vary from 1 to 7 pounds [*0.5 to 3.7 kg*] with 2 pounds [*0.9 kg*] being average. Like the rainbow trout, this species has an olive-green back and whitish belly. It is typically rosy-striped on each side and spotted over its entire body except for the belly. The name cutthroat derives from the rosy patches near its jawbone.

Photo opposite: Commercial fishing can be a cold and lonely pastime, yet fishermen, a unique and individualistic group, seem to prefer such an existence.

JIM REARDEN

Cutthroat trout rise readily to an artificial fly and are good fighters. This species inhabits numerous freshwater locations, including Eshamy Lake, Granite Lake (south of Eshamy Bay), an unnamed lake 1.5 miles [*2.4 km*] south of Miner's Bay in Unakwik Inlet, and an unnamed lake northwest of Wells Bay.

Herring

Herring *(Clupea pallasii).* This species, ranging in size from 10 to 12 inches [*25 to 31 cm*] and silver in color, is abundant in the sound. Herring are an important forage fish for porpoises, seals, numerous species of larger fish and sea birds.

From the 1920s to the 1940s, commercial fishermen with seines harvested up to five million tons of herring annually. The herring were rendered into oil and fish meal. Abandoned herring processing plants may be seen at Crab Bay and Port Oceanic.

The recently revived herring fishery concentrates on harvesting herring for bait and sac roe (eggs). This fishery centers around spawning areas near Glacier Island, Columbia Bay, Montague Island, Green Island and Knight Island between mid April and the end of May. Herring are caught with seines, and the catch is transferred to tenders for delivery to processing plants. Some fish are frozen, while others are placed in large containers and allowed to soften for three to four days. The egg sac (roe) is then removed by hand, salted, packed in barrels and shipped to the Orient. Fishermen in 1973 harvested 14 million pounds [*6.4 million kg*] of roe in the sound, a catch worth nearly one million dollars.

Herring Roe on Kelp. Demand for herring roe attached to seaweed has resulted in a new fishing industry. The herring's sticky eggs often adhere to edible kelps, which are harvested by grappling hooks or scuba divers. The kelp, together with the herring eggs, is salted and packed in barrels for shipment to the Orient. From late April to early May, this fishery operates in shallow waters of the northeastern part of the sound, particularly around Tatitlek Narrows, Landlocked Bay and Boulder Bay.

Shellfish

Dungeness Crab *(Cancer magister).* Many gourmets consider dungeness crab the tastiest of all crabs found in Alaskan waters. The female dungeness lays millions of eggs each summer, which hatch into tiny creatures

Photo opposite: King crabs inhabit deeper waters, although one may occasionally wander into a dungeness crab pot in shallow waters.
DENNIS BROMLEY

resembling small spiny mosquito larvae. The developing crabs undergo many molts (shedding of their shells) before attaining maturity in three years. In four years they reach over 6.5 inches [*16.5 cm*] in shell width and may weigh 2 to 3 pounds [*0.9 to 1.4 kg*].

A small commercial dungeness crab fishery exists in the sound, with an annual harvest of about 250,000 to 300,000 pounds [*113,000 to 136,000 kg*]. Fishermen use a circular wire pot about 40 inches [*102 cm*] in diameter and 14 inches [*36 cm*] deep, usually baited with herring, salmon heads or razor clams.

Sport anglers harvest dungeness crab with crab pots or with crab rings (a piece of net braced with two wire rings, one inside the other, and fastened on the edges with line), which are easier to stow.

Dungeness crab, named for the coastal fishing village of Dungeness, Washington, are usually found in less than 60 feet [*18 m*] of water in bays throughout the sound. Consistently good catches are taken from coves along Port Wells, in Sheep Bay and Simpson Bay north of Cordova, along the edges of Unakwik Inlet, and in Orca Inlet.

King Crab *(Paralithodes camtschatica).* King crabs, with long, spiny legs containing pounds of tasty meat, reach 24 pounds [*10.9 kg*], but commercially caught males average 7 pounds [*3.2 kg*] and are eight or nine years old. The "blue king," a smaller blue-tinted subspecies *(Paralithodes platopus),* inhabits College Fiord, Harriman Fiord and Unakwik Inlet.

Commercial fishermen are allowed a relatively insignificant 500,000 pound [*226,800 kg*] annual quota for Prince William Sound and nearby Gulf of Alaska waters. Major Alaska king crab fisheries are near Kodiak Island, along the Aleutian Chain and in the eastern Bering Sea. Fishermen use crab pots 6 to 8 feet [*1.8 to 2.5 m*] square weighing as much as 700 pounds [*318 kg*]. King crabs are more readily caught and are in best condition during fall months.

Water depths and bulky equipment restrict sportfishing of this crab, although an occasional king crab wanders into a dungeness crab ring or pot.

Tanner Crab *(Chionoecetes bairdi).* The tanner crab, also called commercially the queen or snow crab, has long spiny legs like the king crab but is considerably smaller. Tanner crabs measure about 2.5 feet [*0.8 m*] from leg tip to leg tip. Newcomers to the commercial market, tanner crabs in the Prince William Sound region were first processed in 1968 but have since become the most important commercial crab species in the area. Fourteen million pounds [*6.4 million kg*] were caught during the 1972-1973 season with a value of $1.4 million. Most tanner crabs are caught in the Gulf of Alaska, but many are taken in Hinchinbrook Entrance and Orca Bay.

A limited sportfishery for this deepwater species exists in Orca Bay, Port Fidalgo and Valdez Arm.

Shrimp and prawns are common near tidewater glaciers. Distantly related to lobsters, shrimp are caught with pots or trawls.
M. WOODBRIDGE WILLIAMS
NATIONAL PARK SERVICE TASK FORCE

Shrimp *(Pandalus spp.).* Several species of shrimp inhabit the sound. Spot shrimp *(P. platyceros)* and coonstripe shrimp *(P. hypsinotus),* "prawns" 4 to 10 inches [*10 to 25 cm*] long, are taken in deep water in Unakwik Inlet, Port Wells and Kings Bay in fine-mesh pots fished on long lines. Trawling, which involves dragging a funnel-shaped net, is used to catch the 3 to 5 inch [*8 to 12 cm*] long humpy and pink shrimp *(P. borealis).* These "cocktail" shrimp are common in deep water near tidewater glaciers. Trawling, however, is often restricted by sharp rocks and irregular bottom contours which tangle or destroy the net. Pleasure boaters occasionally use pots to catch shrimp that frequent rocky areas, particularly around the north end of Knight Island.

Mollusks

Clams and Mussels. Edible clams are found in abundance on gravel beaches and mud flats, though shoreline uplift caused by the 1964 Good Friday earthquake destroyed much clam habitat. Clam beaches often may be recognized by their lacing of old clamshells.

Unfortunately, a form of flagellated phytoplankton produces a poison, which very occasionally may be concentrated in clams and mussels feeding on the plankton. The chances of such paralytic shellfish poisoning occurring

are negligible. The Alaska Department of Fish and Game, however, keeps close checks for paralytic shellfish poisoning in the two certified areas near Cordova where clams are harvested commercially. These areas are the southwest half of Orca Inlet and the mud flats from Strawberry Reef to Kanak Island off the Bering River Delta and Copper River Delta.

Humans contracting paralytic shellfish poisoning experience numbness and tingling of lips, tongue, face and extremities, followed by nausea, vomiting and respiratory paralysis. (Use these first aid measures: give artificial respiration if necessary, induce vomiting, give a rapid-acting laxative, elevate the feet and treat for shock, allow no alcohol, and get the victim to a doctor as soon as possible.)

Razor Clam *(Siliqua patula).* This large and tasty bivalve is well named, for its thin shell will shatter into sharp fragments under the shovel of an over-enthusiastic clam digger. Dig from the seaward side of a dimple in the sand made by the clam's siphon. Razor clams, found a foot or two below the surface of a wave-pounded beach during a minus tide, will quickly go deeper upon sensing a disturbance. This species is most abundant near Cordova and the Copper River Delta. Cordova, once known as "Razor Clam Capital of the World," no longer claims this status. The clam beds were overdug and populations declined with destruction of clam beds during the 1964 Good Friday earthquake. High labor costs of digging and processing razor clams also contributed to the decline of this industry.

For a recreational digger, the tasty reward of clam fritters or chowder makes the hard physical task of digging worthwhile. Razor clams may be dug legally for personal use with a valid Alaska sportfishing license. Digging is best in late spring and early summer before spawning begins.

Steamer Clams. Two common clams fall into this category. Butter clams *(Saxidomus giganteus),* found a few inches below the surface of gravel beaches during low tide, have a heavy, strongly ridged shell. Littleneck clams *(Venerupis staminea)* live in the same areas and, although similar in size and shape, have shells with both radiating and concentric striations. These clams are "steamed" by cooking in boiling water until they open.

Blue mussels *(Mytilus edulis),* numerously clustered on rocks in intertidal zones, are also cooked as steamers. Unfortunately, blue mussels concentrate paralytic shellfish toxins even faster and to a greater degree than clams. Mussels have been responsible for most of the paralytic shellfish poisoning deaths along the West Coast of the United States. Unless you are certain that blue mussels are free of possible shellfish poisoning, it is advisable not to eat them.

Photo opposite: Razor clams are among the best-tasting of clams. These mollusks are found in abundance near Cordova and the Copper River Delta. Prior to the 1964 Good Friday earthquake, when the clam beds were extensively damaged, Cordova was called the "Razor Clam Capital of the World."

© NANCY SIMMERMAN, 1973

Plant Succession: Evolution of Forest and Tundra

Continuous Change. Constant, dynamic change characterizes the plant communities of Prince William Sound. Glaciers retreat, leaving areas of barren rock ready for plant colonization; violent windstorms flatten centuries-old forests; snow avalanches and landslides sweep down mountainsides, uprooting long-established trees. Cataclysmic uplifts, such as those produced by the 1964 Good Friday earthquake, expose new land areas.

Valdez Glacier: An Example of Plant Succession. The outwash plains of Valdez Glacier, accessible from Valdez by highway, are a natural laboratory for observing the process of plant succession, the orderly sequence by which plant communities vegetate a barren area. Since 1900, Valdez Glacier has retreated several miles, exposing extensive areas of bare rock and gravel. Near the present terminus of the glacier, pioneer plants, such as lichens, are taking hold. Weak acids produced by this lichen growth slowly attack the rock surfaces. Cracks, widened by this process and by the freeze-thaw action of water, catch windblown dust. Over a period of time, a thin layer of soil and decaying plant growth, called humus, accumulates. Utilizing this layer of new soil, larger lichens establish themselves, soon followed by mosses. Plant succession continues, as fireweed, a flower which needs few nutrients and is common in recently cleared areas, begins to flourish. Alders are the next plant growth stage. Attached to their root systems are specialized nodes containing bacteria that convert gaseous nitrogen from the atmosphere into forms useable by plants. Grasses and small willows soon follow. Later, larger trees find rootholds and nutrients necessary for survival. It may take more than a century for plant succession to reach its "climax." Climax vegetation, such as cottonwoods, spruce and hemlock, is stable, self-perpetuating and in equilibrium with the environment.

Photo opposite: False hellebore and ferns typify the lush rainforest vegetation of the sound. Although false hellebore is poisonous to eat, young fern shoots, called fiddleheads, are delicious after boiling for a few minutes.

M. WOODBRIDGE WILLIAMS
NATIONAL PARK SERVICE TASK FORCE

Variety of Vegetative Zones

From Tideline to Treeline. Visitors to the sound are immediately struck by the wide contrast in vegetation between the shoreline and the skyline. Shoreline seaweeds are overshadowed by moss-draped rainforests. At the upper limit of the rainforests, trees are stunted and wind-shaped, while at higher elevations only alpine tundra grows. On windswept mountain peaks, only lichens survive on exposed rocks below regions of permanent glacial ice.

Intertidal and Sublittoral Zones. Two distinct marine algal habitats occur in the sound: the intertidal zone (area between high and low tide), and the sublittoral zone (area below low tide). Intertidal plants must twice daily endure the advance and retreat of salt water. Myriad forms of seaweed, from smooth sea lettuce to huge bullwhips, range in color from brown to iridescent blue-green. Most seaweed does not grow in water deeper than 150 feet [*45 m*] due to lack of sunlight. Glacial silt from streams and rivers further reduces the amount of sunlight that can penetrate. Several species of yellow-brown seaweed *(Fucus spp.)* are very common on rocks in the intertidal zone. These species are edible as a salad green, make excellent soup and are a good source of protein and iodine.

One of the most widely distributed seaweeds is the large kelp found in water depths of 35 to 50 feet [*11 to 15 m*]. In April and May certain species of kelp are harvested commercially for the Oriental market. Herring roe (eggs), which adhere to the kelp, and the seaweed are salted, packed in barrels and shipped to the Far East, where the product is considered a delicacy.

Rainforest. Continuing from tideline to timberline, mountainsides of the sound are covered by rain-drenched, coastal forests interspersed with boggy, treeless areas. Although occurring at elevations as high as 2000 feet [*615 m*], climatic and soil conditions generally restrict rainforests to narrow coastal strips and river valleys. Saturated by as much as 180 inches [*460 cm*] of annual precipitation, these forests contain tall, closely spaced stands of Sitka spruce *(Picea sitchensis),* western hemlock *(Tsuga heterophylla)* and mountain hemlock *(Tsuga mertensiana).* Sitka spruce, with its scaly, purplish-brown bark and thick, prickly-sharp needles, is the dominant species in the sound. Western hemlock is also abundant, though this species is scarce in the western sound. Alaska yellow cedar *(Chamecyparis nootkatensis)* occurs, usually mixed with spruce. Trees range from 1 to 2 feet [*30 to 60 cm*] in diameter and average 45 feet [*14 m*] in height, though many stands exceed 100 feet [*30 m*]. Limited logging takes place in the sound (see History chapter).

The rainforest is luxuriant with ferns, mosses and shrubs. Blueberry bushes *(Vaccinium ulignosum),* lowbush cranberry *(Vaccinium vitis-idaea)* and trailing raspberry vines *(Rubus pedatus)* are among many shrubs producing delicious berries which ripen in late summer. Watch out, however, when hiking through such areas, for the thorny devil's club *(Oplopanax horridus)* with its large, maple-shaped leaves, and for the odorous skunk cabbage *(Lysichitum americanum).*

Shrub Thickets. Above the rainforests and below alpine tundra areas, summertime cross-country travel is tedious, as the way is frequently blocked by dense thickets of Sitka alder *(Alnus sitchensis),* willow *(Salix spp.),* salmonberry *(Rubus spectabilis),* mountain ash *(Sorbus aucuparia)* or Pacific red elder *(Sambucus callicarpa).* Such plant communities are widespread, particularly in disturbed areas typical of recent glacial retreat, earthquake-uplifted beaches, old river benches, logged-over areas and avalanche tracks.

Open areas occur where drainage is impeded. Although spruce-hemlock forests cannot flourish in such swampy areas, bogs, such as these near Hell's Hole, proliferate with wildflowers in summer.

CHARLES D. EVANS

Muskeg. Where drainage is impeded, such as on areas underlain by bedrock or compacted glacial till, trees are stunted or nonexistent. Viewed from a distance, these areas appear to be meadows between stands of rainforest. Closer inspection, however, reveals that some of these boggy areas are composed of brownish-orange sphagnum moss, which can hold many times its weight in water. Sphagnum moss often intrudes along the edges of small ponds, reaching depths of 5 to 10 feet [*1.5 to 3 m*] in a few places. Nearly all boggy areas in the sound, however, are composed of comparatively young sedge peat which is black or brown in color. Wildflowers proliferate in these open areas. The tiny insect-eating sundew plant *(Drosera angelica Huds.)* is an unusual and often overlooked plant resident.

Alpine Areas. Low-matted vegetation known as tundra generally occurs above 1500 feet [*450 m*]. At this elevation climatic conditions are severe; snow and ice cover plants for as long as nine months of the year. Brief growing seasons produce hardy plants such as crowberry *(Empetrum nigrum),* dwarf blueberry *(Vaccinium ulignosum)* and mountain heather *(Cassiope tetragona).* In some areas poor drainage (due to underlying bedrock) results in wet tundra composed primarily of sedges which resemble thick-stemmed grasses, usually not exceeding 3 feet [*1 m*] in height. Rocks and open areas are often covered with lichens, which serve to break down rock into nutrients and soils useable by higher forms of plant life.

Reference Works. The Appendix contains a listing of publications useful for identifying plants and trees found in the sound.

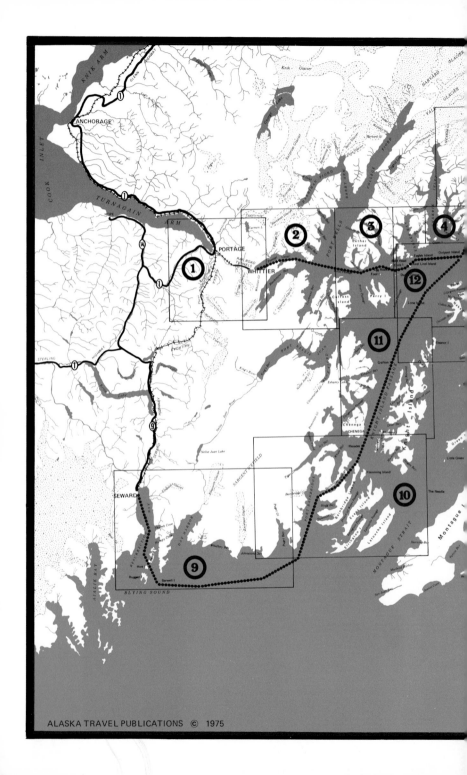

ALASKA TRAVEL PUBLICATIONS © 1975

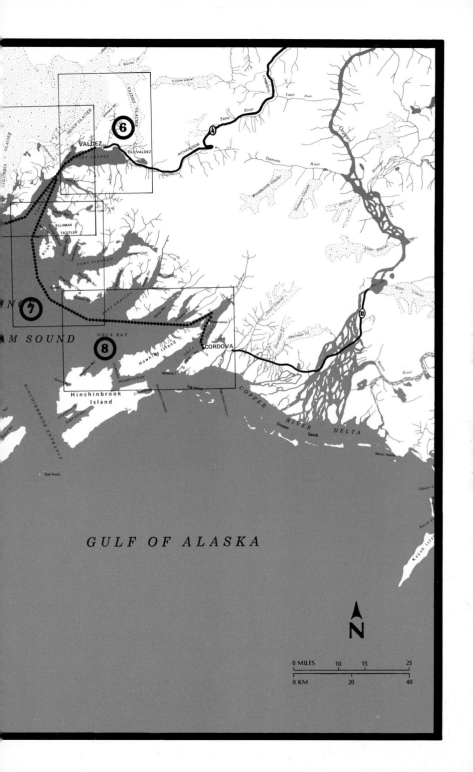

GULF OF ALASKA

Traveling the Marine Highway Across Prince William Sound

Popular Means of Transportation. The Alaska Marine Highway System provides opportunities for visitors to see at close hand the waterways, islands and glaciers of Prince William Sound. The ferry trip between Whittier and Valdez, highlighted by a short stop at Columbia Glacier, has become one of the most popular excursions in Alaska.

Information on access and addresses of the various Marine Highway offices are listed in the Gateways chapter. In the following pages, three ferry routes (Whittier-Valdez, Valdez-Cordova and Seward-Valdez), supplemented by thumbnail descriptions of major Prince William Sound communities, are delineated. Highlights of these voyages are pinpointed by numbers on accompanying maps. Ferry routes are described from west to east. Passengers embarking at Valdez or Cordova and traveling from east to west should thus read the route descriptions in reverse order.

Photo opposite: The ice cliff of Columbia Glacier, up to 300 feet [100 m] *high, frequently splinters gigantic chunks into Columbia Bay.*
NEIL AND ELIZABETH JOHANNSEN

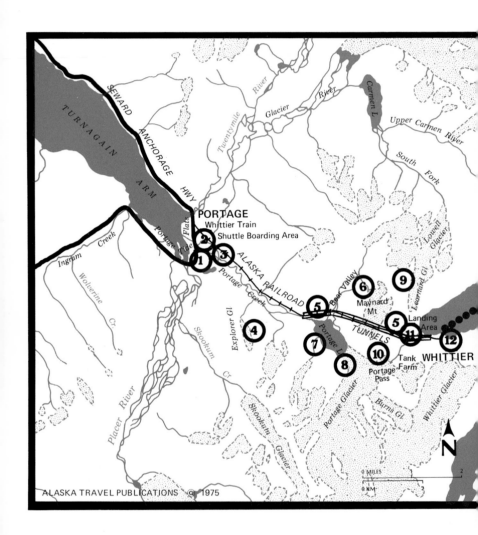

ALASKA TRAVEL PUBLICATIONS © 1975

Portage-Whittier Train Shuttle Guide

Access to Portage. To reach Portage, visitors may either drive the Seward Highway or take the train from Anchorage. If driving, follow the Seward Highway *(Alaska Route 1)* 48 miles [*60 km*] to Portage at the head of Turnagain Arm. The turbulent tides in this arm of Cook Inlet are the second highest in the world, reaching 36 feet [*11 m*], and are exceeded only by those of Nova Scotia's Bay of Fundy. These glacially silted waters do not support permanent populations of marine life, though salmon and other species of fish enter this arm to spawn in streams and rivers that drain the surrounding mountains.

The Seward Highway, following the north shoreline of the arm, traverses the edge of Chugach State Park, largest state park in the United States, passing en route the historic mining settlement of Girdwood and the modern resort community of Mt. Alyeska. There visitors may ride the resort's chairlift to the observation platform, 3994 feet [*1217 m*] above sea level, for a spectacular panoramic view of Turnagain Arm, Girdwood Valley and the snow-capped Chugach Mountains. Weather permitting, at least six glaciers are visible from this vantage point.

Ferry Route Map 1

1. Portage. The 1964 Good Friday earthquake all but destroyed this small village, when land subsided nearly 6 feet [*1.8 m*]. Stands of dead trees, their root systems killed by the invading salt water, surround the former town. Following the earthquake, Portage was relocated on higher ground next to the highway. Today Portage has a cafe, gas station and railroad section house, all built on fill elevated above the high tide zone. Since their old wells now contain only salt water, Portage residents haul their drinking water from nearby streams.

2. Whittier Train Shuttle. A waiting area for foot passengers and loading ramp for driving vehicles on the Portage-Whittier shuttle train are located about 1 mile [*1.6 km*] before reaching the Portage Glacier access road. The two turn-offs, approximately 46 miles [*74 km*] from Anchorage, are well-marked by highway signs. Visitors may ride as coach passengers or drive their vehicles onto railroad flatcars and ride in their vehicles. During summer months the train shuttles several times daily between Portage and Whittier. Check with The Alaska Railroad in Anchorage (telephone: (907) 265-2685, 265-2688 or 265-2494) for times of operation and tariffs.

3. Portage Tide Flats. As the train pulls out of the Whittier Shuttle loading area, look for arctic terns diving for fish. These delicate-appearing birds, which nest in the surrounding saltwater marshes, are abundant between May and early August. They are Alaska's most distant visitors, annually migrating more than 25,000 miles [*40,000 km*] roundtrip from the tip of South America.

No highway connects Whittier with the contiguous state highway system. Vehicles are transported on flatcars on The Alaska Railroad, while foot passengers ride in an enclosed coach. The train passes along Portage Creek, shown here, and through two long tunnels during the 13 mile [21 km] *trip.*
STEVE MC CUTCHEON

Cow moose and their calves summer in the Portage Valley, while bulls seek out the higher valleys and mountain slopes. Look for willows along the railroad right-of-way that appear to have been trimmed about 3 to 4 feet [*1 to 1.2 m*] above ground level. This trimming is the work of wintering moose, which eat the willow branches protruding above snow cover. Snow depths of 3 to 4 feet [*1 to 1.2 m*] are common in Portage Valley.

4. Explorer Glacier. This small, hanging glacier, 1.5 miles [*2.4 km*] long, was so named because Explorer scouts once practiced their glacier climbing techniques here. The glacier has remained virtually stagnant since observations began. Visitors may get a closer view of this glacier and several others from the Portage Glacier access road. The delicate blue color of glaciers results from air bubbles at the bottom of the snowpack being compressed by the constantly accumulating weight of snow at the top of the glacier. The six-sided crystals resulting from such compression of the snow absorb most colors of the spectrum but refract blue.

Major General Simon Bolivar Buckner, Jr., Commanding General of the Alaska Defense Command during World War II, makes a speech prior to blasting open the longer of the two Whittier tunnels in 1942. The construction of The Alaska Railroad spur between Whittier and Portage provided an alternate deepwater port to Seward.
U.S. ARMY PHOTOGRAPH

5. Railroad Tunnels. The first tunnel is about 1 mile [*1.6 km*] in length; the second, 2.5 miles [*4 km*]. Military construction crews hewed out these tunnels in 1941 and 1942 to create an alternate port to Seward. Construction started from both Portage and Whittier. The two holes on the longest tunnel were only ⅛ inch [*0.3 cm*] out of alignment when they met. The "holing-through" ceremony was held the same day that the ribbon was cut on the Alcan Highway. The tunnels withstood the 1964 Good Friday earthquake; the only damage was a small amount of rockfall. The tunnel roofs are covered with icicles which may drip copiously during the summer.

6. Bear Valley. A small bridge crosses Placer Creek, outlet for Bear Glacier, visible at the head of the valley. This valley supposedly gained its name because "Alaska Nellie" Lawing of Moose Pass used to hunt black bear here. Strong winds funneling through Portage Pass have blown empty freight cars off the railroad tracks in this valley.

7. Portage Lake. Portage Glacier covered the entire lake bed in 1914, but the terminus has since receded more than 2 miles [*3.2 km*]. Today the lake, 656 feet [*200 m*] deep, is often filled with beautifully sculptured icebergs calved from the face of the glacier. The silty water is caused by "glacial milk," composed of microscopic glacier-ground rock particles held in suspension.

8. Portage Glacier. This 6 mile [*9.7 km*] long glacier curves out of view to the south so that its upper reaches are not visible from the railroad shuttle route or from the Portage Visitor Center. Subject of countless photographs and paintings, Portage Glacier is currently receding at a rate greater than 100 feet [*30 m*] per year. A smaller glacier, which flows into Portage Glacier from a low saddle to the east, is named Burns Glacier after Scottish poet Robert Burns.

9. Learnard Glacier. This glacier, seen on the left as the train emerges from the second tunnel, has a terminus so covered by morainal debris as to be almost unrecognizable. This glacier was named for Lieutenant Learnard, a member of the Army-sponsored Glenn Expedition, which explored parts of the sound in 1898.

10. Portage Pass. Natives, Russian fur trappers and gold seekers used this 600 foot [*183 m*] high pass for travel between Turnagain Arm and Prince William Sound. Today the retreat of Portage Glacier and ensuing creation of Portage Lake have made this route almost impassable. Thousands of migrating birds utilize this flyway during spring and fall migrations. Hikers may hike a portion of this old route to the edge of Portage Glacier. (See Hiking chapter for a route description.)

11. Whittier-Anchorage Multiproduct Pipeline. Aviation fuel, diesel and gasoline for military use are shipped to Whittier on barges and stored at this tank farm. The pipeline passes through two 8 foot [*2.4 m*] wide tunnels totalling 4.3 miles [*6.9 km*] in length. The tunnels are situated above the Alaska Railroad tunnels. The pipeline then parallels the railroad tracks to Anchorage. The tank farm and pipeline were built in 1967 primarily in response to the Vietnam War, so that fuel could be piped to military bases in Anchorage.

12. Whittier

Community of Incongruities. Situated at the head of Passage Canal, Whittier is an incongruity of gray monoliths in a wilderness of glaciers and spruce-choked mountainsides. The small community contains few visitor facilities but anticipates a major spurt of growth because of the demand for saltwater recreation close to Anchorage.

Because of its proximity to the city of Anchorage, the community of Whittier is a busy place during the summer. The small-boat harbor is filled to capacity. The state ferry M/V BARTLETT makes a daily stop. Large quantities of freight, much of it carried north on the trainship ALASKA, is transferred from ship to rail.
STEVE MC CUTCHEON

History. Native and Russian fur traders used to rest here while crossing the 13 mile [*21 km*] isthmus between Prince William Sound and Turnagain Arm. Portage Pass was used by gold seekers and as a mail route during the late nineteenth and early twentieth centuries, prior to the completion of port and rail facilities at Seward.

Whittier was named after a nearby glacier, in turn named in 1915 for poet John Greenleaf Whittier (1807-1892). Whittier did not become an established community, however, until World War II, when the U.S. Army drilled railroad tunnels to connect the ice-free seaport with The Alaska Railroad. In 1947, the Army began to make Whittier a more permanent base and ultimately erected more than a score of concrete and steel structures, including two skyscrapers and one of the largest wharf and warehouse systems in Alaska. By 1953, the military had constructed in the sprawling Buckner Building living quarters for hundreds of men as well as offices, cafes, a theater, hospital, morgue, bank, classrooms, bowling alley, barber shop, jail and cold storage area. A 14-story apartment house, the Hodge Building, completed in 1956, had a grocery, cocktail lounge and restaurant. The Army discontinued their Whittier operation in 1960 and declared the wilderness "city" surplus in 1963.

The 1964 Good Friday earthquake temporarily paralyzed the ports of Seward and Anchorage. As port facilities in Whittier remained relatively intact, in a fairly short time the bulk of inbound freight entered through the port of Whittier. Excluding oil, Whittier currently handles more tonnage than any other port in the state. Freight comes north from Seattle, Washington and Prince Rupert, British Columbia, in railroad cars carried on ocean-going barges and on the trainship *Alaska.*

In 1967, military authorities decided the best way to supply petroleum products to Elmendorf Air Force Base was via a pipeline from Whittier to Anchorage. Two tunnels above the railroad tunnels were constructed.

Whittier today is rapidly expanding. A small-boat harbor, completed in 1973, partially fulfills the need for such a facility close to Anchorage. The City of Whittier purchased the surplus military buildings in September, 1973, creating 200 condominiums in the 14-story Begich Towers (formerly the Hodge Building). The city is also selling cabin sites.

Exploring Whittier

... Visit the Whittier Museum, located on the fourth floor of Begich Towers. This museum, though modest in size, contains an excellent collection of Eskimo artifacts from northern Alaska, paintings by Florence Melewotkuk, as well as items of local interest. Upon request, Kay Shepherd, founder and curator of the museum, will show slides of Whittier and Prince William Sound. The city offices, located on the same floor, also have information on this community.

... Railroad cars, arriving by barge or trainship, are offloaded and hauled to Anchorage or Fairbanks several times a week, providing a spectacle for "sidewalk superintendents." (Stay well out of the way!) Whittier is one of the most important transshipment centers in Alaska. A significant percentage of Alaska's supplies enter via this ice-free, year-round, deepwater port. Barges, towed from Seattle or Prince Rupert, take five days to reach Whitter, while the trainship makes the voyage in three days.

... Small boats with outboard motors are available for rent from Cooley's Boat Rental. (Inquire at the fuel dock at the small-boat harbor.) With a boat it is possible to visit a large bird nesting colony of thousands of black-legged kittiwakes (a species of gull), located near waterfalls just across Passage Canal from Whittier. Passage Canal has good fishing for salmon, halibut, red "snapper" (rockfish) and dungeness crab. Charter boats are also available. (See Facilities chapter and Recreational Boating chapter, *Cruise One,* for more details.)

... Take time to hike. The hike to the top of Portage Pass is described in the Hiking chapter. Spawning pink salmon can be seen at the mouth of Cove Creek. To reach this stream, walk from the old boat-launching ramp (situated just past the Sportsman's Inn) about 1 mile [*1.6 km*] on an

Naturalists of the U.S. Forest Service travel aboard the state ferries much of the time during summer months, providing information on scenic highlights, wildlife and history of Prince William Sound. Most of the land areas of the sound are in Chugach National Forest.
NEIL AND ELIZABETH JOHANNSEN

unmaintained trail to a tiny cove, which is filled with salmon in late summer. To get a close look at the lush rainforest vegetation that characterizes the sound, visitors need only walk a short distance up the dirt road that begins to the left of the Buckner Building.

Whittier-Valdez Ferry Log

Summary. The Alaska state-operated ferry M.V. *Bartlett* operates between Whittier and Valdez nearly every day during summer months, making the 95 mile [*150 km*] trip in about 7 hours one way. The privately operated cruise vessel *Glacier Queen* makes daily round trips between these points in about 5.5 hours. As trips across the sound are very popular, visitors should make travel plans well in advance. For information on making reservations, consult the Gateways chapter.

A U.S. Forest Service naturalist accompanies summertime sailings of the *Bartlett.* The naturalist provides a continuing commentary on marine life, vegetation, historic sites and glaciers of Chugach National Forest as the ferry travels between the two ports. Nearly all land seen from the ferry is uninhabited. Excluding the major towns, only a handful of people inhabit the several thousand miles of shoreline in the sound.

Employees of the Alaska Marine Highway System direct foot passengers and automobiles from the railroad shuttle offloading area to the nearby ferry loading area. Upon leaving Whittier, the ferry pauses briefly off a large black-legged kittiwake (seagull) nesting colony near the town. The vessel then travels down Passage Canal past glaciers and steep, forested hillsides before entering the open water of Port Wells. To the north on clear days passengers can see high peaks of the Chugach Mountains and glaciers of Barry Arm and College Fiord. The ferry then cruises through numerous offshore islands and bays before reaching Columbia Bay, into which famed Columbia Glacier discharges. The ferry stops in the bay for about half an hour, negotiating its way through icebergs to reach a point about 0.5 mile [*0.8 km*] from the calving glacier terminus. Passengers often have the opportunity to watch huge masses of ice calve into the bay, accompanied by a thundering roar. The ferry then sails the length of Valdez Arm and Port Valdez before arriving at Valdez, once an important mining town and today terminus of the Trans-Alaska Pipeline.

The following pages describe this cruise route between Whittier and Valdez. Locations are pinpointed by number on accompanying maps. Passengers traveling the reverse route from Valdez to Whittier should read the section below in reverse order.

Ferry Route Map 2

1. Passage Canal. This 14 mile [*22.5 km*] long, 400 to 1200 foot [*120 to 365 m*] deep fiord is ice-free year-round. "Benches," or ledges on the north side of Passage Canal show the path of the large valley glacier that carved this fiord thousands of years ago. In 1794, Captain George Vancouver of the British Royal Navy named this fiord Passage Canal, because it led to the portage connecting Prince William Sound and Cook Inlet.

Several large swaths of trees along Passage Canal have been cut by avalanches. During the winter of 1972-1973, an avalanche directly across Passage Canal from Whittier caused a wave that broke over the top of the Whittier small-boat harbor.

2. Whittier Glacier. Numerous waterfalls cascade from this glacier, named in 1915 for poet John Greenleaf Whittier. From the upper end of Passage Canal there is a good view of Whittier Glacier, Portage Glacier and Portage Pass.

3. Black-Legged Kittiwake Nesting Colony. This kittiwake nesting colony, third largest in the sound (larger ones are located at Boswell Bay on Hinchinbrook Island and Icy Bay in southwest Prince William Sound), contains about 5000 birds. The black-legged kittiwake, a species of seagull, spends its life at sea, coming ashore only to breed. Two eggs hatch in late June or early July. The young are distinguished by black bands on neck and tail. In late August, soon after the young leave the nest, the entire colony disperses and leaves for the open sea.

4. Billings Glacier. This glacier, 4 miles [*6.4 km*] long, is named for Commodore Joseph Billings (1761?-1806), an Englishman in the Imperial Russian Navy who in 1791-1792 commanded an exploring and surveying party in the Bering Sea and North Pacific. Tenning Carlson and Albert Nordstrom made the first gold discovery in western Prince William Sound on Billings Creek in 1896. Mining of gold-bearing quartz near the face of the glacier started in 1911. The area sank 6 to 8 feet [*1.8 to 2.4 m*] during the 1964 Good Friday earthquake, and salt water has killed the trees along the shoreline. The silty light gray water of the glacial outlet stream contrasts markedly with the clear deep blue of the salt water of Passage Canal.

5. Shotgun Cove. This cove provides some shelter for Whittier-bound boats and hydrotrain barges. It is slated for development as a small-boat harbor with a capacity of about one thousand boats. A 5 mile [*8 km*] road is under construction to connect Whittier with Shotgun Cove.

6. Poe Bay. This cove was named for writer Edgar Allen Poe (1809-1849) by the U.S. Coast and Geodetic Survey in 1914. The hillside above Poe Bay was

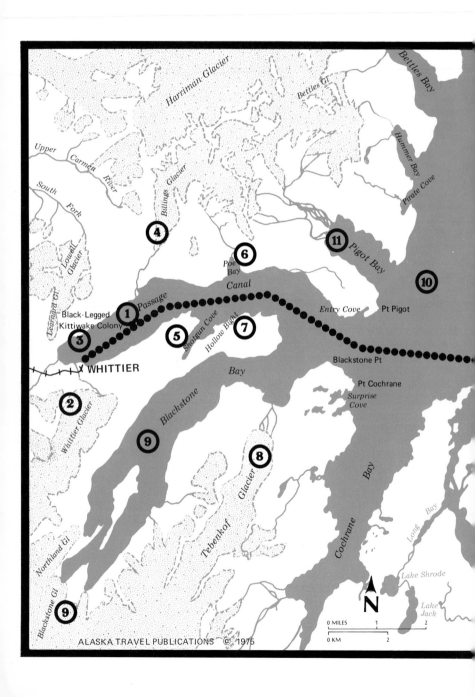

Harriman Glacier

Bettles Gl

Bettles Bay

Upper

Carmen

River

South

Fork

Lowell Glacier

Billings Glacier

Leanard Gl

Hummer Bay

Pirate Cove

④

⑥

Poe Bay

Canal

⑪

Pigot Bay

⑩

Black-Legged Kittiwake Colony

①

Passage

Shotgun Cove

Hollow Bight

Entry Cove

Pt Pigot

③

WHITTIER

⑤

⑦

Blackstone Pt

②

Bay

Pt Cochrane

Surprise Cove

Whittier Glacier

Blackstone

⑨

⑧

Glacier

Tebenkof

Glacier

Cochrane Bay

Long Bay

Northland Gl

Lake Shrode

Blackstone Gl

⑨

Lake Jack

N

0 MILES   1   2

0 KM   2

ALASKA TRAVEL PUBLICATIONS © 1975

the site of a one million board feet "blowdown" of Sitka spruce and western hemlock in the winter of 1969-1970. High winds in excess of 100 miles per hour [*160 km/h*] periodically funnel down Passage Canal and through Portage Pass. Because of high rainfall and thin, unstable soils, the shallow-rooted trees are easily toppled by winds. Seth Glacier, a small hanging glacier, occupies the head of the valley above Poe Bay.

7. Hollow Bight. The hillside to the right of this bight (tiny cove) was logged of two million board feet of timber in 1966. Follow-up studies have shown natural regeneration to be satisfactory. The area also received extensive blowdown in the winter of 1969-1970.

8. Tebenkof Glacier. This glacier, 8 miles [*12.9 km*] long and 1.5 to 2 miles [*2.4 to 3.2 km*] wide, is separated from tidewater by a crescent-shaped terminal moraine and outwash plain. A worthwhile hike leads over the outwash plain along the outlet creek to the terminus of the glacier. The glacier was named for Mikhail Dmitrievich Tebenkov (1802-1872), director of the Russian American Company and governor from 1845 to 1850 of the Russian American colonies. Active in surveying Alaskan coastal waters, he published an "Atlas of the Northwest Coast of America," in St. Petersburg (modern Leningrad) in 1852.

9. Blackstone Bay and Glacier. This large bay, 11 miles [*16 km*] long and 1 to 2 miles [*2 to 3 km*] wide was named for Blackstone Glacier, in turn named for prospector Charles A. Blackstone, who with two companions tried to cross Portage Pass in April, 1896. They became lost in a storm, and all three slowly froze to death on Blackstone Glacier after finding they could not descend the ice cliff to salt water. The glacier, located at the head of the bay, discharges icebergs into tide water, but the ice seldom drifts beyond nearby Willard Island. Black-legged kittiwakes nest near the terminus of the glacier. Only the upper portion of the ice mass is visible from the ferry route.

10. Port Wells. As the ferry rounds Point Pigot, named in 1794 by Vancouver's expedition for midshipman Robert Pigot, a large embayment comes into view. Vancouver named this body of water Port Wells after Edward Wells, mathematician and geographer. Port Wells branches into scenic Harriman Fiord and College Fiord, both explored and named by the Harriman Expedition in 1899. The lofty peaks on the northern horizon culminate in Mt. Marcus Baker, 13,176 feet [*4016 m*], highest peak in the Chugach Mountains. The mountain was named in 1924 by Alfred H. Brooks for his colleague Marcus Baker, a cartographer of the United States Coast and Geodetic Survey. To the right, at the head of College Fiord, passengers may see 24 mile [*39 km*] long Harvard Glacier. The Harriman Expedition named the glaciers on the west side of College Fiord for women's colleges and the glaciers on the east side and at the heads of the fiord for men's colleges. Also visible to the left or west side of Port Wells are

Cascade and Barry glaciers at the head of Barry Arm. Icebergs from the area occasionally drift near the ferry route. Gold mining took place on both sides of Port Wells, particularly at Granite Mine (1915 to the 1960's), north of Hobo Bay, and at the now-vanished mining camp of Golden (1904-1916) on the east side of Port Wells.

11. Pigot Bay. This bay is the site of a U.S. Forest Service public recreation cabin, as well as several abandoned gold mines. Sport anglers may find red "snapper" (rockfish), halibut, pink, chum and king salmon and dungeness crab.

Ferry Route Map 3

1. Culross Passage. Small boats often use this protected, narrow 12 mile [*19 km*] long passage. Impressively scenic, it contains many rocky islets and tiny coves. A short trail leads through weather-shaped, sub-alpine vegetation from Long Bay to Shrode Lake, site of a U.S. Forest Service public use cabin. The outlet stream and lake offer good salmon fishing in late summer.

2. Culross Island. Extensive gold and copper mining took place at the head of Culross Bay on the northeast end of this island in the early 1920s.

Culross Passage, Culross Island, Blackstone Bay and most of western Prince William Sound, as far south as Port Bainbridge, form the Nellie Juan Wilderness Study Area. If this area is set aside as a Wilderness Area as is proposed, the land will remain as unspoiled as it is today.

3. Esther Island. This 12 mile [*19 km*] long island is topped by thousand foot [*300 m*] high peaks of granite. Esther Falls, draining Esther Lake and discharging into the head of Lake Bay, is a recommended 0.5 mile [*0.8 km*] hiking destination (see Hiking chapter). The falls are not visible from the ferry. By Esther Island the ferry turns slightly south during June and July to avoid gill-netters and seiners fishing for red salmon en route to spawning grounds in Coghill River and Lake. The larger boats, called tenders, buy and haul the fish to canneries (see Fishing chapter).

4. Perry Island. This island, 6.5 miles [*10.5 km*] long, was a fox farm around the turn of the century. A commercial fisherman, one of the handful of Prince William Sound residents who live outside established towns, lives at South Bay. The island, like most of the rest of north Prince William Sound, receives very deep snow in winter.

5. Egg Rocks. An arctic tern nesting colony is located here. Ferry passengers often see harbor seals and sea lions. The water is hundreds of feet deep on all sides of these rocks.

6. Esther Passage. Fishing and pleasure boats often use this 11 mile [*17.7 km*] long passage, which is edged by scenic, steep granite cliffs laced with waterfalls. There is good fishing in the area for trout, red and silver salmon, halibut, red "snapper" (rockfish) and king crab. The north end of the passage is currently being logged.

7. Lone Island. This 2 mile [*3.2 km*] long island was used for fox farming in 1896 and in 1925, but the farm was not profitable. The remnants of many fox traps remain on the west shore. Just east of the island the water is 476 fathoms [*2856 feet or 871 m*] deep, the deepest water in the sound and adjacent waters of the Gulf of Alaska.

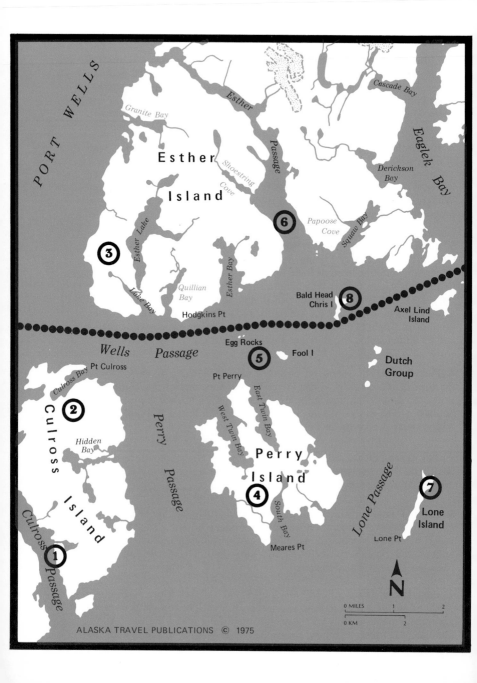

ALASKA TRAVEL PUBLICATIONS © 1975

8. Bald Head Chris Island. Chris Peterson, as "bald as a billiard ball," stocked this island with blue foxes in 1898. It was used as a fox farm intermittently until 1929. In the 1920's, Jefferson, a Valdez postmaster for many years, owned a prosperous fox ranch, which had a cabin, fish house, eight feed houses, a small gas-powered boat, several skiffs and even a milk cow. Today gulls, terns and oystercatchers breed along the shoreline.

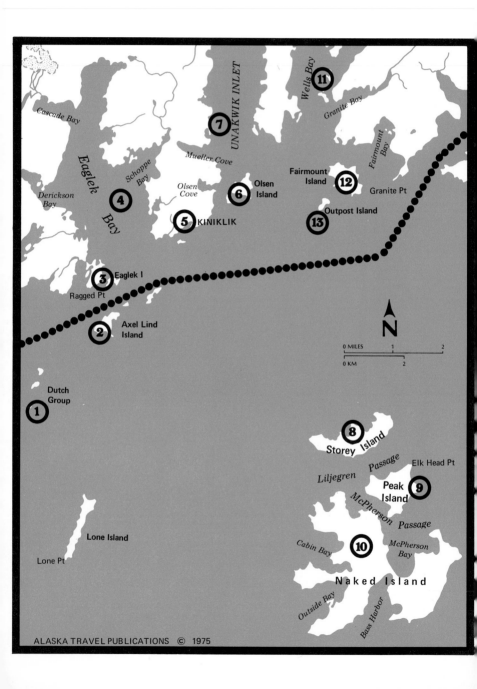

ALASKA TRAVEL PUBLICATIONS © 1975

Ferry Route Map 4

1. Dutch Group. Fred Liljegren and his partner in 1919 stocked the tiny islands of the Dutch Group with blue foxes. In 1946 the Federal Aviation Administration (then the Civil Aviation Administration) built a repeater station, which was abandoned around 1960. This repeater station, still plainly visible, had a boardwalk large enough for a car to drive from the beach to the house. Bird colonies, containing many hundreds of arctic terns and glaucous-winged gulls and lesser numbers of pigeon guillemots and oystercatchers, are scattered throughout these islands.

On a clear day the snow-capped peaks of 50 mile [*80 km*] long Montague Island are visible. In 1778 Captain James Cook, R.N., named the island for his patron, John Montagu, the Fourth Earl of Sandwich and First Lord of the British Admiralty at the time of Cook's voyage. Montague Island protects the sound from the heavy swells of the open Pacific Ocean. Brown bear and Sitka black-tailed deer are common on the island, and many sea otters live in the shallow waters off the northwest coast. Kenai Lumber Company is cutting timber near several bays on the leeward side of the island.

2. Axel Lind Island. Abandoned fox farm buildings are clearly visible on this island, named in 1908 for a local resident. Louie Van stocked the island in 1916 with four pairs of blue foxes and harvested ten pelts two years later. He eventually built a large log house, two fish houses, a large warehouse, eleven feed houses and a dock. At one time the ranch even had a couple of milk goats. Fishermen still occasionally use a sauna bath located behind the house. Fox farms operated on dozens of islands throughout the sound until fur prices dropped in 1926. Bald eagles commonly perch on snags in this area.

3. Eaglek Island. Tiny Eaglek Island, only 0.5 mile [*0.8 km*] long, was also the site of a fox farm. An eagle nest on this island is visible from the ferry. A bird colony on nearby Eaglek Rock is crowded with black-legged kittiwakes, glaucous-winged gulls and arctic terns.

4. Eaglek Bay. This scenic area contains many islands and coves. Cascade Falls (not visible from the ferry), at the head of Cascade Bay, is 75 to 100 feet [*23 to 31 m*] high. Silver, red, pink and chum salmon, abundant in the area, occasionally are seen clearing the water next to the ferry in silvery leaps. Enterprising clam diggers can find several beaches in which to sink a spade. Archeologist Frederica de Laguna, who made an extensive survey of the sound in 1933, reported several old Chugach Eskimo village sites in this area.

5. Kiniklik. This Native village was abandoned in the 1890s. A few old people in Tatitlek remember living here when they were children. Old pilings and some debris mark the former site of a Russian Orthodox log church and seven or eight frame houses.

6. Olsen Island. This 1 mile [*1.6 km*] long island was named for an early fox farm operator who lived here during the 1920's. In his still-standing cabin, the U.S. Forest Service in 1969 found an attic full of bald eagle tails, suggesting that the last occupant supplemented his income by killing bald eagles. Eagle claws brought $2.00 at the time the bounty was nullified by federal decree in 1952.

7. Unakwik Inlet. Meares Glacier, one of the two glaciers in the sound that are advancing slightly (the other is Harvard Glacier at the head of College Fiord), discharges icebergs at the head of this 19 mile [*31 km*] long inlet. At Cannery Creek halfway up the east side, only concrete footings today mark the site of a salmon cannery that operated from 1918 until the 1930s. Commercial fishing takes place in Unakwik Inlet for large shrimp and blue king crab. Sport anglers take dungeness crabs and steamer clams. Bird experts theorize that the estimated 10,000 Kittlitz's murrelets found throughout the inlet nest in upland rock screes away from the water. Few nests have ever been found, though this is one of the most common birds in the sound.

The epicenter of the Good Friday earthquake of 1964 was beneath Miner's Lake, just east of Unakwik Inlet. The earth tremors, strongest ever recorded on the North American continent, lasted up to five minutes and registered between 8.4 and 8.6 on the Richter scale. Land to the west of Unakwik Inlet sank as much as 8 feet [*2.4 m*], while land to the east rose about 6 feet [*1.8 m*]. Portions of Montague Island rose almost 38 feet [*11.5 m*]. Huge sea waves accounted for most of the loss of life and damage to property. The Geology chapter contains a description of the devastating earthquake and its aftermath.

8. Storey Island. This 4 mile [*6.4 km*] long island was the site of the most successful fox farm in Prince William Sound, operating from 1895 to the late 1920s. The island was named for Walter Storey of San Francisco, one of the fox farm operators. Improvements on the island included two houses, employee quarters, a blacksmith shop, carpenter shop, goat barn, 16 feed houses, several boats and a wharf. In the garden grew raspberries, currants and apple trees. Sitka black-tailed deer are found here. The edges of the island contain nesting areas for tufted and horned puffins, pigeon guillemots and rhinoceros auklets.

9. Peak Island. This island, named after a high point of land and occasionally referred to as Little Naked Island, was used as a fox farm from

1895 to the late 1920s. Mrs. Alice Clocke, whose husband was a fox farmer, spent most of her life here before her death in 1973. She lived in a home made of wreckage salvaged from the 1964 Good Friday earthquake.

10. Naked Island. This island was so named because Natives supposedly found an insane, naked woman here. James McPherson operated a fox farm on this island around the turn of the century. A few sea otters live in waters surrounding the island. During the winter, Sitka black-tailed deer forage along the south shore.

11. Wells Bay. The precipitous Yosemite-like shoreline of this bay is composed of granite. One of the major concentrations of western yellow cedar in the sound grows in this area. Many birds, including bald eagles, seagulls, arctic terns and ducks, inhabit the bay. Canada geese winter on the flats near the head of the bay.

12. Fairmount Island. William Beyers, a founder of the town of Valdez, operated a fox farm on the southwest side of the island with the help of his Native wife and numerous children. At nearby Fairmount Point, a freezing plant, open most of the year, processes salmon, crabs, herring and herring roe-on-kelp. Seafood from this plant may be purchased at 10th and M Lockers in Anchorage.

13. Outpost Island. The ferry makes a wide swing around this area of shoals. Large ocean swells entering the sound through Hinchinbrook Entrance, 42 miles [67 km] to the south, are often felt along this part of the ferry route.

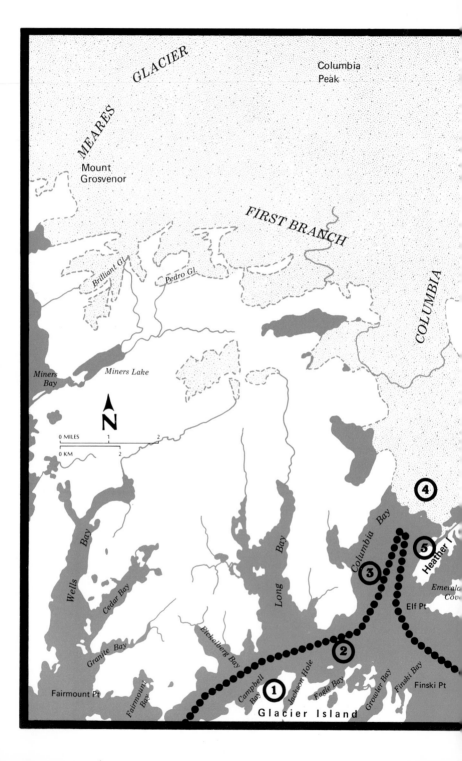

GLACIER

MEARES

Columbia
Peak

Mount
Grosvenor

FIRST BRANCH

Brilliant Gl.   Pedro Gl.

COLUMBIA

Miners Lake

Miners
Bay

N

0 MILES   1   2
0 KM   2

④

⑤

Columbia
Bay

Heather I

③

Emerald
Cove

Wells
Bay

Long
Bay

Cedar Bay

Eichelberg Bay

Elf Pt

Granite Bay

②

Growler Bay

Finski Bay

Fairmount Pt

Fairmount
Bay

Campbell
Bay

①

Jackson Hole

Eagle Bay

Finski Pt

Glacier Island

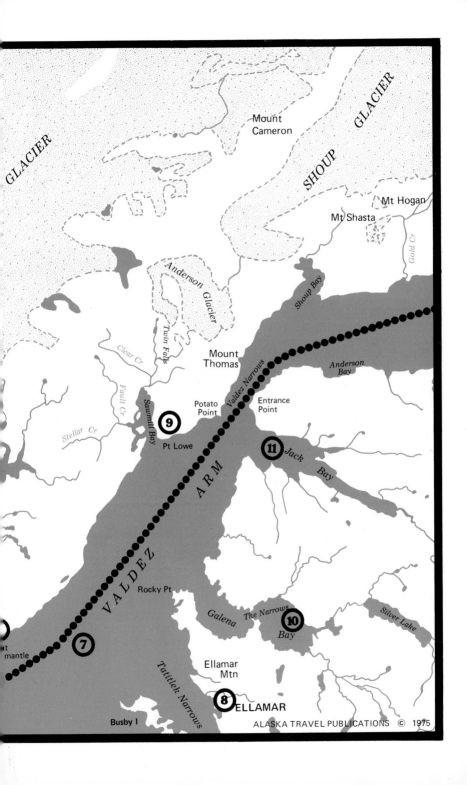

GLACIER

Mount
Cameron

SHOUP GLACIER

Mt Hogan

Mt Shasta

Gold Cr

Anderson Glacier

Twin Falls

Clear Cr

Shoup Bay

Anderson Bay

Mount Thomas

Fault Cr

Sawmill Bay

Stellar Cr

Valdez Narrows

Potato Point

Entrance Point

(9)

Pt Lowe

(11) Jack Bay

ARM

VALDEZ

Rocky Pt

Galena

The Narrows

(10) Bay

Silver Lake

(7)

mantle

Ellamar Mtn

(8) ELLAMAR

Tatitlek Narrows

Busby I

ALASKA TRAVEL PUBLICATIONS © 1975

Ferry Route Map 5

1. Glacier Island. Fox farms operated on this island from 1900 through the late 1920s. A few buildings of an abandoned fox farm on the edge of Irish Cove are visible from the ferry. Many of the old fox feed pens are still in good condition.

Boats and floatplanes often make the numerous bays of this beautiful island their destination. Jackson Hole, a bay which takes its name from Jackson Hole, Wyoming, has a very narrow entrance affected by swift tidal currents. Toward the head of Eagle Bay is a "skookum chuck," a tide funnel passable only at high slack tide. At other times this area has an appearance of fast-running river rapids. About a 12 foot [*3.7 m*] difference between high and low tide occurs in the sound.

Glacier Island, composed mostly of granite, is the site of an unusual geologic phenomenon: pillow lava, found on the south shore, was created by lava bubbling up on the floor of the ocean, forming banks of puffy rock hemispheres marked by radiating fracture lines.

Sea lions occasionally seen swimming near Outpost Island or Point Freemantle come from a haul-out area at Bull Head on the south shore of the island.

2. Icebergs. Ice of all shapes and sizes, common in the channel north of Glacier Island, calves from the active tidewater terminus of Columbia Glacier. Because all the air bubbles have been compressed out of them, the ice chunks are a vivid blue color and take a long time to melt. More than nine-tenths of their mass is submerged in salt water. Geologists estimate that some of the ice that makes up these icebergs fell as snow more than 2000 years ago.

3. Columbia Bay. This 5.5 mile [*8.9 km*] long bay is dominated by awesome Columbia Glacier. Icebergs choke the bay in front of the tidewater terminus of the glacier, often extending about 2 miles [*3 km*] into the bay. Unless icebergs are too numerous, the ferry approaches within 0.5 mile [*0.8 km*] of the face. As the ferry nears the glacier, two peaks just above the glacier disappear from view. These peaks, 3652 feet [*1113 m*] and 3404 feet [*1308 m*] high, are 8 miles [*13 km*] to the north of the face of the glacier. Where the ferry pauses to allow passengers to sightsee, the water beneath the ship is over 80 fathoms [*480 feet or 146 m*] deep, while at the face of the glacier water depths vary from 12 to 40 feet [*4 to 14 m*].

Hundreds of harbor seals rest on icebergs in the bay. Sea life is abundant here, because cold water promotes the growth of various plankton (microscopic water plants and animals). A thermocline, a middle layer of warm water found in most bodies of water, is less prominent here because of constant agitation from icebergs. Thus, plankton, which thrives in cold water, has uninhibited passage to the top, aided by this turbulence. Small fish eat the plankton and in turn are eaten by large fish, bald eagles, black-legged kittiwakes, glaucous-winged gulls and harbor seals. Commercial fishermen harvest thousands of tons of herring in Columbia Bay in April and May.

4. Columbia Glacier. This active glacier, named by the Harriman Expedition in 1899 for Columbia University in New York, reaches about 41 miles [*66 km*] back into the Chugach Mountains. Its area is around 440 square miles [*708 sq km*]. The terminus in the west arm of Columbia Bay as seen from the ferry is about 2 miles [*3.2 km*] wide and up to 300 feet [*100 m*] high.

Columbia Glacier has its sources in the Chugach Mountains where large amounts of snow fall annually. The snow, compressed into dense ice under the weight of successive snowfalls, creeps downhill in response to gravity. Because of the lack of air bubbles, glacial ice appears blue, absorbing other colors. Columbia Glacier advances as rapidly as 10 feet [*3 m*] a day. Visitors can sometimes anticipate an icefall by looking for a section of the ice cliff that is leaning out and has small trickles of ice falling from behind on both sides; an icefall may occur at that spot within a few minutes. For additional information on Columbia Glacier, see the Geology chapter.

5. Heather Island. This 3 mile [*4.8 km*] long island was named by the Harriman Expedition in 1899 for a species of heath *(Calluna vulgaris)* that grows here. Readily evident on the side of Heather Island nearest the glacier is a trimline, or area empty of vegetation, which was scoured when the glacier made a slight advance in the 1930s and then retreated.

6. Point Freemantle. Vancouver named this point in 1794. The ferry may roll here due to the swell coming through Hinchinbrook Entrance from the Gulf of Alaska. A significant herring roe (egg) harvest takes place in this area in the spring.

7. Valdez Arm. Sport anglers travel by small boat from Valdez to take advantage of the good fishing for pink and silver salmon and halibut. Ferry passengers should watch for Dall porpoises, common in this area.

8. Ellamar. This old copper mining town, situated at the foot of massive Copper Mountain, was established around 1898 to develop a large lens of chalcopyrite (copper ore) located just offshore. Some ore was removed through underground shafts, while surface ore was removed after construction of a 400 foot [*122 m*] cofferdam. Active mining continued until about 1919. In succeeding years, fish canneries operated here: Western Fisheries until 1940 followed by Ellamar Packing Company. Many of the virtually abandoned old buildings, visible from many miles away with the aid of binoculars, are still standing.

Southwest of Ellamar is steep-sided Bligh Island, named by Captain George Vancouver for Royal Navy Captain William Bligh (1754-1817).

This is the same Captain Bligh who was commander of the mutiny-struck H.M.S. *Bounty* in 1789.

A few miles south of Ellamar is the Native village of Tatitlek. The ferry makes a flag stop near Tatitlek en route between Valdez and Cordova. The town, with a year-round population of about 60, consists of some 15 frame buildings. In the center of the village is a beautiful white Russian Orthodox church, visible from the ferry on clear days. The primary livelihood of the villagers is commercial fishing. Under terms of the Native Claims Act, Tatitlek Natives are selecting from Chugach National Forest over 69,000 acres [*27,925 hectares*] in the vicinity of their village.

9. Sawmill Bay. Sportfishing boats from Valdez often travel to this bay for silver and pink salmon, halibut, dungeness crab and clams. A U.S. Forest Service public recreation cabin is located here. Bill Jackson, "mayor" of Sawmill Bay, reports that during the 1964 Good Friday earthquake the bay emptied and filled three times, ruining an attempt at oyster-seeding that he and a friend had begun in 1960.

10. Galena Bay. This 5 mile [*8 km*] long bay is a favorite destination of recreationists, with good fishing for silver and pink salmon. The U.S. Forest Service maintains two public recreation cabins on the edges of the bay. Named for lead ore deposits found in the vicinity, the bay was also the location of extensive copper mines. An abandoned dirt road, constructed about 1910, leads into the hills past old mining equipment.

11. Jack Bay. Captain Abercrombie, a U.S. Army explorer who aided many of the first gold miners in the region and who later pioneered the Richardson Trail to the Interior, named this 7 mile [*11 km*] long bay in 1898 for a local prospector named W. G. Jack. Russian traders once cut timber here, as evidenced by recently discovered old stumps. Harbor seals, brown and black bears and land otters are relatively common in the area. Sport anglers fish for silver and pink salmon.

Ferry Route Map 6

1. Valdez Narrows. This cliff-lined passage, about 2 miles [*3.2 km*] long and 3000 feet [*915 m*] wide, supports a limited commercial tanner crab fishery. Cascades of water throughout this area turn in winter to gigantic blue-tinged icicles.

2. Middle Rock. A Coast Guard day beacon and light are located here. Several additional markers have been added on both sides of Valdez Narrows in anticipation of the oil tankers that will be traveling between the Valdez Trans-Alaska Pipeline Terminal and West Coast ports.

3. Anderson Glacier. Look for the glacier and waterfall outlet stream on the cliffs directly above Valdez Narrows. Anderson Glacier is one of three major glaciers within the city limits of Valdez. The others are Shoup and Valdez glaciers.

4. Port Valdez. This bay, the northernmost year-round ice-free port on the Pacific Coast of North America, is about 12 miles [*19 km*] long and 2.5 to 3 miles [*4 to 4.8 km*] wide.

5. Shoup Glacier. This 17 mile [*27 km*] long glacier was probably named for one of the first U.S. Marshals assigned to Alaska, a colorful and well-known character. Ferry passengers can see the terminus of the glacier, which was one of the main tributaries to the extensive valley glacier that carved out Valdez Arm and Port Valdez thousands of years ago. For a few years early in this century, a commercial operation supplied ice from Shoup Glacier to Valdez and Fort Liscum in the summertime. During the 1964 Good Friday earthquake, an undersea slide from the submerged moraine of this glacier created a wave 170 feet [*52 m*] high, which toppled trees 100 feet [*30 m*] above the bay and deposited silt and sand 220 feet [*67 m*] above waterline. This wave is listed in the *Guinness Book of World Records*.

6. Cliff Mine. This was the most productive gold mine in the sound. Located in 1906 by "Red" Ellis, it operated until World War II. The Shoup Glacier seismic wave, mentioned above, destroyed most of the buildings of this mine, but wharf pilings and some of the debris are still visible. The mine shaft tunneled under the bay, and the ferry route passes over the end of the now-flooded tunnel.

7. Gold Creek. Gold Creek waterfall, visible from the ferry, during rainy weather resembles a faucet pouring out of a mountain. Several gold mines operated along this creek, and the remains of a gold dredge still lie on the beach. One Gold Creek mine, the Happy Day mine, was worked by two partners, Charley Fleur and Scot MacAndres. During the winter of 1911,

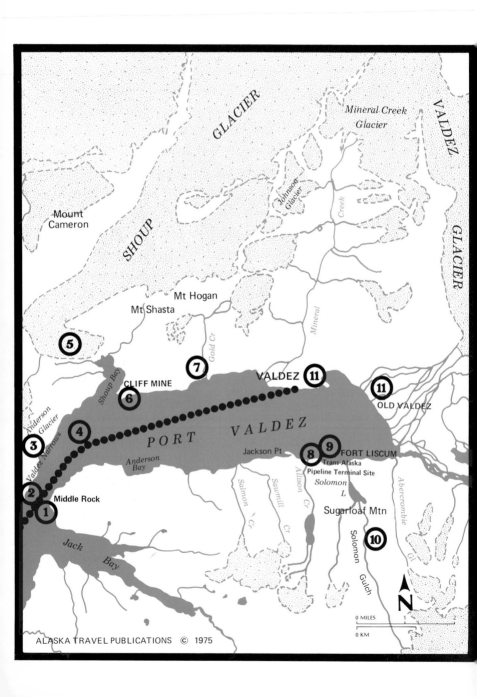

GLACIER

Mineral Creek
Glacier

VALDEZ

Johnson
Glacier

Creek

SHOUP

Mount
Cameron

GLACIER

Mt Hogan

Mt Shasta

Gold Cr

⑤

⑦

VALDEZ ⑪

⑪
OLD VALDEZ

CLIFF MINE

⑥

Shoup Bay

Mineral

Anderson
Glacier

③

Valdez Narrows

④

PORT   VALDEZ

Anderson
Bay

Jackson Pt

⑧ ⑨ FORT LISCUM
Trans-Alaska
Pipeline Terminal Site
Solomon
L

②

① Middle Rock

Salmon
Cr

Sawmill
Cr

Allison Cr

Abercrombie

Sugarloaf Mtn

Jack
Bay

Solomon
Gulch

⑩

N

0 MILES   1   2

0 KM

ALASKA TRAVEL PUBLICATIONS © 1975

when they were imprisoned in their tiny cabin by snow, Scot went berserk and threatened Charley, so Charley shot Scot. At his trial in Valdez, Charley was defended by Tony Dimond, a young lawyer who subsequently became mayor of Valdez and one of Alaska's Territorial delegates to Congress. Dimond persuaded the judge to let the court adjourn to the tiny cabin where the murder had taken place. The jury agreed that anyone imprisoned in such a place for a winter would be likely to go crazy. The jury found Charley not guilty.

8. Trans-Alaska Pipeline Terminal Site. The cluster of buildings and cleared area on the south side of Port Valdez is the site where tankers will eventually take on their cargo of oil. "Black gold" will flow through a 48 inch [*122 cm*] wide, 798 mile [*1283 km*] long pipe from Prudhoe Bay on Alaska's North Slope. Tank farm facilities are planned to include five loading berths and up to 14 million barrels of crude oil storage in 32 tanks. Large tankers, weighing from 45,000 to 150,000 deadweight tons and from 800 to 1000 feet [*240 to 300 m*] long, will transport crude oil from Valdez.

The U.S. Army established Fort Liscum near Valdez at the turn of the century to provide assistance to prospectors trying to reach the Klondike. Later it became a base for the building of telegraph lines to the Alaskan Interior. The Trans-Alaska Pipeline Terminal now occupies the land where the fort once stood.

KEN HINCHEY — ALAGCO COLLECTION

9. Fort Liscum (Dayville). Fort Liscum was established as Fort Valdez at the time of the Gold Rush to maintain order and was officially named Fort Liscum in 1900 after Colonel Liscum, commander of the United States Army 9th Infantry during the Boxer Rebellion. The fort later became the Signal Corps station for the telegraph cable that connected Valdez and Sitka. As many as 250 men were garrisoned here. Old photographs show neat white buildings surrounded by expansive lawns. The Army band gave regular summer concerts at the Valdez courthouse and became an important part of the social life of Valdez. Dances and card parties were frequent. Steam launches made regular trips between the fort and Valdez, carrying passengers and supplies and transporting children to school. The Army abandoned the fort during World War I. In 1930, the Day family homesteaded part of the land and began using the Army buildings as a salmon cannery and sawmill which operated until 1952. The site suffered extensive damage during the 1964 Good Friday earthquake, and as the deteriorated buildings were located too close to the pipeline terminal site, they have been dismantled in preparing the site for construction.

10. Solomon Gulch. This steep canyon, located to the right or down-bay side of Sugarloaf Mountain, is the site of the 5.25 mile [*8.4 km*] aerial tramway which at the time it was in operation was the longest in Alaska. Completed in 1915, it contained a total of 22 miles [*35 km*] of cable and 77 tram towers and brought copper ore from the Midas Mine to waiting ships, which then sailed with their cargo to smelters in Tacoma, Washington.

11. Valdez

History. Valdez (pronounced *Val-DEEZ*), a seacoast settlement ringed by spectacular snow-capped peaks, is aptly nicknamed the "Switzerland of Alaska." Not the least of Valdez's colorful attractions is its rich and colorful past. Spanish explorer Lieutenant Salvador Fidalgo, in his search for the Northwest Passage, became on June 16, 1790, the first European to enter Port Valdez. He named it for Antonio Valdes y Basan, a celebrated Spanish naval officer who had approved plans and financing for Fidalgo's voyage. Captain George Vancouver, R.N., who explored this portion of Prince William Sound in 1794, adopted this name, but changed the spelling to Valdez.

The town of Valdez had modest beginnings as a trading center in the 1870s. In the 1890s, the Pacific Steam Whaling Company based its operations here, harvesting whales that were attracted by large schools of herring in the sound. A three-story company dormitory became a permanent town structure, later housing a succession of businesses.

Major changes took place in 1897. Gold was discovered in the faraway Klondike in the Yukon Territory, and promoters advertised an overland route from Valdez to the gold fields. Ships disgorged thousands of miners at

The community of Valdez experienced its first big growth during gold mining days at the beginning of the century. Now the "black gold" that will soon pour through the Trans-Alaska Pipeline has given the town an even larger economic boost.
NEIL AND ELIZABETH JOHANNSEN

the foot of Valdez Glacier, but few of these stampeders conquered its icy wastes. Nearly all turned back to Valdez, and many whiled away the time prospecting the cliffs and gullies of the sound. Valdez soon evolved into a prosperous and permanent mining center. Mining for copper and gold peaked between 1900 and 1910, resulting in a pre-World War I population of more than 6000 persons.

The military played an important role in the development of Valdez. In 1898 the U.S. Army established a military post on the moraine of Valdez Glacier for the hordes of prospectors seeking a way over the glacier. A larger military reservation was established across the bay the same year, to serve as a base for the building of telegraph lines and to keep order on the Thompson Pass Trail, the route that later became the Richardson Highway.

After the mining boom, Valdez maintained its economic base as a transshipment center. Vessels of the Alaska Steamship Company offloaded goods here which were then shipped to the Interior. During World War II, Valdez was an important receiving center for raw materials to build the Alcan Highway.

Valdez is both an old and new city. The 1964 Good Friday earthquake and ensuing seismic sea waves destroyed much of the original town. Subsequent investigation by geologists confirmed pre-earthquake theories that the town was built on unstable glacial sediments. Following the 1964 disaster, the townspeople moved to a new location on more stable bedrock, several miles to the west. The Mineral Creek Subdivision, or "new Valdez," is now one of the fastest growing communities in Alaska.

Exploring Valdez

. . . Stop by the Valdez Chamber of Commerce at the corner of Egan Drive and Chenega Street, (open during summer months). The recently remodeled centennial building houses a collection of memorabilia from early Valdez.

. . . From Old Valdez eleven glaciers can be seen. Drive to Valdez Glacier, a short distance beyond Valdez Airport, or go a couple of miles beyond the top of Thompson Pass (Mile 28 on the Richardson Highway) to Worthington Glacier.

. . . Drive and hike up rough but scenic Mineral Creek Canyon. An old stamp mill, reached by an 8 mile [*13 km*] road and trail, is a reminder of once widespread gold mining. During August red and orange salmonberries abound in the canyon.

. . . Take a look at the hundreds of miles of 48 inch [*122 cm*] pipe stacked at the old Valdez townsite for the 798 mile [*1283 km*] long Trans-Alaska Pipeline. Construction is underway at the pipeline terminal site and at many points along the pipeline route. Visitors may view pipeline construction from a number of points along the Richardson Highway. To get a close look at the pipeline terminal site, look through the telescope at the visitor center next to the ferry dock. An artist's conception of the finished terminal plus general information on the pipeline project are also available here. During summer months in the Chamber of Commerce building, Alyeska Pipeline Service Company sponsors films about the northland followed by a slide presentation about the pipeline.

. . . Visit Keystone Canyon, location of many scenic waterfalls. An old tunnel in the canyon is all that remains of an attempt in 1905 to build a railroad from Valdez to the Interior. After fierce controversy the railroad was routed from Cordova through the Copper River Canyon. The disputes and drama of this era are described in Rex Beach's novel, *The Iron Trail.* The proposed Keystone Canyon State Park encompasses about 310,000 acres [*125,000 hectares*] of this spectacular area.

. . . Try fishing. Freshwater Robe Lake contains dolly varden char and cutthroat trout. There is good fishing for salmon, halibut and a variety of shellfish, particularly in the vicinity of Sawmill Bay and Galena Bay in Prince William Sound. The Valdez Silver Salmon Derby, held annually from the beginning of August to Labor Day, offers a substantial cash prize and smaller daily and weekly prizes. A number of charter fishing boats are available.

. . . Take a sightseeing tour. Kennedy Air Service offers flightseeing tours of Columbia Glacier and of Prince William Sound. Charter boats are available for trips to Columbia Glacier and across Prince William Sound. (The Sheffield House has up-to-date information on some of these charters.)

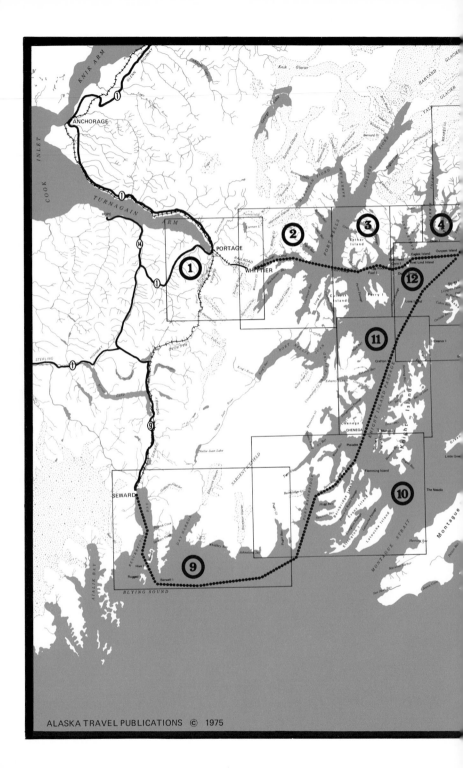

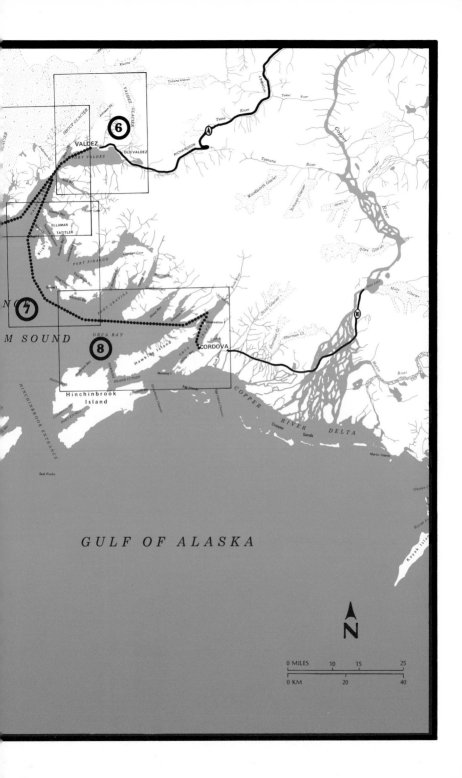

GULF OF ALASKA

Fiords and Fishing Boats

Summary. The state ferries M.V. *Tustemena* and M.V. *Bartlett* operate between Valdez and Cordova during the summer season, making the 85 mile [*137 km*] trip one way in about six hours. The M.V. *Bartlett* makes this run several times a week during the remainder of the year.

The first leg of the voyage, through Port Valdez and Valdez Arm, is identical to that of the last portion of the trip between Whittier and Valdez and is described in the Whittier to Valdez ferry log section. From the abandoned town of Ellamar on the mainland northeast of Bligh Island, the ferry turns south and skirts several headlands before reaching Cordova. On this route passengers frequently see whales, sea otters, bald eagles and sea birds. Passengers traveling from Cordova to Valdez should read the following route description in reverse order.

Valdez to Galena Bay. See the Whittier to Valdez ferry log section for a description of this part of the route.

Photo opposite: The state ferry occasionally makes a flag stop for passengers from the Native village of Tatitlek. Situated near the base of Copper Mountain, the region contained dozens of copper mining claims at the turn of the century. Now a herring-roe-on-kelp fishery thrives in shallow waters of the vicinity each spring.

GIL MULL

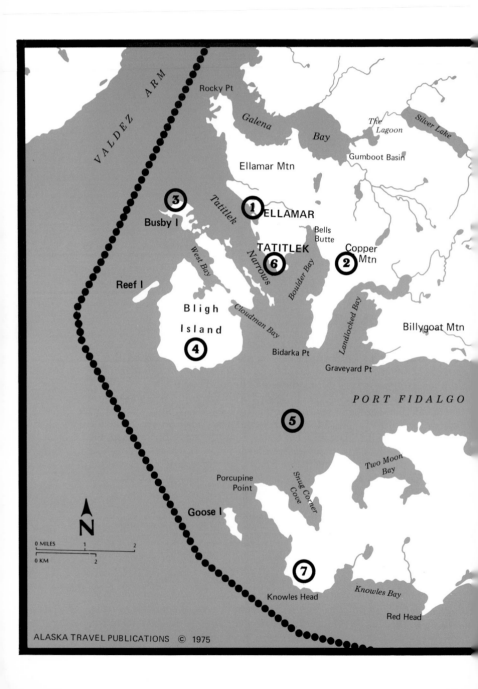

ALASKA TRAVEL PUBLICATIONS © 1975

Ferry Route Map 7

1. Ellamar. This old copper mining town, north of Tatitlek Narrows and visible from the ferry, was started around 1900 to mine a huge lens of chalcopyrite (copper ore) located just offshore. Much of the ore was removed after construction of a 400 foot [*122 m*] cofferdam. Active mining continued until around 1920. In succeeding years, fish canneries operated here. Many of the old buildings are still standing.

2. Copper Mountain. This spectacular landmark, 3858 feet [*1175 m*] high and 6 miles [*9 km*] southeast of Ellamar, was the site of dozens of copper claims around the turn of the century.

3. Busby Island. Fox farms operated on this island in the late nineteenth century and in the 1920s. On March 20, 1908, the S.S. *Saratoga* was wrecked here. Part of the fleet of the Alaska Steamship Company, the iron steamship departed Ellamar in clear weather but was soon caught in a heavy snowstorm. As she approached Busby Island, she slowed to half-speed. Despite this precaution, she struck the southwest part of the island, tearing a large hole in her hull amidships and flooding all compartments. The tug *Elsie* of the Valdez Dock Company removed the passengers, who subsequently signed an affidavit acquitting the captain of all blame and praising the officers and crew for courage and good judgment. Although there was no loss of life, and most of the cargo, baggage and mail was saved, the *Saratoga* broke up and became a total loss. Bits and pieces of rusting machinery, visible at low tide, mark the remains of this ship.

4. Bligh Island. Captain George Vancouver, R.N., named this mountainous island for William Bligh, who visited the sound in 1778 as a midshipman with Captain Cook and who later gained lasting fame as captain of the H.M.S. *Bounty.*

5. Port Fidalgo. Vancouver named this 25 mile [*40 km*] long bay after Salvador Fidalgo, the Spanish explorer who in 1790 explored much of eastern Prince William Sound. Captain James Cook, first European to enter the sound, anchored in Snug Corner Cove for eight days in 1778. Numerous abandoned copper mines, dating from the turn of the century, dot hillsides near Port Fidalgo. Few of these mines are still visible.

The region near the head of the bay harbors much wildlife, including numerous waterbirds, harbor seals, sea otters, mountain goats, brown and black bears, and bald eagles.

An important herring roe-on-kelp fishery takes place each spring in shallow waters near the mouth of Port Fidalgo. Fishermen also take king and tanner crab from deeper waters.

6. Tatitlek. The ferry makes a flag stop near this Native village, which has a summer population of about 160 (winter population about 63). The ferry stops near the old town of Ellamar, because the water at Tatitlek is too shallow for such a large vessel. As there is no safe dock, the stern ramp of the ferry is lowered, and a boat from the village takes passengers to and from shore. The village consists of about 15 homes clustered around a picturesque Russian Orthodox church. Most of the villagers fish commercially, primarily for salmon. Under terms of the Native Land Claims Act, Tatitlek is selecting about 69,000 acres [*27,925 hectares*] of land from the surrounding Chugach National Forest.

7. Knowles Head. Boats use this steep mountainous headland, jutting out between Port Fidalgo and Port Gravina, as a navigational landmark. Near this point boats often encounter ocean swells that come through Hinchinbrook Entrance from the tempestuous Gulf of Alaska. Ferry passengers should watch for sea otters, common around Knowles Head and Port Gravina, and for occasional sea lions.

Photo opposite: Officers on the bridge of the state ferry M/V BARTLETT *maintain careful watch for navigational hazards. They often report sightings of whales over the public address system to passengers.*

NEIL AND ELIZABETH JOHANNSEN

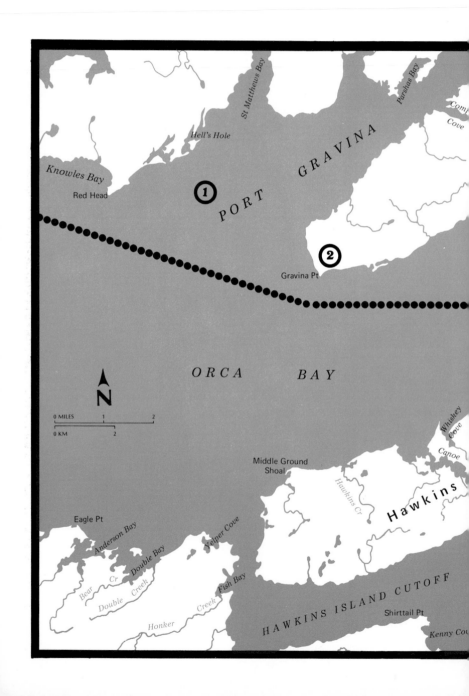

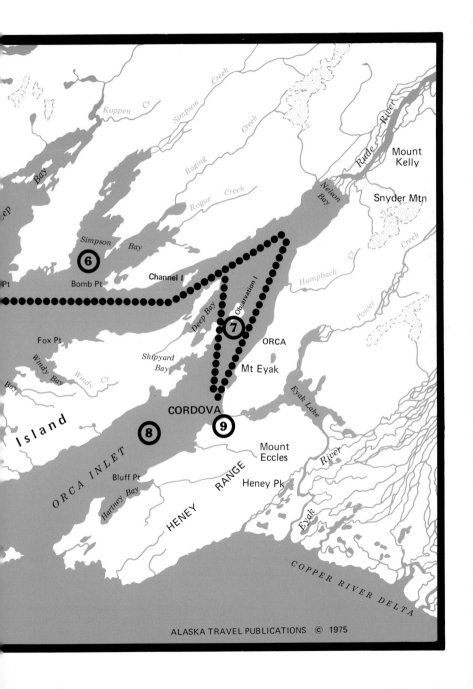

Ferry Route Map 8

1. Port Gravina. In 1790, Salvador Fidalgo named this 9 mile [*14.5 km*] wide bay for Frederico Gravina, a prominent Spanish naval officer of the day. Humpback whales, killer whales and occasional sei whales are seen here. Brown and black bears and mountain goats inhabit the land at the head of the bay. Birdlife includes bald eagles and ducks; trumpeter swans nest at the confluence of Gravina River and Dead Creek. Fishermen harvest kelp roe and catch pink and chum salmon, king crab, halibut and herring.

2. Gravina Point. The ferry passes close by this point of land. Black bears and Sitka black-tailed deer may be seen foraging on the shore in spring. In July and August, salmon fishermen successfully use this "hook point" for their seine nets.

3. Hawkins Island. Vancouver named this 20 mile [*32 km*] long island in 1794. Several prehistoric village sites have been found on its southern and western shores. Most famous of these is Palugvik, location of extensive digging by archeologist Frederica de Laguna in 1933. Her investigations show that the Chugach Eskimos had resided in the sound for thousands of years. Today the Palugvik site is a national historic landmark, but because it is difficult to reach, the plaque commemorating Palugvik is on display in the Cordova museum.

4. Orca Bay. The name of this 14 mile [*23 km*] wide bay is derived from the Orca Cannery of the Pacific Steam Whaling Company, which was named for one of the company's vessels, named in turn for the killer whale, *Orcinus orca.* Orca Bay is a good place to watch for these carnivorous marine mammals, particularly in fall.

5. Sheep Bay. Brown and black bears, sea otters and harbor seals inhabit the head of the bay. Deer forage on beaches in late winter and spring. Recreationists find dungeness crabs and butter clams. Herons, geese and arctic terns nest at the head of the bay.

6. Simpson Bay. Brown and black bears are regularly observed here, particularly in August and early September when silver salmon spawn. In late summer sport anglers also find silver salmon and dungeness crabs in this relatively shallow bay. The U.S. Forest Service maintains a public recreation cabin on the south side of the bay.

7. Observation Island. The ferry passes on either side of this scenic island, depending on the level of the tide. The eastern route passes close to the huge New England Fisheries cannery. The shallower western route is the more direct.

8. Orca Inlet. Razor clams dug from the mud flats at the southern end of this 15 mile [*24 km*] long body of water helped Cordova earn the title, "Razor Clam Capital of the World." In the early 1960s, however, the clam beds were overdug and further depleted by land uplift during the 1964 Good Friday earthquake. Clams may still be dug at low tide from approved beaches. Cordova residents use crab pots to capture dungeness crabs, which are attracted by cannery wastes. Millions of shorebirds and waterfowl, landing on the tidal flats during spring and fall migrations, are most numerous between May 5 and May 20 of each year.

9. Cordova

History. With an area population of about 2500, this fishing town has picturesque old buildings and a friendly Alaskan atmosphere. It offers a range of visitor services, including hotels, restaurants, laundromats, ice and propane. (See the Facilities chapter for more detailed information.)

Once-bountiful runs of Pacific salmon and abundant clams attracted the first inhabitants, the Eyak Indians, who frequently camped at the west end of Eyak Lake. About 1893, white settlers began to arrive and soon built a

The fishing community of Cordova, nestled among fluffy clouds, had its origins as saltwater terminus of the Copper River and Northwestern Railway.

CHARLES D. EVANS

cannery at Orca, a few miles northeast of the present town. This cannery employed Chinese workers from San Francisco. A few years after the establishment of the cannery southeast of Observation Island, a second cannery was established on Odiak Slough. This was a floating cannery, served by fishermen who caught red salmon in Copper River and hauled their catches up Eyak River, across Eyak Lake, then via mule-drawn carts on a tramway to the cannery.

The name of the town is probably derived from the original Spanish name given to the area, "Puerto Cordova" (Port Cordova), by Spanish naval explorer Salvador Fidalgo, who made a reconnaissance of eastern Prince William Sound in 1790.

In 1906, Michael J. Heney, the founder of Cordova, began construction of a railroad from Cordova to the Alaskan Interior. In what became an epic struggle in both a harsh political and physical climate, Cordova finally bested the towns of Valdez and Katalla to become the enviable saltwater terminus of the Copper River and Northwestern Railway.

In May 1911, hundreds of angry Cordovans staged a latter-day Boston Tea Party. The event became the nationally publicized "Coal Party." The federal government had withdrawn the nearby Bering River coal fields from public entry, forcing Alaskans to buy expensive Canadian coal. The president of the local Chamber of Commerce led a group of townspeople who pitched several hundred tons of Canadian fuel into the bay. The effort eventually resulted in the reopening of the coal fields.

For the next two decades railroad cars hauled copper ore from the Kennecott Mines to waiting ships at Cordova, which then sailed to smelters in Tacoma, Washington. Mining ended in 1938 with the closing of the mines and the railroad, but by then Cordova had gained a foothold as an important fishing port.

Major fires have destroyed many of the old buildings. The most recent fire, in 1963, destroyed almost half of the Cordova business district. Although much of the town has been rebuilt, a special "old-Alaska" charm remains.

Exploring Cordova

. . . Visit the recently renovated Cordova Centennial Museum for insights into the history of Prince William Sound. Visitors will find a three-hole baidarka (kayak) of the Chugach Eskimos, old Russian and Native implements from the abandoned sea otter hunting center at Nuchek-Fort Constantine on Hinchinbrook Island, newspapers and other memorabilia from the days of the Copper River and Northwestern Railway, and a large exhibit devoted to the life of Captain Joseph F. Bernard, a pioneer Alaskan who participated in the Nome Gold Rush and later traded and explored along the Arctic coast from 1903 to 1925. He then lived near Cordova for many years, working as a fisherman and boat builder.

. . . Visit the Cordova Chamber of Commerce (Box 99, Cordova, Alaska

99574), located on Main Street next to the First Bank of Cordova. This center provides free information on visitor facilities.

. . . Explore the town. Photograph the picturesque old wood frame buildings on Main Street, such as the Alaskan Hotel and Cordova House, both built in 1908, or the homes of "Railroad Row" near Eyak Lake, built about 1910 for key personnel of the Copper River and Northwestern Railway. One of the first buildings in Cordova was the Red Dragon, now a private residence. Painted with red paint donated by railway construction crews, it became a community center and library for miners, railway men and fishermen and was used for Sunday church services prior to the construction of the Episcopal Church. Alaskan artist Eustace Ziegler was an early leader of this church. Visit the Alaska Airlines office on Main Street and look at bush pilot memorabilia.

. . . Tour the canneries, mainstay of Cordova industry. By advance arrangement, you may watch workers process salmon, dungeness, king and tanner (snow or queen) crabs, halibut and herring roe. The seafood processing season is one of the longest and most diversified in the state, operating nearly year-round, primarily on salmon or tanner crab.

. . . Absorb the sights, sounds and smells of the small-boat harbor. Watch boats leave for salmon, crab and halibut fishing grounds. Overhead, bald eagles, seagulls and crows circle, looking for scraps. The harbor was extensively redredged following the 1964 Good Friday earthquake, when the land rose about 6 feet [1.8 m]. Spike Island, a tiny spruce-covered islet near the entrance to the harbor, was the scene of World War II gun emplacements for harbor defense.

. . . Try local fishing. Tasty halibut and dungeness crab, feeding on cannery wastes, may be caught from Cordova docks. Silver and red salmon in Eyak River challenge anglers. Dolly varden char, cutthroat trout and arctic grayling abound in many nearby freshwater lakes and streams. Tasty razor clams may be dug on tidal flats of Orca Bay. Cordova restaurants serve appetizing fresh seafood; a local specialty is fresh, steaming razor clams.

. . . Ride a 3000 foot [914 m] long, 75-chair ski lift. The challenging new ski area on Tripod Hill, with an 800 foot [244 m] vertical rise, has runs for beginning, intermediate and advanced skiers. A small lodge, located at the bottom of the slope, is within walking distance of downtown Cordova. Cordova winters are characterized by relatively mild temperatures and abundant snow. Visitors may ride the chairlift in summer to enjoy a sweeping view of Cordova and the offshore islands of Prince William Sound. Cross-country skiers find good slopes between Tripod Hill and Eyak Lake.

. . . Take part in the Iceworm Festival, a three-day extravaganza annually held in February, featuring dances, sports competition, a talent show, a king and queen pageant, and a 150 foot [46 m] long multi-legged "Iceworm" which marches down Main Street during the parade which highlights the festival.

... Hike on the network of trails maintained by the U.S. Forest Service. Stop by the Forest Service office in the Federal Building for detailed and up-to-date information on trail conditions.

The Copper River Delta

Important Wildlife Habitat. The Copper River Delta, located east of Cordova and containing some of the most significant wildlife concentrations in Alaska, stretches along the seacoast some 45 miles [*73 km*] from Eyak River to Point Martin. The delta contains approximately 300 square miles [*500 sq km*] of tidal marshes interspersed with brush and patches of spruce, hemlock and cottonwood. The region is spotted with numerous freshwater lakes, ponds and marshes, some of which are linked by extensive intertidal sloughs and streams. The 1964 Good Friday earthquake brought about numerous changes on the delta, when the area rose an average of 6 feet [*1.8 m*], draining many former tideland areas.

The delta is traversed by the Copper River Highway, which generally follows the alignment of the former Copper River and Northwestern

The Copper River Delta is the only known nesting area of the dusky Canada goose.

JULIUS REYNOLDS, ALASKA DEPARTMENT OF FISH AND GAME

Railway. An Eyak Indian village once was situated near Alaganik Slough. In 1971, the flats on the seaward side of this highway were closed to use by off-road vehicles (ATVs, etc.) to protect valuable nesting habitat.

The best time to observe wildlife along the 27 miles [*43 km*] of highway between Cordova and the Copper River is just after sunrise or at dusk. Binoculars, a camera and a bird guide will add to your enjoyment of the trip.

The delta provides habitat for numerous species of animals. Beaver lodges indicate the presence of this large member of the rodent family. Mountain goats are visible as white dots on steep mountainsides to the north of the delta. Although often obscured by dense thickets of alder and willow, both brown and black bears roam the delta and during late summer and early fall may be seen eating spawning salmon. Moose are common on the delta. Not native to the area, the present population of over 500 animals developed from a transplant of 26 animals made by the U.S. Fish and Wildlife Service between 1949 and 1959.

Large concentrations of ducks, geese, swans and shorebirds indicate the importance of the Copper River Delta as a major waterfowl nesting area. Nearly two million birds use the delta for nesting during the summer and for resting and feeding during spring and fall migrations. The grass flats and ponds bordering the tidal beaches support populations of ducks, majestic trumpeter swans and imperiled dusky Canada geese.

Near Mile 8 on the highway is a favored nesting area for the dusky Canada goose, although these birds are not often seen from the highway during their nesting period. During this time, adult dusky Canada geese molt their flight feathers, forcing them to remain earthbound for two or three weeks with their young. During August, as summer wanes, these birds are frequently seen taking short flights between their nesting grounds and nearby feeding areas. In late fall, they migrate to the Willamette Valley in Oregon to winter, returning to the Copper River Flats in spring. Although dusky Canada geese presently number a healthy 19,000 to 30,000, deterioration of either of these only known habitats could pose a serious threat to the survival of this species.

Just beyond the Alaganik Slough access road, at approximately Mile 17 [*27 km*], is a trumpeter swan nesting area. This graceful white bird, largest of all North American waterfowl, has a wingspan of almost 8 feet [*2.4 m*]. Forty years ago, the trumpeter swan, so named for its characteristic call, faced extinction. This swan is now making a comeback. In 1969, the species was removed from the federal list of rare and endangered birds. The largest known concentration of trumpeter swans in the world breeds throughout the Copper and Bering River deltas; ornithologists estimate that about one-fourth of the known world population of this species, numbering about 4500 birds, breeds within a 50 mile [*80 km*] radius of the mouth of the Copper River. Nesting areas should not be disturbed, particularly in light of the relative scarcity of this species.

Management for Wildlife and Recreation. To conserve this rich wildlife and birdlife area, the U.S. Forest Service, in cooperation with the Alaska Department of Fish and Game and the Alaska Department of Natural Resources, in 1967 established the 330,000 acre [*134,000 hectares*] Copper Delta Game Management Area. In addition, the U.S. Forest Service maintains a number of public recreation cabins on the delta. (Refer to the Facilities chapter for more information on these cabins.) Additional information on the Copper River Delta may be obtained from the U.S. Forest Service (Federal Building, Cordova), or from local offices of the Alaska Department of Fish and Game (adjacent to the Cordova small-boat harbor).

Copper River. This river, one of the largest in Alaska, supports an important commercial fishery. Many thousands of sockeye, king and silver salmon spawn in tributaries, though sportfishing is poor in the glacially silted lower reaches of the river. Watch for harbor seals in the Copper River at Mile 27.

Mountains and Glaciers. Scott, Sheridan and Sherman glaciers, all named for Civil War generals, add to the imposing mountain backdrop of the Copper River Delta. A 4 mile [*6.4 km*] spur road leads from Mile 14 to Sheridan Glacier. Mountain goats are fairly common here; the area also offers good hiking. During the 1964 Good Friday earthquake, approximately 10 million cubic yards of rock, carried on a cushion of air, slid across nearby Sherman Glacier.

The Copper River Delta, east of Cordova, is one of the richest biological habitats in the world. Thousands of ducks, geese and swans nest in the area. Brown bear, black bear and moose are common. Glaciers and rugged peaks form a dramatic backdrop.
WILLIAM QUIRK

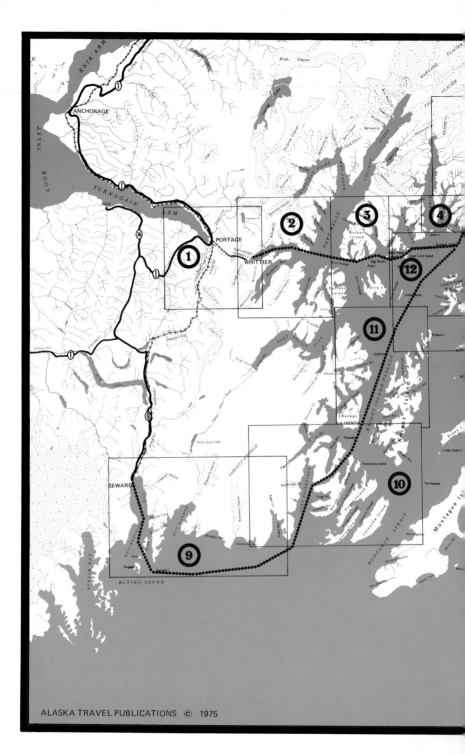

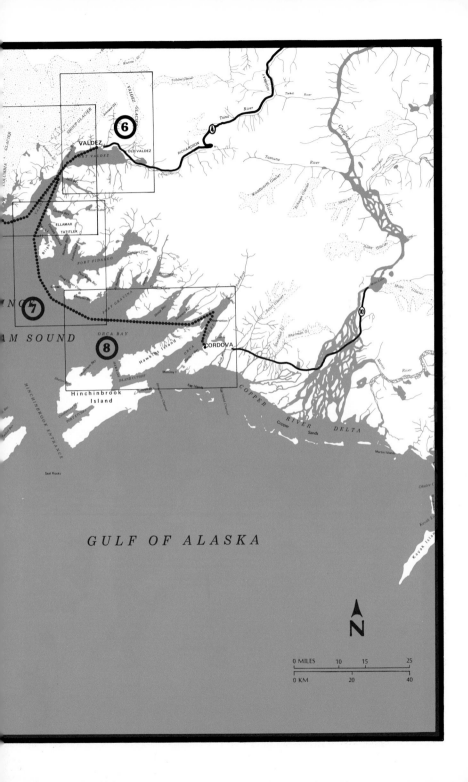

Ferry Route Map 9

1. Seward

General Information. Seward lies about three hours driving time southeast of Anchorage via the 127 mile [204 km] long Seward Highway, a paved two-lane road. The highway parallels Turnagain Arm for about 50 miles [80 km] before winding across the mountainous spine of the Kenai Peninsula to reach the seaside community of Seward. Sandwiched between sheer glacier-covered peaks at the head of Resurrection Bay, Seward is a gateway to the Gulf of Alaska and, indirectly, to Prince William Sound. The town has an area population of about 2300 and an economy based on tourism and fishing. A full range of service facilities includes lodging, campgrounds, restaurants, gift shops, dumping stations, ice, propane and laundromats.

History. Aleksandr Baranov, chief manager of the Russian American Company, sailed into Resurrection Bay in 1792, calling it "Voskresenskaya Gavan," meaning "Resurrection (Sunday) Harbor." Observing fine stands of timber in the vicinity, he chose the bay as the site for building the *Phoenix*, first European ship constructed on the West Coast of North America. In spite of labor and supply problems, the vessel was completed in 1794 under the direction of Englishman James Shields. The *Phoenix* sailed Alaskan waters until foundering in a Gulf of Alaska storm in 1800.

For nearly a hundred years after the building of the *Phoenix*, Resurrection Bay remained almost uninhabited. In 1884, a family named Lowell settled on the present Seward townsite. In May, 1902, a party of surveyors landed at Seward in search of a railroad route to Interior Alaska. Their findings were promising. Settlers followed in 1903, and in 1904 a post office was established. The city was named for William H. Seward, U.S. Secretary of State (1801-1872), who promoted the purchase of Alaska from Russia in 1867.

The Alaska Central Railroad, organized as a private stock company, had completed 71 miles [114 km] of track starting from Seward by 1915, when the federal government purchased the line. Organized as The Alaska Railroad, the route was completed in 1923 to Fairbanks. The ice-free port of Seward experienced considerable growth during railroad construction. The Iditarod Trail, a winter route to Nome and the Seward Peninsula, had its

Photo opposite: The M/V TUSTEMENA *makes Seward its home port. The community, situated at the head of mountain-fringed Resurrection Bay, has an economy based on tourism and fishing. The southern terminus of The Alaska Railroad is located here.*
STEVE MC CUTCHEON

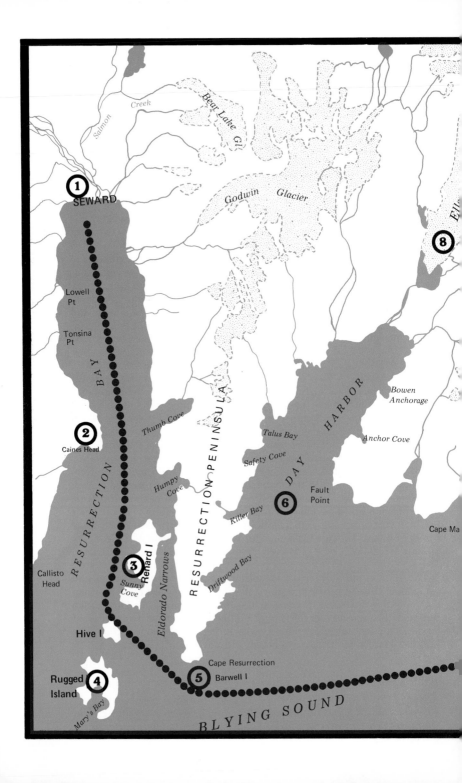

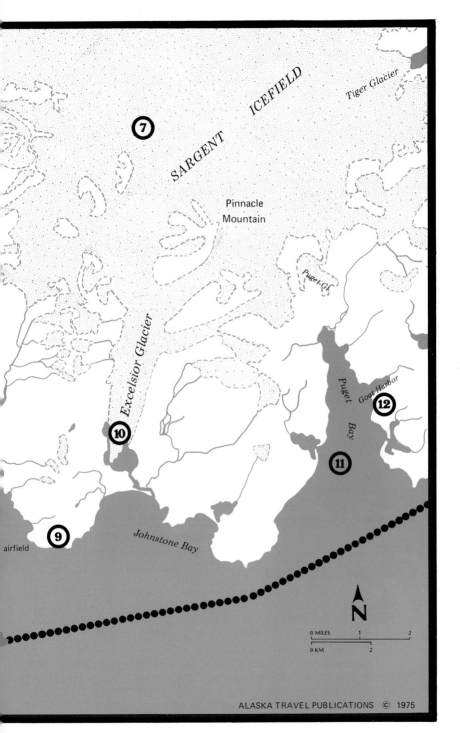

SARGENT ICEFIELD

Tiger Glacier

⑦

Pinnacle
Mountain

Puget Gl.

Excelsior Glacier

Puget
Bay

Goat Harbor

⑫

⑩

⑪

⑨

Johnstone Bay

airfield

N

| 0 MILES | | 1 | | 2 |
| 0 KM | | | 2 | |

ALASKA TRAVEL PUBLICATIONS © 1975

southern terminus at Seward. Dog teams pulled sleds to and from gold mining camps near Cook Inlet and in the Alaska Interior. For many years after the completion of The Alaska Railroad, Seward remained the busiest port in Alaska.

The Jesse Lee Home, a large building overlooking the city, operated between 1916 and 1966, providing care for orphans. Funded by the Methodist Church, the Jesse Lee Home had its beginnings in 1890 in Unalaska in the Aleutian Chain. The home was moved to Seward, as that town grew into an important population center. In 1926, Bennie Benson, a thirteen-year-old Aleut orphan at the home, won the contest sponsored by the American Legion to create the design for the Alaska state flag.

During World War II Seward remained a busy port, as ships unloaded vast quantities of supplies destined for military bases in Anchorage, Fairbanks and for the construction of the Alcan Highway. The U.S. Army built elaborate gun emplacements and fortifications along Resurrection Bay to protect this vital port.

After World War II, Seward attracted new businesses by building better dock and harbor installations and thus gained the designation "All-America City" in 1963.

The Good Friday earthquake drastically altered Seward. The most intense earthquake ever recorded on the North American continent, this cataclysm created a destructive tidal wave which leveled port facilities and took the lives of 13 people. Seward made a dramatic comeback, however, cleaning up the wreckage and building new freight loading facilities, including a dock worth 10 million dollars, thus earning a second "All-America City" accolade in 1965.

Recent expansions of the Port of Anchorage and the Port of Whittier have diminished the status of Seward as a transshipment center. Today the economy centers around tourism and processing of scallops, salmon, halibut, shrimp and crab. In addition, the Alaska Skill Center provides training for unemployed or underemployed Alaskans in a variety of adult educational programs. Kenai Lumber Company processes lumber from trees cut on Montague Island.

Exploring Seward

. . . Visit the Chamber of Commerce Information Cache, open during the summer season and housed in the railroad car "Seward," which in 1923 carried President Harding to the ceremonies that marked completion of The Alaska Railroad. The Information Cache's summer telephone number is (907) 224-3046.

. . . Visit Saint Peter's Episcopal Church. In 1925 church members commissioned Dutch artist Jan van Emple, then living in Seward, to paint a picture of the Resurrection. Visitors may view this unique painting in which the traditional scene of onlooking Apostles has been replaced by people of Alaska standing against a background of Resurrection Bay.

. . . Visit the Resurrection Bay Historical Society Museum located in the basement of the state and city office building. Artifacts include old mining equipment, furniture of early settlers, a collection of Attu baskets and many old photographs and newspaper clippings. Check with City Hall or the Chamber of Commerce for hours of operation. Photographs of the disastrous Good Friday earthquake are located on the first floor of the same building.

. . . View the slide presentation: "Seward Is Burning," in the City Hall basement. Tape recordings of accounts by local residents graphically portray the ordeal of the 1964 Good Friday earthquake. The show, accompanied by color slides, is given most afternoons during summer months for a nominal admission fee.

. . . Sample the fishing in Resurrection Bay. Try your luck from the shoreline or local docks. Several shops, located near the small-boat harbor, sell ice, fishing equipment and bait, and act as agents for charter boats from which anglers may catch silver salmon, halibut, cod, black "sea bass" (rockfish) and red "snapper" (rockfish).

. . . Enter the Seward Silver Salmon Derby, held annually for eight days starting the second Saturday in August. The excitement of catching one of these fighting fish is heightened by $30,000 in prizes given to lucky anglers. First prize for the largest fish is $3,000. A specially tagged fish is worth $10,000. The largest salmon ever caught during the Derby weighed 19 pounds, 8 ounces [8.8 kg].

. . . On the Fourth of July, watch, or take part in, the grueling Mt. Marathon race. The event started around 1909 when two sourdoughs scurried up the 3022 foot [912 m] peak to settle a wager. Since then the annual race has attracted contestants, many of Olympic caliber, from all over the world. The rugged course starts downtown and ascends Mt. Marathon over rock-strewn gullies, rocky bluffs and, often, snow and ice. Bill Spencer set the record time of 44 minutes, 11 seconds in 1974.

. . . See Gateways and Facilities chapters for more specific information on access and accommodations.

Seward to Valdez Ferry Route

A Way to See Southwestern Prince William Sound. The state ferry M.V. *Tustemena* makes one round trip each weekend during summer months between Seward, Valdez and Cordova. The vessel also travels between Seward, Kodiak, Port Lions, Seldovia and Homer. The voyage between Seward and Valdez, a distance of about 150 miles [241 km], takes approximately twelve to thirteen hours.

From Seward the ferry sails the length of Resurrection Bay before turning east south of Renard Island. The ship then travels through the often rough waters of the Gulf of Alaska on a course several miles south of the open coastline, finally entering through Bainbridge Passage the protected waters of Prince William Sound. The *Tustemena* then continues through Knight Island Passage, where whales are seen more often than anywhere else in the sound. This passage is flanked by mountainous Knight Island and hundreds of tiny islets. Occasionally the ferry follows an alternate route through Elrington Passage. Highlight of the voyage is the side trip to Columbia Glacier, where passengers may view tremendous icefalls and hundreds of harbor seals resting on icebergs.

The Seward-Valdez route is described in detail in the following pages. The ferry route from Glacier Island to Valdez, including Columbia Glacier, is identical to the Whittier-Valdez ferry route and is described in a previous chapter. Areas of interest are pinpointed on accompanying maps.

Ferry passengers traveling from Valdez to Seward should read the route description in reverse order.

2. Caines Head. Sailing from Seward, the ferry passes, on the right, Caines Head, which during World War II was the site of extensive gun emplacements and ammunition storage bunkers, now all but concealed by brush. A small military base was situated on a cove south of Caines Head. The Caines Head State Recreation Area, to be developed in the future, will feature a campground, a network of trails and a boat dock.

3. Renard (Fox) Island. Rockwell Kent, famous New England artist and author, and his young son spent the winter of 1918-1919 with an old Swedish fox farmer, Olsen, in a cove on the northwest side of the island. Kent recorded his experiences in a sensitively illustrated journal, *Wilderness: A Journal of Quiet Adventure in Alaska.* Today only a few moss-covered logs mark the site of his cabin.

4. Rugged Island. Descriptively named, the steep, rocky headlands of this island attract harbor seals and sea lions. Sport anglers take red "snapper" (rockfish), ling cod and black "sea bass" (also a species of rockfish) on the wave-battered eastern shoreline. The U.S. Army installed gun and searchlight emplacements on several points of the island during World War II.

5. Cape Resurrection — Barwell Island. Thousands of marine birds, including species of puffins, kittiwakes and murres, nest on the steep headlands of Cape Resurrection and nearby Barwell Island. The U.S. Army installed searchlights and several buildings on the summit of Barwell Island during World War II. The sturdily built structures, somewhat resembling an old European castle, are easily visible on the southwest coast of the island. Watch for sea lions in this area.

6. Day Harbor. English sea captain Nathaniel Portlock named this bay in 1787. Mountain goats range the slopes on the west side of Day Harbor.

Harbor seals are common near the head of the bay. Boats often anchor in protected Bowen Anchorage and Anchor Cove on the east side of Day Harbor.

7. Sargent Icefield. This mass of snow, ice and glaciers was named in 1952 for Rufus Harvey Sargent (1875-1951), a topographer of the United States Geological Survey, who extensively explored and mapped the Kenai Peninsula. There is no documented crossing of the Sargent Icefield on foot.

8. Ellsworth Glacier. On a clear day, ferry passengers may see at the head of Day Harbor this conspicuous 18 mile [29 km] long glacier, which begins in Sargent Icefield and terminates about 2 miles [3.2 km] from tidewater. Two small mountain peaks, called nunataks by glaciologists because they are "islands" surrounded by flowing ice, may be seen in the middle of the glacier.

9. Cape Fairfield. Stark outlines of Pinnacle Rock mark this precipitous, unprotected section of coastline, which was witness to a tragic drama on February 3, 1946. The Alaska Steamship *Yukon,* carrying 495 people, was caught in a severe Gulf of Alaska storm. The vessel struck the rocks, and the stern section, wrenched off by huge seas, overturned, killing eleven people. The survivors huddled in the forward section of the remainder of the wreck, which was caught on the rocks, in freezing weather without food, heat or water. Sixty foot [19 m] seas and steep terrain made rescue operations extremely difficult and hazardous. It was several days before all the passengers were safely removed. The huge rusting hull was a landmark for passing ships for many years but has been battered into near invisibility today.

10. Excelsior Glacier. Like Ellsworth Glacier, this glacier heads in Sargent Icefield and terminates in a lake not far from tidewater. On a clear day, ferry passengers may see the tips of the large icebergs that dot the lake.

11. Puget Bay. Cape Puget was named in 1794 by Joseph Whidbey, a member of Vancouver's expedition, to honor Lieutenant Peter Puget, R.N., a fellow officer. The names Puget Bay and Puget Glacier derive from the name for the cape. Puget Glacier, so steep that it resembles a frozen waterfall, ends several miles from tidewater.

12. Goat Harbor. This cove, laced with waterfalls and surrounded by towering cliffs and moss-draped forests, is the first safe small-boat anchorage after leaving Day Harbor. The U.S. Coast and Geodetic Survey named the area in 1928 because of "numerous wild goats." Mountain goats are still common along the steep headlands between Seward and Prince William Sound.

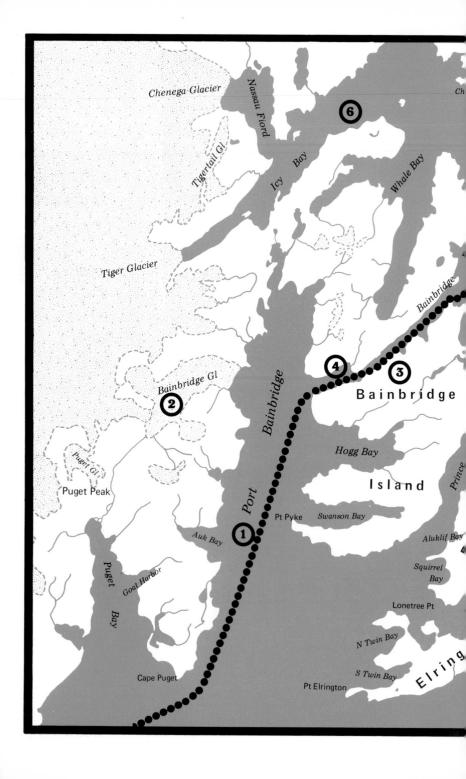

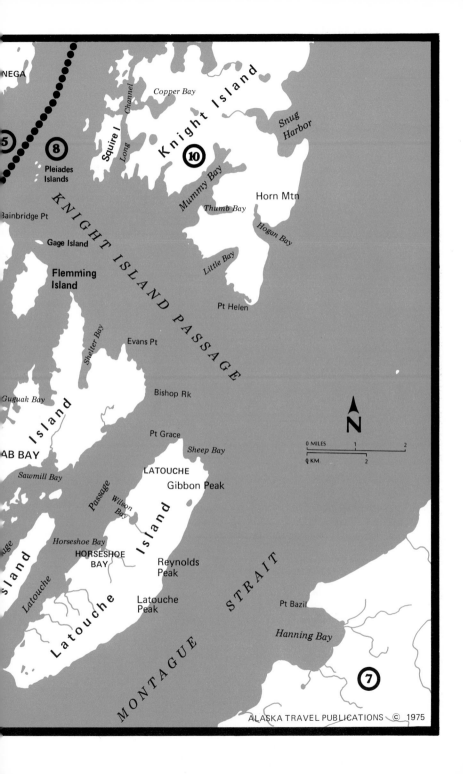

NEGA

⑤

⑧
Pleiades
Islands

Squire I

Long Channel

Copper Bay

K n i g h t   I s l a n d

Snug
Harbor

⑩

Mummy Bay

Horn Mtn

Thumb Bay

Hogan Bay

Bainbridge Pt

Gage Island

Little Bay

Flemming
Island

Pt Helen

Shelter Bay

Evans Pt

Guguak Bay

Bishop Rk

I s l a n d

AB BAY

Pt Grace

Sheep Bay

Sawmill Bay

LATOUCHE

Gibbon Peak

Passage

Wilson Bay

I s l a n d

Horseshoe Bay

HORSESHOE
BAY

Reynolds
Peak

S T R A I T

Latouche

Latouche
Peak

Pt Bazil

L a t o u c h e

Hanning Bay

⑦

M O N T A G U E

K N I G H T   I S L A N D   P A S S A G E

N

0 MILES   1   2
0 KM   2

ALASKA TRAVEL PUBLICATIONS © 1975

Ferry Route Map 10

1. Port Bainbridge. Vancouver named this bay in 1794 after a seventeenth century astronomer. Many large rock slides mark the west side, apparently a result of the 1964 Good Friday earthquake. The port is exposed to ocean swells from the Gulf of Alaska, and tide rips, treacherous to small boats, occur in the southern portion. Ferry passengers should watch for sea otters along the route from Port Bainbridge to north of Knight Island. Sea lions, coming from Point Elrington, an important haul-out area, are common near Cape Puget. Many sea birds also nest at Point Elrington, including numerous horned and tufted puffins, glaucous-winged gulls, common murres, red-faced and pelagic cormorants and pigeon guillemots. Look for these birds in the water near the ferry route.

Much of the western sound, from Port Bainbridge north to Decision Point (near Passage Canal), is included in the Nellie Juan Wilderness Study Area.

2. Bainbridge Glacier. Although it has since receded, this large glacier, 16 miles [*26 km*] long, reached salt water at the beginning of the century. Ducks, gulls and horned puffins nest in the vicinity.

3. Bainbridge Island. Natives used the abundant greenstone of this island for adzes (stone axes). The southern half of the island contains many beautiful subalpine meadows. Numerous sea otters inhabit the shallow waters near the rocky shoreline.

4. Bainbridge Passage. This narrow passage extends to the northeast about 14 miles [*22 km*]. Watch for sea otters, numerous in the area, and for occasional black bears. Snow slides and snow bridges linger on the south side of the passage throughout the summer.

Tidal currents through this passage often reach three or four knots in certain places, sometimes forcing small boats to wait for slack water at either end of the passage.

5. Knight Island Passage. As the ferry emerges from Bainbridge Passage, it passes Point Countess on the northwest and enters the comparatively open waters of Knight Island Passage. Watch for a steamy spout of water or a black triangular "sail-like" dorsal fin; Knight Island Passage is the best place in the sound to view whales, particularly humpback and killer whales.

6. Icy Bay. Two active tidewater glaciers, the Chenega (visible from the ferry route) and the Tiger, discharge icebergs so numerous that Icy Bay is often impassable by boat. A few icebergs drift close to the ferry route. Near the glaciers four bird-nesting colonies contain a total of some 6000 to 7000 black-legged kittiwakes.

7. Montague Island. Looking south from Knight Island Passage, 50 mile [*81 km*] long Montague Island, topped by a line of snow-covered 3000 foot [*915 m*] peaks, is visible. At the south end of Montague Island, land near Cape Cleare rose 38 feet [*12 m*] during the 1964 Good Friday earthquake. Extensive wave-pounded beaches, littered with beachcombing treasures, characterize the seaward side of the island. Sitka black-tailed deer and brown bear roam the spruce-hemlock rainforests. A hunting lodge is located at McLeod Harbor. Cook named this island "Montagu" in honor of his patron John Montagu, the Fourth Earl of Sandwich and First Lord of the British Admiralty at the time of Cook's third voyage.

8. Pleiades Islands. The ferry passes close to this picturesque chain of seven tiny wooded islands, named in 1908 for the seven daughters of Atlas, who, according to Greek mythology, were transformed into a group of stars.

9. Chenega. A village of the Chugach Eskimos was situated on a small cove on the south shore of Chenega Island. On March 27, 1964, seismic waves, generated by the strongest earthquake ever recorded on the North American continent, destroyed most of the village and killed 23 of the 80 inhabitants. Most survivors moved to Tatitlek on the eastern shore of the sound.

10. Knight Island. Vancouver named Knight Island in 1794 after Sir John Knight, R.N., who had been a Colonial prisoner in America during the Revolutionary War. Although the island is only 26 miles [*42 km*] long, its coastline is so convoluted that it has more miles of shoreline than larger Montague Island. The steep and scenic island contains little timber but offers much high alpine country. The three highest peaks, 2600 to 2800 feet [*793 to 853 m*], at the head of Drier Bay, were nicknamed the "Three Giants" by geologists at the beginning of the century. Arctic terns nest on rocky islets off the west shore of the island.

Abandoned copper mines pocket the slopes of the island, particularly at Drier Bay, site of an old tramway, and at Rua Cove on the east side of the island, where networks of tunnels riddle the mountainside.

Prince William Sound Inn operates during the summer at the site of a colorful former herring saltery in Thumb Bay. Several canneries once operated in Drier Bay.

Photo following pages: These purse seiners near Chenega Island are netting pink salmon. The snow-capped peaks of Knight Island loom in the distance.

CHARLES D. EVANS

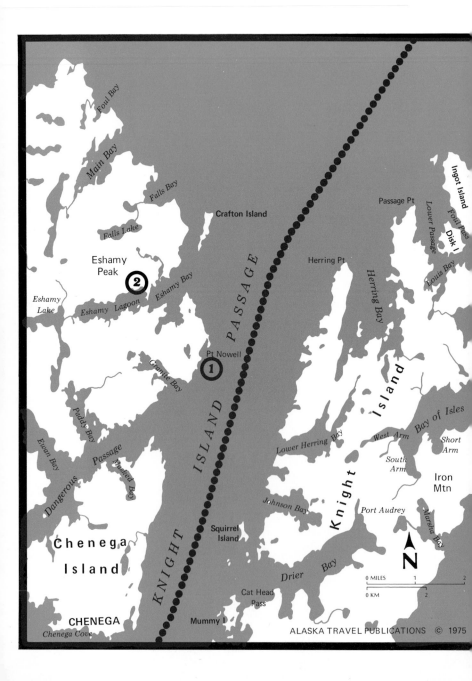

Foul Bay

Main Bay

Falls Bay

Crafton Island

Falls Lake

Eshamy
Peak

②

Eshamy
Lake

Eshamy Lagoon

Eshamy Bay

Passage Pt

Herring Pt

Ingot Island

Lower Passage

Disk I

Foul Pass

Louis Pass

PASSAGE

Herring Bay

Pt Nowell

①

Granite Bay

Paddy Bay

Ewan Bay

Dangerous Passage

Masked Bay

K N I G H T   I S L A N D

Lower Herring Bay

West Arm

South Arm

Bay of Isles

Short Arm

Iron
Mtn

Knight Island

Marsha Bay

Johnson Bay

Port Audrey

Chenega
Island

Squirrel
Island

Drier   Bay

N

CHENEGA

Cat Head
Pass

Mummy I

0 MILES   1   2

0 KM   2

Chenega Cove

ALASKA TRAVEL PUBLICATIONS   © 1975

Ferry Route Map 11

1. Point Nowell. Set nets, which are gill nets with one end anchored to shore, are used near this point during July and August to catch sockeye and silver salmon. Ferry passengers should scan the water for killer and humpback whales, relatively abundant in the area.

2. Eshamy Bay, Lagoon and Lake. This area is one of the most important salmon fishing grounds in the sound. Four species of salmon (pink, chum, sockeye and silver) are found in abundance. In the early decades of this century Eshamy Lagoon contained a floating cannery. Ferry passengers may see fishing boats and tenders going to and from this busy area. Eshamy Bay is also a favorite fishing spot for sport anglers (see Fishing chapter). The name Eshamy is reputedly a Chugach Eskimo word signifying "good fishing grounds."

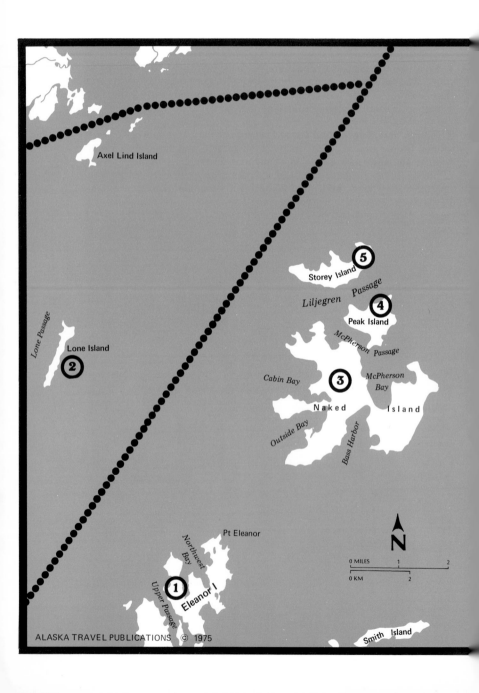

Axel Lind Island

Lone Passage

Lone Island
②

Storey Island
⑤

Liljegren Passage

Peak Island
④

McPherson Passage

Cabin Bay

Naked
③

McPherson Bay

Island

Outside Bay

Bass Harbor

Northwest Bay

Pt Eleanor

Upper Passage

Eleanor I
①

N

0 MILES 1 2
0 KM 2

Smith Island

ALASKA TRAVEL PUBLICATIONS © 1975

Ferry Route Map 12

1. Eleanor Island. Named by Vancouver in 1794, this island became a fox farm early in the twentieth century. One of the fox farmers was named Shumaker. While on the island, his wife wrote a series of nature essays that were published in a Valdez newspaper and later as a book, *Do You Know?* The book is a good local-color account of life in the sound. Shumaker later operated a steamer on Prince William Sound. Until 1942, he carried groceries and other supplies to fox farms and hunting camps.

The rocks east of Eleanor Island contain a black-legged kittiwake colony and a glaucous-winged gull colony. Harbor seals and sea lions are relatively common near Eleanor Island.

2. Lone Island. This 2 mile [*3.2 km*] long island was used for fox farming in 1896 and again around 1925 but was never profitable. Remains of fox traps are found on the western shore. Water depths in a trench east of the island reach 476 fathoms [*2850 feet or 869 m*], the deepest point in the sound and adjacent Gulf of Alaska waters.

3. Naked Island. This island was named because Natives supposedly found an insane, naked woman here. James McPherson operated a fox farm on this island around the turn of the century, but few buildings remain. A scattering of sea otters live in surrounding waters. Deer feed on kelp on south-facing beaches during winter and early spring.

4. Peak Island. This island was used as a fox farm beginning in 1895. Mrs. Alice Clocke, whose husband was a fox farmer, spent most of her life on this island. She raised most of her own food and had a comfortable home made of wreckage salvaged from the 1964 Good Friday earthquake. Her descendants still live on the island. Only a handful of people inhabit the wilderness islands of the sound.

5. Storey Island. The sound's most successful fox farm, owned by Fred Liljegren, operated here on a large scale from 1895 until the late 1920s. The farm included many buildings and a garden of raspberries, currants and apple trees.

Sitka black-tailed deer inhabit the island. Tufted puffins, pigeon guillemots and rhinoceros auklets nest along the shore.

Storey Island to Valdez. The ferry goes north passing between Granite Point and the west end of Glacier Island. From this point the ferry route is the same as that traveled by the M.V. *Bartlett* between Whittier and Valdez. See previous sections for this route description.

Alternate Route of the Tustemena. During periods of limited visibility, the *Tustemena* travels through Elrington Passage instead of Bainbridge Passage.

Elrington Passage is protected, deep and well marked by navigation aids. The passage is one of the best places to observe sea otters. This corner of the sound is steeped in history. Three abandoned canneries are situated on the edges of shallow Sawmill Bay on Evans Island. San Juan Cannery, the largest, is visible from Latouche Passage. San Juan Cannery, Port Ashton Cannery and what little remains of the Crab Bay herring saltery are very rickety and in dangerous condition. The canneries operated from the 1920s until the early 1960s processing locally caught salmon and herring. Today, because of improved fish preservation techniques and transportation, fish processing operations are centered in the larger towns. A handful of people still make their homes near Sawmill Bay.

The crumbling rust-red buildings of Latouche, on the north shore of Latouche Island, are a landmark visible for miles. Now abandoned, the town had its beginnings with the discovery of copper at Beatson Mine in 1903. By World War I, under the ownership of the Kennecott Mining Corporation, the town boasted a hospital, large bunkhouses, a movie theater, a reading room, bowling alleys and warehouses. The mine closed in 1930.

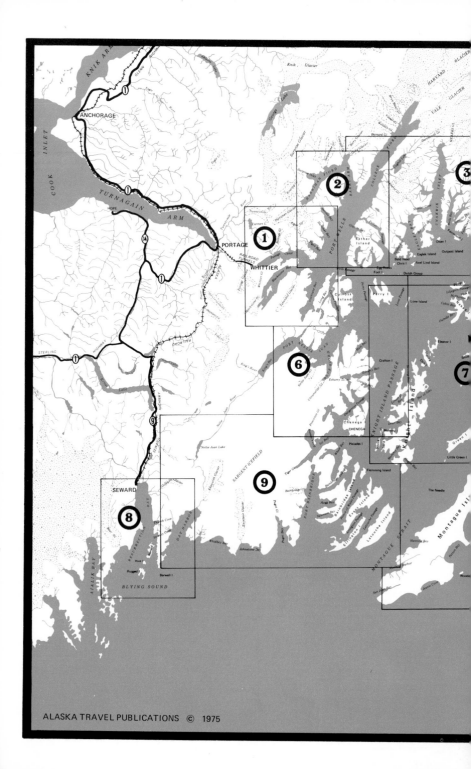

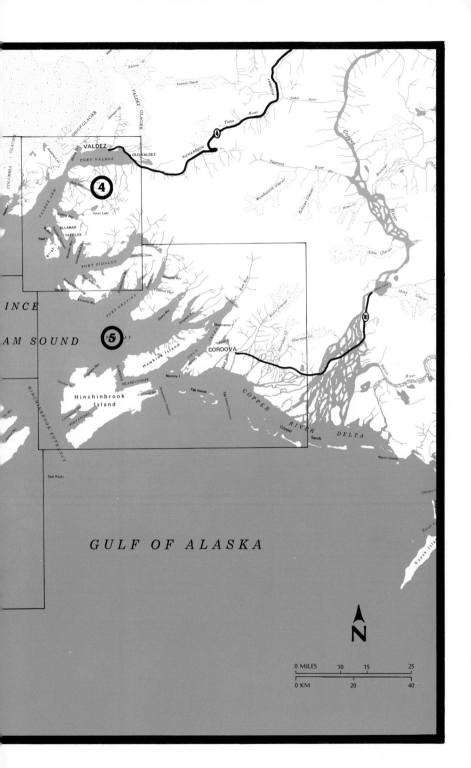

GULF OF ALASKA

VALDEZ
OLD VALDEZ
PORT VALDEZ
VALDEZ GLACIER
SHOUP GLACIER
COLUMBIA GLACIER
Silver Lake
ELLAMAR
TATITLEK
PORT FIDALGO
PORT GRAVINA
RICHARDSON
Tsina River
Tiekel River
KLUTINA GL.
Tonsina Glacier
Tazlina River
Copper River
Woodworth Glacier
Schwan Glacier
Heney Gl.
Allen Glacier
Miles Glacier
Bremner River

PRINCE
WILLIAM SOUND

Hawkins Island
ORCA BAY
Observation I.
Scott Glacier
Sheridan Gl.
Sherman Gl.
CORDOVA

HAWKINS ISLAND CUTOFF
Mummy I.
Egg Islands
Hinchinbrook Island
HINCHINBROOK ENTRANCE
PORT ETCHES

COPPER RIVER DELTA
Copper Sands
Martin River
Martin Islands
Kayak Island
Okalee C.

Seal Rocks

N

0 MILES   10   15   25
0 KM   20   40

A Way to the Wilderness

Boating for the Adventurous. Rugged shorelines of Prince William Sound have precluded highway construction, but lack of roads need not deter visitors from exploring the sound. The region offers a variety of boating possibilities; shallow, protected coves are suitable for kayaks while larger vessels may sail the open waters and find anchorages in dozens of scenic harbors. In Whittier, Valdez and Cordova, small-boat harbors are equipped to handle many types of vessels.

In this region of quickly changing weather, take sufficient fuel and carry safety equipment. Make certain you have foul-weather gear. (Refer to the Climate chapter for a few suggestions.)

This boating guide will enhance your appreciation of the sound; it is intended, however, only as a supplement to government charts and publications.

Safety Tips

Coast Guard Information and Suggestions. The United States Coast Guard Auxiliary offers a 12 lesson study course entitled *Boating Safety and Seamanship.* For a nominal fee, the Auxiliary will provide expert instruction in nautical rules of the road, aids to navigation, use of charts and compass, judging weather and use of radiotelephones. For information on the course in Alaska, contact:

> *Director of Auxiliary*
> *Seventeenth Coast Guard District*
> *Box 3-5000*
> *Juneau, Alaska 99801*

Photo opposite: The authors' sailing sloop, the NELLIE JUAN, *finds shelter from the stormy Gulf of Alaska in peaceful Goat Harbor.*
NEIL AND ELIZABETH JOHANNSEN

Safety Checklist. Refer to this safety checklist before your next cruise. Should you encounter difficulties while cruising the sound, it may be days or weeks before anyone else happens by.

1. Owner's manual for boat, engine, other equipment aboard?
2. Critical spare parts aboard?
3. Basic tools aboard and handy?
4. Hose clamps for engine and through-hull fittings tight and in good shape?
5. Fuel and water filters clean?
6. Fuel and oil ample?
7. Battery(s) fully charged?
8. Lights and electrical equipment in good operable shape ?
9. Cables, wires, belts A-OK?
10. Charts and compass aboard?
11. Lines and ground tackle (anchors) up to snuff?
12. Radiotelephone working properly?
13. Required safety equipment aboard? ... first aid kit, full fire extinguishers, floatcoats or life jackets for everyone?
14. Checked local weather forecasts?
15. Filed a float plan in the harbormaster's office?

Regulations. The Federal Boating Safety Act of 1971 establishes mandatory regulations for registration and numbering of all vessels equipped with mechanical propulsion. The Coast Guard issues numbers for the bow of each vessel and a validation sticker good for three years. Alaska currently has no state registration requirements.

In addition to registering your craft, the law requires Coast Guard approved personal flotation devices (lifejackets) for all passengers. For boats 16 feet [*4.6 m*] in length or over, at least one throwable flotation device (such as a life-ring) is also mandatory. Regulations vary according to vessel length and type and include requirements for fire extinguishers, back-fire flame arrestors, ventilation, audio signaling devices and lights. These regulations are summarized in a free booklet, *Federal Requirements for Recreational Boats,* available from the Coast Guard.

Radiotelephone Communications. This equipment, though not at present legally required on personal pleasure craft, is highly recommended for safety reasons. Coast Guard cutters, fixed stations, and many commercial craft monitor emergency frequencies. Radios, though expensive, usually represent a small percentage of the total cost of most pleasure craft.

Regulations established and enforced by the Federal Communications Commission (FCC) govern the use of radiotelephone equipment. Boats currently using AM equipment must convert to VHF-FM by January 1, 1977. After a boat is equipped with VHF-FM radio equipment, boaters may wish to add longer range single sideband radios, since VHF-FM is "line of sight" with an effective range of 30 miles [48 km] or less and due to intervening mountains is impractical to use in many areas of the sound. A mandatory radiotelephone operator's license is available upon application and payment of a fee. For information on radio licensing and equipment, contact:

Alaska District Office
Federal Communications Commission
P.O. Box 644
Anchorage, Alaska 99510
Telephone: (907) 272-1822

Radio Frequencies. The Coast Guard has 24 hour monitoring service of emergency frequencies 2182 KHz (AM) and 156.8 MHz (FM). Personal radio sets should be tuned to these frequencies to intercept possible distress calls from other boats. Coast Guard vessels are stationed at Kodiak, Seward, Cordova and Valdez, and rescue helicopters are at Kodiak.

Commercial fishing vessels operating in the sound use 2638 KHz and 2738 KHz in ship-to-ship AM calls and 2512 KHz and 2430 KHz in ship-to-shore AM calls.

Tides. Tides (the diurnal rise and fall of the sea) create three areas of concern to skippers of small boats: tidal currents in narrow passages, fluctuating water depths and currents while traveling and anchoring, and rip tides.

Tidal currents, periodic horizontal movements of waters, can be swift and turbulent, particularly near narrow, restricted passages. Boaters should time their trips through such areas as Bainbridge Passage during high or low slack water periods, and then proceed cautiously. Not only are currents weaker, but navigational hazards such as rocks and shoals are either covered with maximum water or are visible due to low water. Boaters should carry the National Ocean Survey's *Tidal Current Tables* (see Reference section) and a tide time booklet (available from private businesses such as banks and service stations) to aid in predicting currents and slack water (one-half hour before and after high and low tide).

Maximum measured currents for selected sound waters are:

Area	Average Velocities in Knots per Hour	
	Flood	Ebb
Culross Passage	Too weak and variable to measure	
Wells Passage	Too weak and variable to measure	
Valdez Narrows	Too weak and variable to measure	
Cordova, Orca Inlet	1.8	1.0
Bainbridge Passage	3.1	2.4
Elrington Passage	1.6	1.3

When anchoring, tide phase is important. Boaters must consider the depth of water required to float the craft and provide ample "swing room" at anchor. Diurnal tide ranges in the sound are approximately 12 feet [*3.7 m*]. Thus a boat anchoring in 2 fathoms (1 fathom = 6 feet or 1.83 meters) at high tide will find itself on the rocks at low tide. In addition, too much anchor rode length (length of chain and line) allows a craft to swing toward shore and onto the rocks when the tide drops, while too little anchor line may permit a boat to drift away at high tide. When anchoring, keep in mind the boat's draft, amount of scope (length of anchor line paid out), and current tide phase. A depth sounder or fathometer is a valuable aid in selecting anchorages.

Rip tides, occurring where tidal currents meet, are pronounced near headlands or at narrow outlets to embayments. At certain stages of the tide such areas have strong currents and, in extreme cases, may resemble steep, fast-running river rapids. Rip tides often occur near headlands between Resurrection Bay and Prince William Sound, in Port Bainbridge, and in Hinchinbrook Entrance. Hinchinbrook Entrance, exposed to winds and storms blowing into the sound from the Gulf of Alaska, is particularly dangerous during outgoing tides. During such periods, fishermen have reported overhanging seas as high as 60 feet [*20 m*].

Violent storms may appear with little warning, lashing the open coast for days at a time. Only large, seaworthy craft should travel open waters, such as the Gulf of Alaska.

M. WOODBRIDGE WILLIAMS
NATIONAL PARK SERVICE TASK FORCE

Handling in Rough Weather. Piloting a small craft in rough weather is a harrowing experience that usually can be avoided by keeping an eye on the weather. Although disagreements exist, some safety techniques are listed below:

... Never "drive" a boat through rough seas. Reduce power to prevent pounding and steer the boat so the bow takes heavy waves slightly to one side or the other. The same tactics should be used with the wakes of large ships.

... A boat with high stern freeboard sufficient to prevent waves from swamping the craft might find it safe to turn the stern to the oncoming waves and steer for shelter.

... Avoid taking seas "on the beam" or into the boat's side.

... Best rule of all is to avoid heavy weather. Skill, not courage, generally gets you home safely.

Marine Weather Forecasts. Marine weather forecasts are broadcast by the Kodiak Coast Guard station and by the National Weather Service from Seward and Anchorage. The Coast Guard announces the upcoming broadcast on the emergency channel of 2182 KHz, and the actual weather forecast follows on 2670 KHz. The scheduled broadcast times, subject to change without notice, are at 4:00 a.m., 6:45 a.m., 1:00 p.m., 4:00 p.m., 6:45 p.m. and 11:00 p.m. For local daylight savings time, add one hour. National Weather Service transmissions are repeated taped messages, updated every two to three hours and broadcast continually every four to six minutes. Messages include wind velocity and direction, visibility and sea conditions. These stations transmit on 162.550 MHz.

Some AM broadcasting stations also give marine forecasts. KFQD, KHz 750 in Anchorage, with an output of 50,000 watts, gives a marine forecast for the sound at 3:00 a.m., 6:00 a.m., noon, 7:00 p.m. and 10:00 p.m. A Cordova AM radio station, KLAM, operating on 1450 KHz with an output of 500 watts, frequently broadcasts weather forecasts during morning and evening.

Anchorage residents may also obtain a marine forecast for Resurrection Bay and Passage Canal by telephoning 936-2626 for a taped message, updated every few hours.

Broadcasts warn mariners of the following weather classifications:

... Small craft advisory: indicates forecast winds as high as 33 knots and sea conditions considered dangerous to small craft operations.

... Gale warning: indicates forecast winds in the range of 34 to 47 knots.

... Storm warning: indicates forecast winds 48 knots and above.

The mariner's experience and type and size of boat should determine degree of danger and necessary action. Boaters should keep in mind that any time there is a wind warning, one may expect winds blowing near mountainous terrain to be stronger than indicated in the forecast.

Nautical Charts. Aids to navigation, offshore reefs and rocky headlands are mapped in remarkable detail on charts (maps used at sea) issued by the National Ocean Survey. Although areas are surveyed with extreme care, navigational hazards are sometimes missed or change with time. Bottom contours changed significantly during the 1964 Good Friday earthquake. On deeper-draft boats, charts should be used in conjunction with a reliable fathometer.

Charts are classed according to scale, amount of detail and area covered. Harbor charts are on a scale of 1:50,000 or less, or 0.7 nautical miles to the inch (1 nautical mile equals 6076 feet or 1852 meters). Coast charts are 1:50,000 to 1:110,000 or a maximum of 1.4 nautical miles to the inch. General charts are between 1:100,000 to 1:600,000 or a maximum of 8.2 nautical miles to the inch. In addition to the general chart *No. 8551 (16700)* of *Prince William Sound,* boaters should also obtain the following regional charts: *Seward No. 8528 (16682), Whittier No. 8517 (16705), Valdez No. 8519 (16708), Cordova No. 8520 (16709)* and *Montague Strait No. 8515 (16701).*

Boaters should purchase *Chart Number One, Nautical Chart Symbols and Abbreviations.* Also obtain *Nautical Chart Catalogue Three, Alaska,* and determine which charts cover the area you plan to visit. Charts cost between $1 and $2. They are available from the following sources in Southcentral Alaska:

Alaska Map Service
723 West 6th Avenue
Anchorage, Alaska 99501

Chart Sales and Control Data Office
National Ocean Survey
Room 303, 632 6th Avenue
Anchorage, Alaska 99501

Durant's Hardware
236 Fourth Avenue
Seward, Alaska 99664

Hammersmith's Hardware
Main Street
Cordova, Alaska 99574

Marine Ventures, Inc.
Valdez, Alaska 99686

Photo opposite: Aids to navigation mark narrow passages such as Valdez Narrows and Elrington Passage. Information about these aids is indicated on charts of Prince William Sound.
NEIL AND ELIZABETH JOHANNSEN

Coast Pilot. The most important reference book for boaters is the *United States Coast Pilot 9*, available for $2.50 from the chart distributors listed above. This U.S. Government publication details nautical landmarks, anchorage peculiarities, dangers, weather, ice, freshets, routes, pilotage and port facilities. The *Coast Pilot* is updated every two years.

Fuel. Distances in the sound can be deceiving. Diesel fuel and gasoline are available only in Whittier, Valdez, Cordova and Seward. Although emergency fuel may be available from other craft, do not depend upon this source! Carry enough fuel to travel one and a half times the distance of planned travel.

Small-Boat Harbors

Summary. Small-boat harbors, located in Whittier, Valdez and Cordova, provide about 600 boat slips. In addition, the small-boat harbor in Seward contains about 700 boat slips. These harbors feature adjacent or nearby fuel, water, ice, some supplies, launching ramps, overnight accommodations, restaurants and transportation services. Moorage should be confirmed before purchasing a boat.

Whittier Small-Boat Harbor. This harbor opened in 1973. Reception to the new facilities was overwhelming, and a reported three to five year waiting list now exists. Lack of rented moorage, however, need not restrict use of this harbor. Facilities for boats on trailers are provided, including two launching ramps, boat trailer parking space and boat lift. Boaters reach Whittier from Anchorage by trailering their craft to the Whittier Train Shuttle at Portage (Mile 46.5, Seward Highway), then traveling by railroad flatcar to Whittier. For information on rates, schedules and size limitations, contact:

> *Tourist Information*
> *The Alaska Railroad*
> *Pouch 7-2111*
> *Anchorage, Alaska 99510*
> *Telephone: (907) 265-2685*

or visit The Alaska Railroad passenger and freight depot at First and "C" streets in Anchorage.

Gasoline, diesel and heating fuel are sold at the harbor. Two hundred feet [*61 m*] of transient open side-tire moorage is also available. For information, contact: Harbormaster, Whittier, Alaska 99502.

Photo opposite: The small-boat harbor in Whittier has capacity for about 100 boats. Trailerable boats may be stored in an adjacent parking lot.
STEVE MC CUTCHEON

A larger small-boat harbor, with moorage for more than 1000 boats, is planned for Shotgun Cove, several miles east of Whittier. A road from Whittier to Shotgun Cove is presently under construction.

Valdez Small-Boat Harbor. About 180 moorage spaces for boats from 20 feet [*6.1 m*] to 60 feet [*18.3 m*] long are provided in this harbor. The harbormaster is on seasonal duty beginning in May, and boaters are urged to rent their slips early in the season. Transient visitors have free moorage for up to 72 hours. Gasoline and diesel fuel are available from the Sheffield House dock. For information, write: Harbormaster, Valdez, Alaska 99686.

Cordova Small-Boat Harbor. About 325 stalls for boats from 24 feet [*7.3 m*] to 70 feet [*21.3 m*] long are located in this important commercial fishing port. Gasoline and diesel fuel are available at the small-boat harbor and for large vessels at the ocean dock 0.5 mile [*0.8 km*] north of the harbor. Transient moorage is available. For information, contact: Harbormaster, P.O. Box 938, Cordova, Alaska 99574.

Seward Small-Boat Harbor. Although located on Resurrection Bay facing the Gulf of Alaska, this harbor, with a capacity of about 700 boats, also serves the sound. Large seaworthy boats regularly travel 35 miles [*56 km*] east from Seward to the sound. Due to the increase in recreational boating in recent years, about 85 per cent of the boats in this harbor are pleasure craft. Moorage is available for boats from 17 feet [*5.2 m*] to 75 feet [*22.9 m*] long. Transient moorage is also available. Gasoline and diesel fuel may be purchased at the harbor. For information, contact: Harbormaster, Seward, Alaska 99664.

Small-Boat Cruising Areas

Introduction. Each year, hundreds of boats, some no larger than single-person kayaks, venture over protected waters of the sound. Larger and more seaworthy craft travel in less protected areas such as Blying Sound between Seward and Prince William Sound, or across Hinchinbrook Entrance between Montague and Hinchinbrook islands.

Prince William Sound and Resurrection Bay, with thousands of miles of isolated coastline, offer numerous cruising possibilities for recreational boaters. The following pages describe ten cruising areas in detail. Suggested anchorages are pinpointed on accompanying maps. Be aware, however, that there is no such thing as an absolutely safe anchorage; also be aware that anchor-holding qualities may vary widely from descriptions.

With knowledge of this wildland comes responsibility to see that it retains its pristine character for the next visitor. Confine garbage, particularly plastics and metals, to your boat; too many styrofoam cups already litter the otherwise untouched beaches of the sound. Anglers should keep no more fish than can be eaten.

1. Passage Canal and Blackstone Bay

General Description. Majestic deepwater fiords are surrounded by steep mountains and spectacular glaciers. Passage Canal, 25 miles [*40 km*] long and 1 to 2.5 miles [*1.6 to 4 km*] wide, has depths from 96 fathoms [*177m*] at the head of the fiord to 200 fathoms [*366 m*] at the entrance. Passage Canal is ice-free year-round. Whittier lies at the head of Passage Canal. Some local fishermen and recreational boaters consider Blackstone Bay, 11.5 miles [*18.5 km*] long, 1 to 2 miles [*1.6 to 3.2 km*] wide, and up to 200 fathoms [*366 m*] deep, to be one of the most impressive areas in the sound.

Anchorages. *(1) Shotgun Cove* and *(2) Entry Cove* are protected from most winds and offer good mud holding bottoms. Blackstone Bay lacks good anchorages.

Fishing. During late summer pink and chum salmon spawn in virtually every stream. Between October and June "white" king salmon may be caught near Point Pigot. Good fishing for red snapper may be found near Billings Glacier in Passage Canal, and dungeness crab are found near the kittiwake nesting colony opposite Whittier and in Shotgun Cove.

Birds. The third largest black-legged kittiwake nesting colony in the sound (abokt 5000 birds) is on Passage Canal opposite Whittier. Kittiwakes, pigeon guillemots, and glaucous-winged gulls also nest just north of the terminus of Blackstone Glacier.

Mammals. Dall and harbor porpoise are often seen in the entrance of Passage Canal. Harbor seals are found in Shotgun Cove and Blackstone Bay. Black bears are sometimes seen on the north side of Passage Canal.

History. Captain George Vancouver, R.N., named Passage Canal in 1794, because Natives and Russian fur traders used this passage and Portage Pass as a travel route between the sound and Cook Inlet. Blackstone Bay and Glacier owe their names to a prospector who became lost while attempting to cross Portage Pass in a storm in April, 1896. Blackstone and his two companions froze to death on Blackstone Glacier. Tebenkof Glacier is named for Mikhail Tebenkof, director of the Russian American Company from 1845 to 1850, who was instrumental in surveying much of the uncharted Alaskan coast. Poe Bay is named for writer Edgar Allen Poe. Billings Glacier commemorates the name of Joseph Billings, an Englishman in the Imperial Russian Navy, who commanded a surveying party in Alaskan waters in the late 1700s. Gold was discovered in Billings Creek in 1896, though active mining of quartz-bearing veins did not begin until 1911. Old mining debris is still visible along the shoreline.

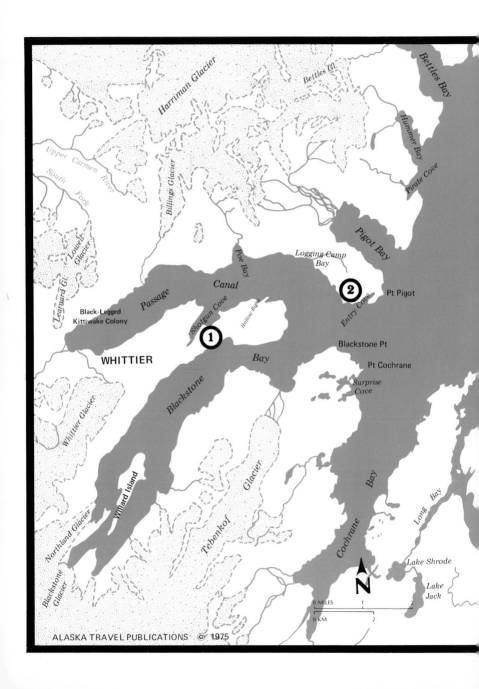

ALASKA TRAVEL PUBLICATIONS © 1975

Whittier Glacier was named in 1915 for American poet John Greenleaf Whittier. The town of Whittier, taking its name from the glacier, was founded during World War II when a spur line of The Alaska Railroad, connecting Whittier to the main Seward-Anchorage line, and several large military buildings were constructed. A 40 foot [*12 m*] high seismic wave caused by the 1964 Good Friday earthquake destroyed waterfront structures and killed 13 persons in Whittier.

Special Interest. Skiffs and fishing gear may be rented in Whittier. Lodging and meals are available at the Sportsman's Inn. From Whittier, the state ferry serves Valdez and Cordova, and the railroad shuttle runs to Portage and Anchorage.

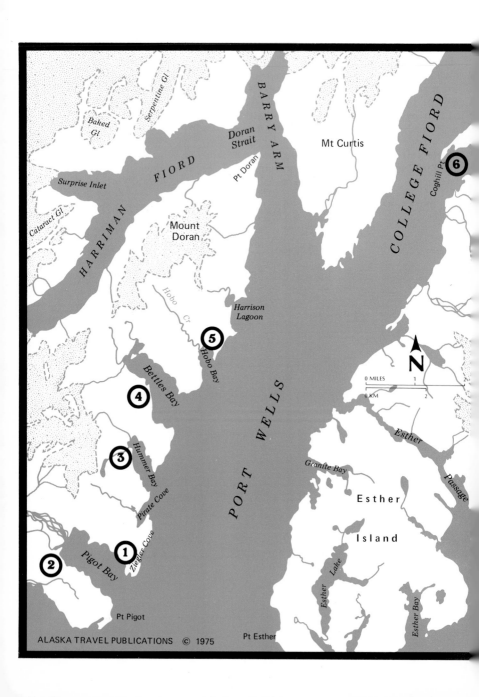

Baked Gl

Serpentine Gl.

Surprise Inlet

Cataract Gl

HARRIMAN FIORD

Doran Strait

Pt Doran

BARRY ARM

Mt Curtis

COLLEGE FIORD

Coghill Pt

⑥

Mount Doran

Hobo Cr

Harrison Lagoon

⑤

Hobo Bay

Bettles Bay

④

Hummer Bay

③

Pirate Cove

Ziegler Cove

①

Pigot Bay

②

PORT WELLS

N

0 MILES   1
0 KM   2

Esther

Granite Bay

Esther Island

Esther Lake

Passage

Pt Pigot

Pt Esther

Esther Bay

ALASKA TRAVEL PUBLICATIONS © 1975

2. Port Wells and College Fiord

General Description: Deep fiords, rugged mountains, and numerous tidewater glaciers characterize this region. Port Wells, exposed to northwest winds and seas, extends north 13 miles [*21 km*] before dividing into Barry Arm and Harriman Fiord to the west and College Fiord to the east. Offshore depths range to about 200 fathoms [*365 m*], though satisfactory anchorages may be found in many small bays and coves.

Anchorages. Well protected *(1) Ziegler Cove* in Pigot Bay has a heavy blue clay holding bottom. *(2) Two other coves,* unnamed, near the head of Pigot Bay are also satisfactory for anchoring. Pirate Cove is unsatisfactory due to exposure to prevailing northwest winds. *(3) Hummer Bay* provides good anchorage, although numerous rocks at the bay's entrance require caution. A cove midway on the south shore of *(4) Bettles Bay* and a lagoon at the head of the bay are excellent small-craft anchorages. A bight in *(5) Hobo Bay* is satisfactory except during strong south winds. Barry Arm, Harriman Fiord and College Fiord contain icebergs and afford no anchorages. A small cove inside of *(6) Coghill Point* provides protection from prevailing northwest winds. The northern entrance to Esther Passage is well-protected, but water is deep. Granite Bay is protected but offers poor holding bottom.

Fishing. Pink and chum salmon angling is good at streams throughout the area but is generally best in Pigot Bay and Coghill River. The area also offers good halibut fishing. Deepwater rock fishing is found along the west shore of Esther Island, particularly for red "snapper" (rockfish). Blue king crab may be taken in deeper waters of Harriman and College fiords. Dungeness crab inhabit shallow bays, particularly Pigot Bay. Butter clams may be dug on the few gravel beaches in the area.

Birds. Cliffs near Yale Glacier form a nesting area for more than 2000 black-legged kittiwakes in addition to numerous glaucous-winged gulls, arctic terns and several pairs of black oystercatchers. Bonaparte's gulls breed to the west of Cascade Glacier, and about 1000 black-legged kittiwakes nest near Surprise Glacier in Harriman Fiord. Shallow waters around Point Pakenham and Harrison Lagoon support thousands of sea ducks. Numerous bald eagles nest in this area.

Mammals. During late summer, black bears congregate along Coghill River and other salmon spawning streams. Harbor seals, occasional sea lions and numerous Dall and harbor porpoises are seen throughout the area. A group of about 20 to 30 sea otters recently have been seen in Harriman Fiord. Sitka black-tailed deer are found on Esther Island.

History. In 1794 Vancouver named Port Wells for Edward Wells, an English mathematician and geographer. The Harriman Expedition of 1899 named many glaciers in the area for American colleges and universities (Harvard, Yale, Vassar, etc.) and discovered Harriman Fiord. Later, gold mining activity centered around Hobo Bay, Pigot Bay, Point Pakenham and Golden, where a mining camp existed from about 1904 to 1916. Only the ruins of a stamp mill now remain. Granite Mine, easily visible on a mountainside between Hobo Bay and Harrison Lagoon, was the last active hardrock gold mine in Prince William Sound. Operations continued intermittently until the mid 1960s.

Special Interest. Mt. Marcus Baker, 13,176 feet [*4016 m*], highest peak of the Chugach Range, rises behind Harvard Glacier. The mountain was named by Alfred H. Brooks (for whom the Brooks Range is named) in 1924 for Marcus Baker (1849-1903), a cartographer with the United States Geological Survey and the United States Coast & Geodetic Survey. Prior to this naming, the mountain was known as Mt. St. Agnes.

A U.S. Forest Service A-frame cabin is available for public use at Pigot Bay; reservations must be made in advance (see Facilities chapter).

Icebergs are abundant near tidewater glaciers, particularly in Icy Bay, College Fiord and Columbia Bay. Although seals and marine birds often rest on these chunks of ice, boaters should avoid climbing on them as they are very unstable and roll easily.
© NANCY SIMMERMAN, 1975

3. Esther Island to Columbia Glacier

General Description. Dominated by Eaglek Bay and Unakwik Inlet, this region contains numerous small islands and coves. Columbia Glacier is one of the most spectacular glaciers in Alaska. Extensive foul ground throughout this cruising area, much of it uncharted, requires caution.

Anchorages. On Esther Island, the two arms of Granite Bay are rocky with poor holding bottom. A sheltered cove in Lake Bay near the mouth of Esther Creek also has a rocky bottom. *(1) Quillian Bay* is the most protected anchorage on the island, but stay clear of a rock hazard located in the center of the channel leading to the upper half of the bay. *(2) Esther Bay* is extremely rocky, but suitable anchorages are available in small coves. Shoestring Cove in Esther Passage is a protected anchorage, but it probably has a rocky bottom and is iced over most of the year.

Two coves in *(3) Squaw Bay,* an unnamed cove on the east shore, and *(4) Papoose Cove* on the west shore provide adequate small-craft protection. *(5) Derickson Bay* in Eaglek Bay is well protected at the upper end with a good holding bottom. *(6) Cascade Bay* has several well-protected anchorages. A small but protected anchorage exists on the east shore of *(7) Eaglek Bay* north of Schoppe Bay. Several small coves in *(8) Schoppe Bay* are suitable anchorages. *(9) Olsen Cove* in Unakwik Inlet is well protected with a mud bottom. Mueller Cove has no protection from southeast winds. *(10) Siwash Bay* has two protected coves midway up on opposite sides of the bay. Anchorage in Jonah Bay is not recommended due to tidal currents and shallow water. An unnamed cove 2 miles [*3.2 km*] north of Unakwik Point in *(11) Wells Bay* offers good protection and a gravel beach.

The *(12) west fork of Wells Bay* has several good anchorages. *(13) Cedar Bay* has three good anchorages, the best of which is located in a bight halfway up the northwest shore. The best anchorage in *(14) Granite Bay* is midway up the north shore. *(15) Fairmount Bay* is well-protected but has many uncharted rocks.

Jackson Hole on Glacier Island is well protected but has swift tidal currents near the mouth of the bay. *(16) Eagle Bay* and *(17) Growler Bay* are well-protected from wind. The only suitable anchorage in *(18) Long Bay* is the west arm. The upper end of *(19) Useless Cove* gives good protection and has a mud bottom. *(20) Granite Cove* in Columbia Bay is a suitable anchorage but may contain icebergs from nearby Columbia Glacier. *(21) Emerald Cove* is an excellent, scenic anchorage for small boats.

Fishing. Fish for pink salmon during late summer in Siwash Bay. Red salmon may be caught in early summer and silver salmon may be caught in August and September in a stream draining into Miner's Bay. There is fair fishing for red snapper in Esther Passage near Shoestring Cove. Shrimp may

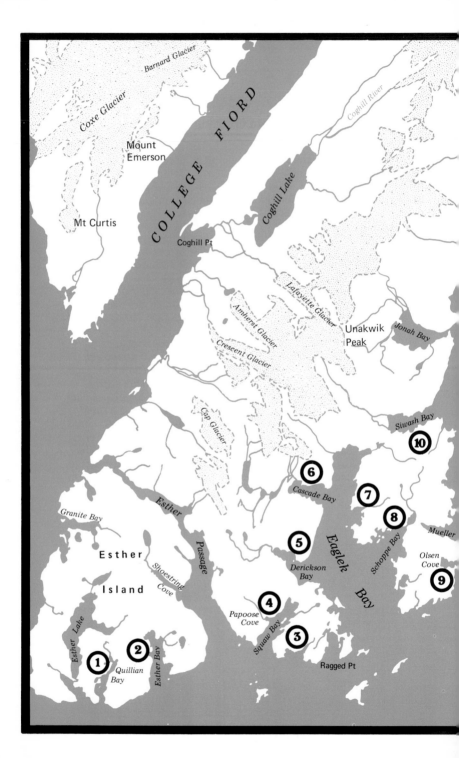

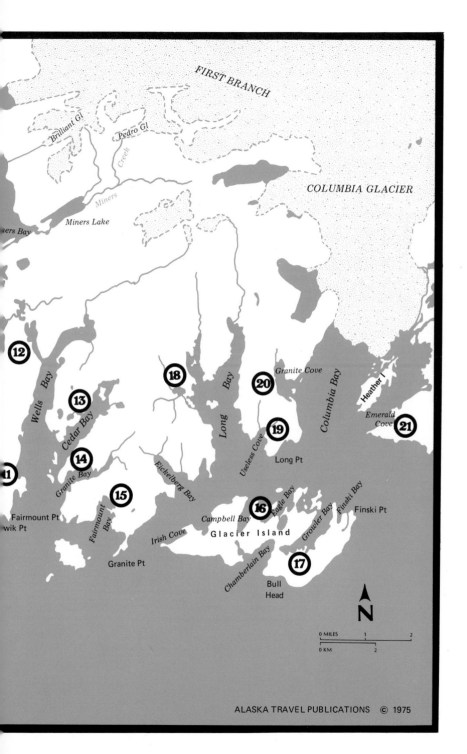

FIRST BRANCH

COLUMBIA GLACIER

Brilliant Gl

Pedro Gl

Creek

Miners

Miners Lake

ers Bay

12

Wells Bay

13

Cedar Bay

18

Long Bay

Granite Cove

20

Columbia Bay

Heather I

Emerald Cove

21

14

Granite Bay

19

Useless Cove

Long Pt

1

Fairmount Pt
wik Pt

Fairmount Bay

15

Eichelberg Bay

Campbell Bay

16

Eagle Bay

Growler Bay

Finski Bay

Finski Pt

Irish Cove

Glacier Island

Granite Pt

Chamberlain Bay

17

Bull
Head

N

| 0 MILES | 1 | 2 |

| 0 KM | 2 |

ALASKA TRAVEL PUBLICATIONS © 1975

be taken in Unakwik Inlet, Siwash Bay and in deep water near Olsen Island. Dungeness crab are found in Siwash Bay and in shallow water of Unakwik Inlet. Blue king crab inhabit Unakwik Inlet. Halibut may be caught throughout the area. Beaches near Siwash Bay and Schoppe Bay offer butter clams.

Birds. The shoreline along Wells Bay is prime bald eagle habitat. Several gull colonies flourish in the region. Upper Unakwik Inlet provides feeding habitat for approximately 10,000 Kittlitz's murrelets, which apparently nest above timberline on adjacent mountain slopes.

Mammals. Harbor seals inhabit Wells Bay and the head of Unakwik Inlet. Black bear congregate at salmon spawning streams along Jonah Bay and Eaglek Bay.

History. Eskimo burial caves once existed on Glacier Island and in Long Bay. Long-vacant fox farms are located on Dutch, Fairmount, Glacier, Olsen, Axel Lind and Bald Head Chris islands.

Special Interest. The 1964 Good Friday earthquake had its epicenter beneath Miner's Lake near Unakwik Inlet. Columbia Glacier is the largest glacier in Prince William Sound (see Geology chapter). Meares Glacier, ending at tidewater and discharging many icebergs, is one of the few in the sound that have advanced slightly in recent years. Cascade Falls, a picturesque sight at the head of Cascade Bay, spills over a ledge to drop about 100 feet [30 m] into salt water. The only large stands of western yellow cedar in the sound are near Wells Bay, Cedar Bay and Long Bay. A seafood processing plant is located on Fairmount Point.

4. Columbia Glacier to Knowles Head, Including Valdez

General Description. Dominated by Valdez Arm, Port Valdez, Jack Bay and Port Fidalgo, this area contains fewer islands and anchorages than the remainder of the sound. The communities of Tatitlek and Valdez are in this area. Valdez has an excellent small-boat harbor and a full range of marine services. Tatitlek has no harbor and no marine services.

Anchorages. *(1) Sawmill Bay* is well protected behind the west entrance point and offers a sticky holding bottom. *(2) Jack Bay* has a small-boat anchorage about 900 feet [*275 m*] west of an islet near the lower end of a flat at the head of the bay. *(3) Galena Bay* is deep except for flats off the mouths of streams. *(4) Landlocked Bay,* past Tatitlek Narrows, affords good protection and a sticky bottom at the eastern end, but submerged reefs require caution. *(5) Irish Cove* is a secure anchorage. The eastern arm of *(6) Two Moon Bay* affords a good anchorage. *(7) Snug Corner Cove* is good except during northwest winds.

Fishing. Valdez hosts its annual Silver Salmon Derby in August. Silver salmon fishing is good throughout the waters of Port Valdez and Valdez Arm. Pink salmon are found during summer months in Sawmill Bay, Snug Corner Cove, Jack Bay, Galena Bay and Boulder Bay. Fishing for halibut is good in Valdez Arm. Tanner crab are found in Valdez Narrows and Port Fidalgo. King and dungeness crab may be caught in Port Fidalgo and Sawmill Bay. Small shrimp inhabit Shoup Bay.

Birds. Bald eagles are common along shores of Port Fidalgo, and thousands of shorebirds are found on tidal flats at the head of the bay. Small colonies of black-legged kittiwakes and arctic terns are located near the terminus of Shoup Glacier.

Mammals. Black and brown bears are relatively common at the heads of Galena Bay, Jack Bay and Port Fidalgo. Mountain goats are found on cliffs surrounding these bays. Harbor seals inhabit most of the bays. Sea otters are found in Port Fidalgo and near Knowles Head. Land otters are common near lakes and streams.

History. Bligh Island is named for William Bligh of *Mutiny on the Bounty* fame who explored these waters in 1778 as a midshipman under the command of Captain Cook. Bligh Island was also once a fox farm. Remains of an old Russian sailing vessel are said to be on one of the outer beaches. Cook stopped and repaired his vessels at Snug Corner Cove, which later

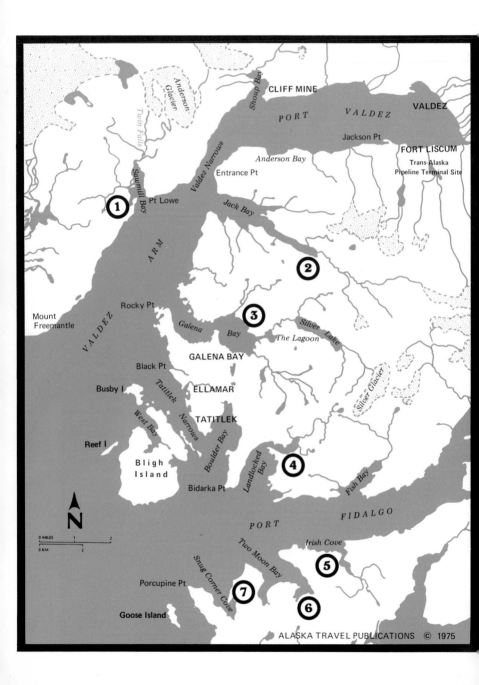

became a favored anchorage for fur traders. Jack Bay is the site of an old Russian timber cutting operation. Galena Bay, location of an old Eskimo village, later became the site of copper mining operations during the first decade of this century. The remains of the old copper mining and cannery town of Ellamar, south of Galena Bay, are visible from a great distance offshore. The steamship *Saratoga* was wrecked on Busby Island in 1908; wreckage is still visible at low tide on the west point of the island. Busby Island and Goose Island had fox farms; a liquor still was located on Goose Island during Prohibition. Thousands of gold and copper mining claims pocket hillsides throughout the cruising area.

Valdez is one of the most historic towns of Alaska; see "State Ferry Log: Whittier to Valdez" and History chapter for information on this community.

Special Interest. The region surrounding the Native village of Tatitlek, located at the foot of Copper Mountain, 3858 feet [*1176 m*], is one of the most scenic spots in the sound. A number of clearcuts from the late 1930s and early 1940s in Boulder Bay, Fish Bay and Irish Cove support thriving young regrowth. U.S. Forest Service public recreation cabins located at Galena Bay and Sawmill Bay require advance reservations (see Facilities chapter). Supplies, fuel and transient boat slips are available only at Valdez.

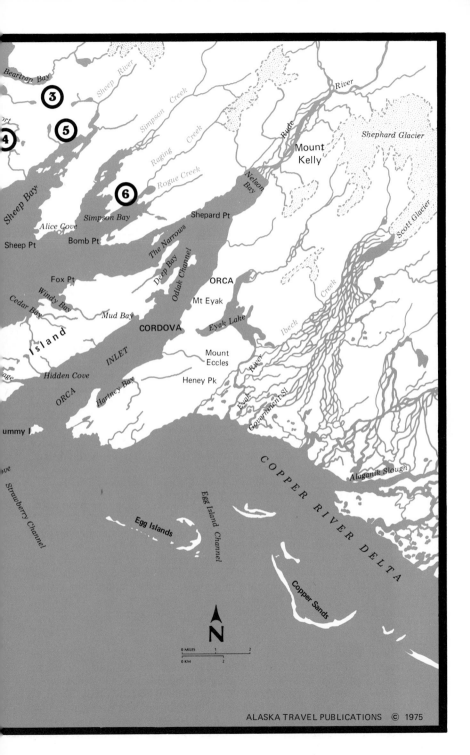

Beartrap Bay

③

⑤

④

Sheep River

Simpson Creek

Raging Creek

Rogue Creek

River

Rude River

Mount Kelly

Shephard Glacier

Scott Glacier

Nelson Bay

Sheep Bay

Alice Cove

Simpson Bay

Shepard Pt

Bomb Pt

⑥

Sheep Pt

The Narrows

Odiak Channel

ORCA

Deep Bay

Fox Pt

Mt Eyak

Windy Bay

Cedar Bay

Mud Bay

CORDOVA

Eyak Lake

Island

INLET

Mount Eccles

River

Tbeck Creek

Hidden Cove

ORCA

Hartney Bay

Heney Pk

Eyak R.

Government Sl.

ummy I

Alaganik Slough

Strawberry Channel

COPPER RIVER DELTA

Egg Island Channel

Egg Islands

Copper Sands

N

0 MILES 1 2
0 KM 2

ALASKA TRAVEL PUBLICATIONS © 1975

5. Knowles Head to Cordova, Including Hawkins and Hinchinbrook Islands

General Description. Hawkins and Hinchinbrook islands, each about 10 miles [*33 km*] long, are mountainous and heavily wooded. Port Gravina and Orca Bay are large deep embayments with several small-craft anchorages. Cordova is a major fishing town with a population of approximately 2500. The nearby Copper River Delta has many sloughs, large salmon runs and is an important waterfowl nesting area. Hinchinbrook Entrance is a major shipping lane from the Gulf of Alaska into the sound.

Anchorages. The northeast arm of Hell's Hole is suitable for shallow-draft boats only. The head of *(1) Saint Matthews Bay* is a good anchorage with a mud bottom. The head of *(2) Olsen Bay* is satisfactory. Parshas Bay is unsatisfactory due to rocks and great water depths. The upper basin of *(3) Beartrap Bay* is satisfactory with a mud bottom. *(4) Comfort Cove* has a narrow entrance, suitable only for shallow-draft small craft. Boats entering *(5) Sheep Bay* should proceed with caution due to shoals, but an anchorage is available at the head of the bay. The upper arm of *(6) Simpson Bay* provides satisfactory anchorage, but the north arm is very shallow at the head. *(7) Boswell Bay* offers a good anchorage although there are rocks at the entrance. *(8) Garden Cove* is the best anchorage for small boats in Port Etches. Parts of *(9) Constantine Harbor* provide adequate anchorage for small boats. *(10) English Bay* is exposed to ocean swells, northerly and westerly winds but has a good holding bottom. *(11) Anderson Bay* and *(12) Double Bay* offer good anchorages, but at low tide portions of the bay are shallow and careful selection of anchoring sites is recommended.

Fishing. Silver salmon fishing is good in August and September in Hell's Hole and Simpson Bay. Pink and chum salmon may be caught during summer months in Anderson Bay, Sheep Bay, and Saint Matthew's Bay. Dungeness crab may be taken in Olsen Bay, Sheep Bay, Simpson Bay and Orca Inlet. King crab are found in Port Gravina and tanner crab in Orca Bay. Throughout the area steamer clams are common on gravel beaches. Dig for razor clams in Orca Inlet and south of the Copper River Delta.

Birds. Bald eagles nest on shorelines throughout this area, with the exception of logged-over and inhabited locations. Several species of pelagic birds nest at Porpoise Rocks near Cape Hinchinbrook, and thousands of tufted puffins nest on cliffs on the south side of Hinchinbrook Island. A nesting colony at Boswell Rocks on Hinchinbrook Island, largest nesting colony in the sound, contains black-legged kittiwakes, glaucous-winged gulls, tufted puffins and pelagic and double-crested cormorants.

The largest concentration of trumpeter swans in North America is found on the Copper River Flats. The only known nesting area of dusky Canada geese is also located here. Millions of waterfowl and shorebirds use the area as a resting and feeding stop during spring and fall migrations.

Mammals. Brown and black bears may be seen at the heads of Port Gravina, Sheep Bay and Simpson Bay. Brown bears inhabit the Copper River Flats and Hinchinbrook Island. Sitka black-tailed deer are found throughout the area, particularly on the larger islands. Moose inhabit the Copper River Delta.

Sea otters are common throughout southeastern Prince William Sound, particularly in shallow waters near Hinchinbrook Island. Killer whales are seen in Orca Bay, most often in autumn. Harbor seals, common throughout the region, are especially abundant at the head of Port Gravina, Sheep Bay and Simpson Bay.

History. Both Chugach Eskimos and Eyak Indians lived in the area. The historic Eskimo village of Palugvik on the south shore of Hawkins Island was excavated by archeologist Frederica de Laguna in 1933. Russians operated a sea otter pelt trading center at Fort Constantine on Hinchinbrook Island from the 1790s until 1867. The fort was presumably named in honor of Grand Duke Constantine, a younger brother of Czar Alexander II. The Native village of Nuchek, a few miles from Fort Constantine, was abandoned in 1930. Cannery operations began near Cordova in the 1890s. A railroad was built a few years later from Cordova up the Copper River. Land in the eastern sound uplifted at least 6 feet [*1.8 m*] during the 1964 Good Friday earthquake.

Special Interest. Cordova has fuel, marine supplies and a small-boat harbor. Strong tidal currents occur through Hawkins Island Cut-off. Hinchinbrook Entrance during an outrunning tide and strong southerly winds is extremely hazardous for small craft. A hunting lodge is located at Nuchek on Hinchinbrook Island.

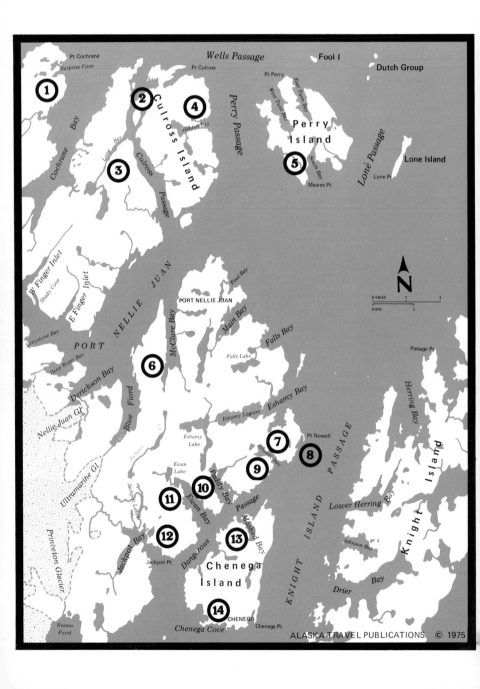

Pt Cochrane
Surprise Cove
Wells Passage
Pt Culross
Fool I
Dutch Group
Pt Perry
West Twin Bay
East Twin Bay

① ② Culross Island ④
Hidden Bay
Perry Passage
Perry Island
Lone Island

Cochrane Bay
Louis Bay
③
Culross Passage
⑤
South Bay
Lone Passage
Lone Pt
Meares Pt

W Finger Inlet
Shady Cove
E Finger Inlet
NELLIE JUAN
PORT NELLIE JUAN
Fool Bay
Main Bay
Falls Bay
Passage Pt

Greystone Bay
PORT
Deep Water Bay
McClure Bay
Falls Lake
Herring Bay

Nellie Juan Gl
Derickson Bay
Blue Fiord
⑥
Eshamy Lagoon
Eshamy Bay

Ultramarine Gl
Jackpot
Eshamy Lake
⑦ Pt Nowell
⑧

Ewan Lake
Charlie Bay
⑨
KNIGHT ISLAND PASSAGE
Knight Island

⑪
⑩
Paddy Bay
Passage
Lower Herring Bay

Jackpot Lakes
Ewan Bay
⑫
Mustang Bay
Johnson Bay

Princeton Glacier
Jackpot Pt
Jackpot Bay
Dangerous
⑬
Chenega Island
Drier Bay

Nassau Fiord
⑭
CHENEGA
Chenega Cove
Chenega Pt

N

0 MILES   1   2
0 KM   2

ALASKA TRAVEL PUBLICATIONS © 1975

6. Cochrane Bay to Chenega Island

General Description. This region is characterized by extensive areas of open alpine vegetation, numerous bays and islands. Major islands are Culross, Perry and Chenega. Important small-craft routes include Wells, Culross, Perry, Dangerous and Knight Island passages. The large fiord of Port Nellie Juan dominates this cruising area.

Anchorages. The southwest arm of *(1) Surprise Cove* in Cochrane Bay is a suitable anchorage. *(2) Culross Passage* has a good anchorage in an unnamed cove on the east side 1 mile [*1.6 km*] from the north entrance and in *(3) Long Bay*. *(4) Hidden Bay* on Culross Island is a good small-craft anchorage. East and West Twin bays on Perry Island are poor anchorages; use *(5) South Bay* except during southerly, rough weather. Port Nellie Juan has few anchorages except in the western arms of *(6) McClure Bay*. A good small-craft anchorage is located in the southeast corner of *(7) Eshamy Bay*. The inside hook of *(8) Point Nowell* south of Eshamy Bay is a good anchorage. *(9) Granite* and *(10) Paddy* bays are reported to be good anchorages. The head of *(11) Ewan Bay* is satisfactory but deep. Two northern basins of *(12) Jackpot Bay* are very good anchorages. *(13) Masked Bay* on Chenega Island is an excellent anchorage but use caution in entering. The cove fronting the village of *(14) Chenega* is protected except during southerly winds. An uncharted rock hazard is located off this village.

Fishing. Sportfishing is best at Eshamy Bay and at Long Bay in Culross Passage, where anglers find trout and several species of salmon. Pink and chum salmon are found in streams throughout the area. Gravel beaches contain clams. Small shrimp are found in deep water near tidewater glaciers.

Mammals. Harbor seals and occasional sea otters are seen throughout the area. Mountain goats inhabit the peaks above Cochrane Bay. Sitka black-tailed deer are found on Culross and Perry islands. Sea lions sometimes haul out on rocks south of Perry Island. Black bears and mountain goats are found at the head of Kings Bay. Dall porpoise are often seen in open waters, while harbor porpoises are found near shore.

History. In McClure Bay, Port Nellie Juan Cannery, abandoned in the early 1960s, was established about 1917 to process pink salmon. Twenty-three of the 80 inhabitants of the Native village of Chenega were swept away by a seismic sea wave generated by the 1964 Good Friday earthquake. Many of the survivors now live in the village of Tatitlek south of Valdez. A gold and copper mine operated during the 1920s at the northern end of Culross Island.

Special Interest. The area surrounding Port Nellie Juan is being considered for classification under the Wilderness Act. The 1964 Good Friday earthquake generated seismic sea waves that swept timber from the edge of Kings Bay at heights of 110 feet [*33.5 m*] above waterline. Take a short, scenic hike from Long Bay in Culross Passage to Shrode Lake, or take a 15-minute walk from a small lagoon on the west shore of Paddy Bay to Eshamy Lake.

The Native village of Chenega was swept away by tidal waves during the 1964 Good Friday earthquake. Little remains to mark the site of the village.

© NANCY SIMMERMAN, 1975

These explorers row ashore in an inflatable dinghy to look at the dilapidated ruins of the abandoned copper mining town of Latouche.
NEIL AND ELIZABETH JOHANNSEN

7. Storey Island to Knight Island

General Description. Knight Island, 26 miles [*42 km*] long, has steep mountains with many deeply indented bays. Peaks reach to 3261 feet [*994 m*]. Treeline reaches to about 1000 feet [*305 m*]. Naked, Storey and Peak islands, smaller and not as rugged, are wooded to their summits.

Anchorages. Anchor in bights on the north side of *(1) Storey Island,* but watch for northerly winds. A small bight on the southwest side of *(2) Peak Island* is also suitable. Commercial fishermen use an anchorage on the right side of *(3) Cabin Bay* on Naked Island. The south arm of Northwest Bay on *(4) Eleanor Island* provides a suitable anchorage.

    Many bays on Knight Island are good anchorages, but be on the lookout for williwaws (gusty winds). Anchor at the head of either arm in *(5) Louis*

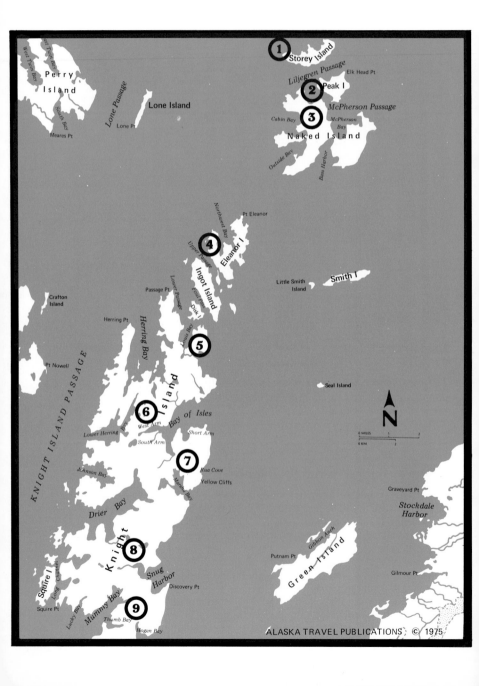

ALASKA TRAVEL PUBLICATIONS © 1975

Bay. A good anchorage is situated at the head of *(6) Bay of Isles*, but beware of rocks when entering. The north end of *(7) Marsha Bay* is a satisfactory anchorage. The west arm of *(8) Snug Harbor* is secure at the head. Hogan Bay is exposed to easterly winds. A deep but well-protected anchorage is located at *(9) Thumb Bay*. Port Oceanic, located in Thumb Bay, has a floating dock. Johnson, Drier, Herring and Lower Herring bays provide anchorages but are notorious for extensive foul ground.

Fishing. Shrimp are fished commercially off the north and south ends of Knight Island. Pink salmon are caught in streams entering the west and south arms of Bay of Isles and in a stream at the south end of Herring Bay. Black cod fishing is good on the northwest end of Knight Island. Halibut fishing is good in Knight Island Passage.

Birds. Black-legged kittiwakes nest on rocks off the east side of Eleanor Island and in Bay of Isles. Tufted puffins nest on Carolyn Island, which is a prominent outcrop south of Naked Island, and on Smith and Little Smith islands. Arctic terns nest on rocks west of Knight Island.

Mammals. Sitka black-tailed deer are found on islands throughout this cruising area. Harbor seals and sea otters, as well as Dall and harbor porpoises, are common. Look for killer whales and species of baleen whales in Knight Island Passage.

History. Vancouver named Knight Island in 1794 for Sir John Knight, R.N., who had been captured by Colonial forces during the American Revolutionary War. During the first decade of the twentieth century, copper mines existed on many areas of Knight Island, including Drier Bay, Hogan Bay and Rua Cove. A herring processing plant operated for many years at Port Oceanic on Thumb Bay. The largest and most successful fox farm in Prince William Sound thrived during the 1920s on Storey Island. Fox farmers also lived on Peak and Eleanor islands.

Special Interest. Knight Island is possibly the most scenic island in the sound. A small rustic lodge, the Prince William Sound Inn, is situated at Port Oceanic at Thumb Cove. Fuel may be available there.

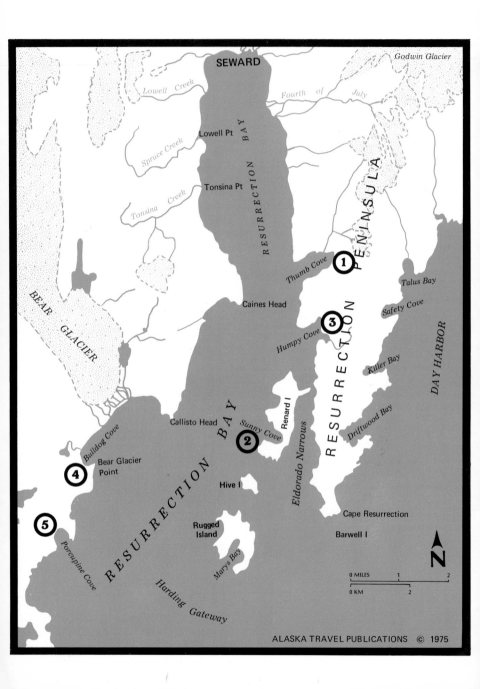

ALASKA TRAVEL PUBLICATIONS © 1975

8. Resurrection Bay

General Description. Resurrection Bay, about 35 miles [*56 km*] west of Prince William Sound, trends south to the Gulf of Alaska. Sixteen miles [*26 km*] long, 2 to 10 miles [*3 to 16 km*] wide and up to 150 fathoms [*274 m*] deep, the bay is edged by steep wooded headlands and mountains up to 4000 feet [*1220 m*]. Three major islands and Bear Glacier are prominent features near the mouth of the bay. South of Caines Head, seas are usually rougher. The community of Seward is at the head of the bay.

Anchorages. *(1) Thumb Cove,* backed by three hanging glaciers, has a soft bottom and fairly good protection. *(2) Sunny Cove* on Renard Island, the best anchorage in the bay, has a good mud bottom. Sandy-bottomed *(3) Humpy Cove* is also satisfactory. With easterly winds, common during late summer and fall, williwaws can occur in these bays. Only in southwesterly weather are *(4) Bulldog* and *(5) Porcupine* coves, on the west side of Resurrection Bay, good anchorages.

Fishing. Red "snapper" (rockfish), black "sea bass" (also a species of rockfish) and ling cod are found on the east side of Rugged Island. The southern tip of Renard Island also has good bottom fishing. Silver salmon fishing is good along the edges of the bay during August but seems best off Caines Head and at Thumb and Porcupine coves. Seward hosts its annual Silver Salmon Derby in August.

Birds. Black-legged kittiwakes, gulls, tufted and horned puffins, and murres nest at Cape Resurrection. Bald eagles also frequent the area.

Mammals. Harbor seals and sea otters are found throughout the bay. Sea lions occur in small groups throughout the bay during winter and spring, and haul out on the east side of Rugged Island and in the vicinity of Barwell Island during summer. Many of these sea lions come from a large colony on the Chiswell Islands. Dall and harbor porpoise are seen frequently.

History. In 1792 Aleksandr Baranov named this bay "Voskresnskaya Gavan" (Resurrection Harbor). The first ship of European design built in Alaska, the *Phoenix,* was built here under Baranov's supervision in 1792-1794. Seward was founded when railroad construction began in 1902. World War II defense installations included large coastal artillery on Caines Head and on the southern tip of Rugged Island, anti-aircraft guns on Point Lowell and searchlights on Barwell Island. Unsafe docks, buildings and trails remain from this era. The 1964 Good Friday earthquake and seismic sea wave destroyed the Seward harbor, adjacent warehouses and oil tanks and killed 13 people.

Special Interest. The small-boat harbor has about 700 slips. Charter boats, gasoline, diesel fuel, supplies, haul-out and repair facilities, bait, ice and tackle are available. Ferry service is available to Kodiak, Valdez and Cordova. Seward is 127 highway miles [*204 km*] from Anchorage.

Prevailing winds blow over the bay from the south during early summer, while during the winter prevailing winds blow from the north. Tidal currents between Rugged and Hive islands set to the northwest. The small-craft route to Prince William Sound usually goes between Renard and Hive islands. A Coast Guard cutter based in Seward makes regular patrols of the bay in summer. Caines Head is slated for development as a state recreation area.

Sea stacks and steep cliffs characterize the Resurrection Bay coastline. The water is often rough south of Caines Head.
RICHARD W. MONTAGUE

9. Cape Resurrection to Knight Passage

General Description. The coast between Cape Resurrection and Cape Puget is characterized by steep headlands intersected by many glaciers. Mountain summits rise to about 5000 feet [*1500 m*]. Few sheltered anchorages exist until the large islands of the western sound are reached. Bainbridge, Evans, Elrington and Latouche islands have rugged forested shores and occasional gravel beaches. Seas in Blying Sound can be rough year-round; only large, seaworthy craft should travel in this cruising area.

Anchorages. *(1) Anchor Cove* in Day Harbor is excellent. *(2) Bowen Anchorage* is the best anchorage in Day Harbor, having a sticky mud bottom. Talus Bay, Safety Cove and Killer Bay should be avoided due to poor holding bottoms. A satisfactory anchorage, found in *(3) Driftwood Bay* in a southern bight, has a rocky to hard bottom. The coastline between Fault Point and Goat Harbor in Puget Bay offers no safe anchorages. Breathtakingly scenic *(4) Goat Harbor* offers good protection and a mud bottom. A smaller, unnamed cove at the eastern side of the head of *(5) Puget Bay* offers a satisfactory anchorage but has quite a bit of kelp. *(6) Auk Bay* is good with a muddy bottom, but watch for rocks and anchor close to the head of the bay.

Fishermen anchor in a bight about 1.2 miles [*1.9 km*] to the southwest of *(7) Point Countess* to wait out strong tidal currents in Bainbridge Passage. Anchorages in the passage are 2.2 miles [*3.5 km*] south of the point. On Bainbridge Island anchor at the head of the northern arm of *(8) Hogg Bay* or at the head of *(9) Swanson Bay*. Best anchorage on Evans Island is *(10) Squirrel Bay,* which has a sand and gravel bottom. Other anchorages are located at *(11) Guguak Bay* and *(12) Iktua Bay. (13) Sawmill Bay* should be used with caution due to numerous rock hazards. Elrington Island contains anchorages at *(14) Fox Farm Bay* and at *(15) North Twin Bay* and *(16) South Twin Bay,* though better shelter is generally found in South Twin Bay. On Latouche Island, anchor at *(17) Horseshoe Bay. In (18) Whale Bay* anchor on the eastern edge of the south arm, where a good mud bottom will be found.

Fishing. Good bottom fishing is found off the entrance of Driftwood Bay. Excellent fishing for black "sea bass" may be found along a mile-long section of coastline north of Fault Point. Both "snapper" and "bass" are found along the open coast but be wary of the weather.

In Bainbridge Passage and at the north end of Icy Bay, pink salmon may be taken. Pink and chum salmon are found in Sawmill Bay. Tasty, small flounders may be caught in Squirrel Bay. Fishing for halibut is good in

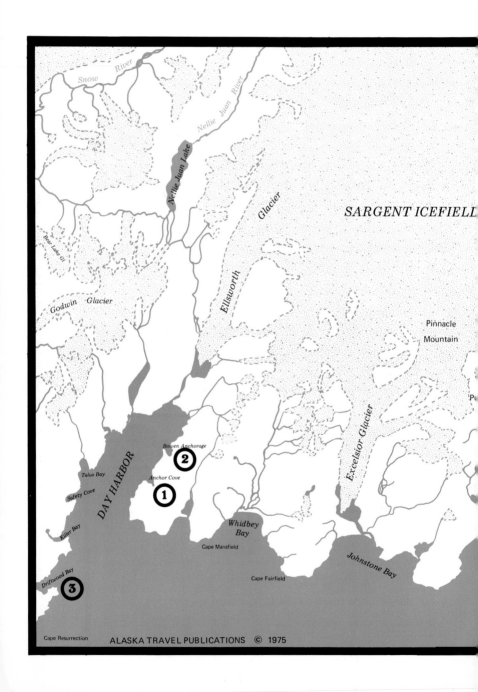

Snow River

Nellie Juan River

Nellie Juan Lake

Glacier

SARGENT ICEFIELD

Bear Lake Gl

Godwin Glacier

Ellsworth

Pinnacle
Mountain

Pi

Bowen Anchorage
②

Anchor Cove
①

Talus Bay

Safety Cove

DAY HARBOR

Killer Bay

Whidbey
Bay

Excelsior Glacier

Cape Mansfield

Johnstone Bay

Driftwood Bay
③

Cape Fairfield

Cape Resurrection

ALASKA TRAVEL PUBLICATIONS © 1975

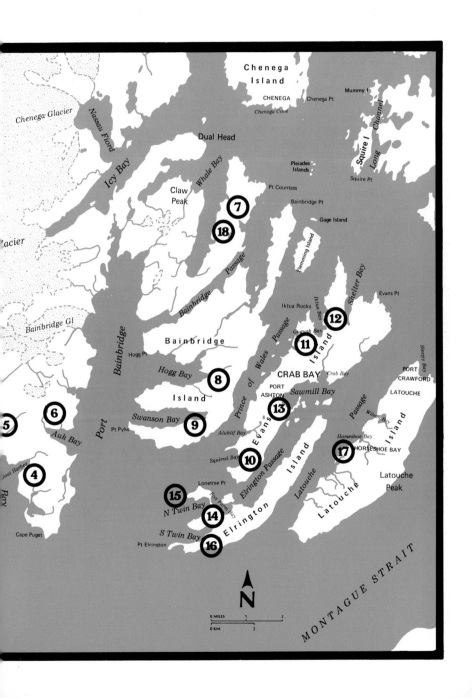

Knight Island Passage. Shrimp may be taken in Icy Bay, Nassau Fiord and at the south end of Knight Island Passage. Dig for clams on gravel beaches throughout the area.

Birds. Puffins, murres, gulls and kittiwakes nest on Cape Resurrection and Barwell Island. Whidbey Bay contains great numbers of sea ducks. A large black-legged kittiwake colony is situated on the north shore of Icy Bay. Point Elrington has a large colony of tufted puffins, horned puffins, glaucous-winged gulls, pigeon guillemots, murres and three species of cormorants.

Mammals. Mountain goats are common on most of the steep headlands. Sitka black-tailed deer are found on major islands. Black bears roam the shorelines in spring, and in summer and fall may be seen near salmon spawning streams. Sea otters are very common throughout the southwestern sound. Harbor seals are also often seen in this area. Large numbers of sea lions haul out on the rocks at Point Elrington.

History. Vancouver explored and named most of this cruising area in 1794. Fox farms operated during the early part of the twentieth century on Flemming Island and near North Twin Bay on Elrington Island. The ghost town of Latouche owed its existence to copper mines, which operated from 1903 until the late 1920s. Port Ashton, Port Benney and Port San Juan are three currently inactive canneries at Sawmill Bay. In 1946, the steamship *Yukon,* carrying 495 people, was wrecked in a winter storm near Cape Fairfield, killing 11 people. Some wreckage is still visible.

Special Interest. Blying Sound can be very rough. Boats traveling to the eastern part of the sound should use Elrington Passage, due to better aids to navigation, protected water and less foul ground than Montague Strait. The 1964 Good Friday earthquake uplifted much of the cruising area, invalidating some information on charts, so mariners should be especially cautious throughout this area.

10.Montague Island

General Description. This 50 mile [*80 km*] long island is mountainous, with peaks rising to about 3000 feet [*915 m*]. Treeline lies at about 1000 feet [*300 m*]. This extremely wild island is seldom visited, but the outer coast, accessible by aircraft, affords excellent beachcombing. It is not recommended that other than ocean-going vessels navigate the outer coast of Montague Island.

Montague Island was subject to uplifting of almost 38 feet [*11 m*] as a result of the 1964 Good Friday earthquake. Mariners should be cautious with all anchorages; use a depth sounder in bays and coves and when traveling near shore.

Anchorages. *(1) McLeod Harbor,* an excellent anchorage protected from all but west winds, has a mud bottom. *(2) Hanning Bay* is satisfactory during easterly winds. *(3) Port Chalmers* and *(4) Stockdale Harbor* should be entered with caution but afford good protection in all winds. Small craft can anchor at the head of Stockdale Harbor, but extensive foul rocky bottom demands careful navigation. Rocky Bay provides suitable anchorage only during good weather. A small cove on the southeast side of *(5) Zaikof Bay,* 1.6 miles [*2.6 km*] from the head of the bay, is well protected except during south and southeast winds. Patton Bay, which provides very limited protection, has a sand and mud bottom and is a poor anchorage during northeast to southerly winds.

Fishing. Pink salmon are found in Jeanie Cove, Zaikof Bay and San Juan Bay. Fish for pink and silver salmon and dolly varden char in Nellie Martin River in Patton Bay from late July to early September. Dungeness crab inhabit Port Chalmers and Stockdale Harbor.

Birds. Huge bird colonies near Patton Bay on Wooded Islands contain tufted puffins, horned puffins, fork-tailed petrels and black-legged kittiwakes, in addition to three species of cormorants. North of Montague Island and east of Knight Island Passage lies a rocky outcrop known as The Needle, which supports a colony of black-legged kittiwakes.

Mammals. Sitka black-tailed deer are common on Green and Montague islands. Brown bears, found on Montague Island, congregate along salmon spawning streams in late summer. Many sea otters inhabit the waters around Green Island and shallow waters near the north end of Montague Island. Whales and porpoises are commonly seen in Montague Strait. Large numbers of sea lions breed on Fish Island near Wooded Islands on the

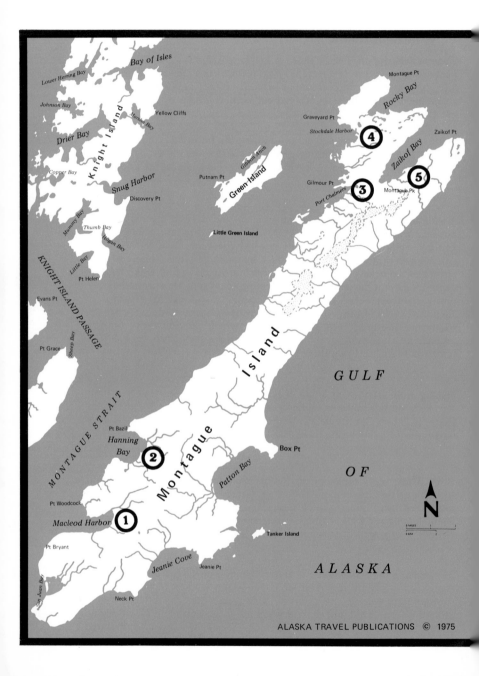

ALASKA TRAVEL PUBLICATIONS © 1975

southeast coast of Montague Island, on Seal Rocks south of Hinchinbrook Entrance and at The Needle in Montague Strait. Harbor seals are found throughout the area.

History. In 1778, Captain James Cook first sighted and named this island in honor of his patron John Montagu, Earl of Sandwich and First Lord of the British Admiralty. A military aircraft warning station was located on the north end of the island during World War II.

Special Interest. Two U.S. Forest Service public recreation cabins are located near Patton Bay. Kenai Lumber Company is logging near bays on the leeward (northwest) side of the island. A hunting lodge is situated at McLeod Harbor.

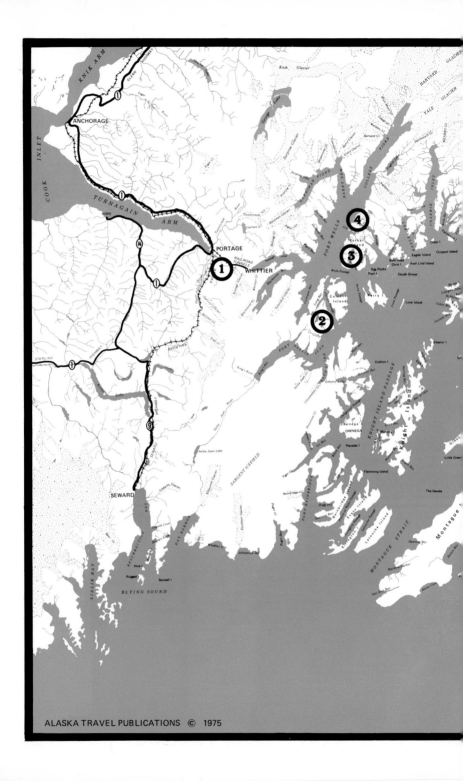

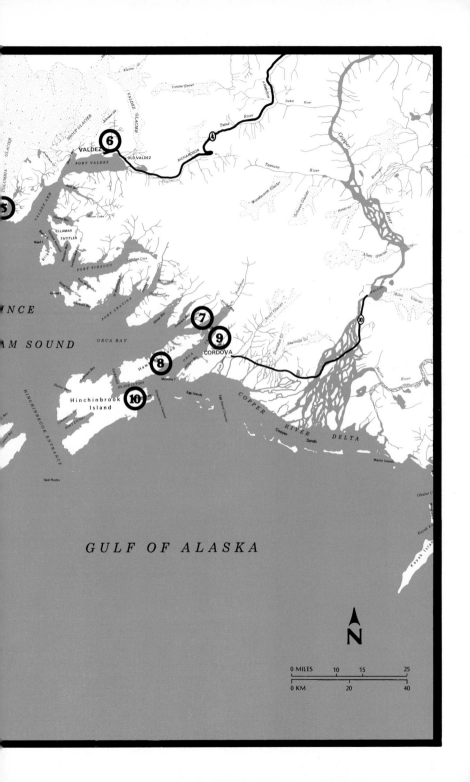

A Closer Look at the Wilderness

Endless Possibilities. As there are few maintained trails around Prince William Sound, hikers must seek open beaches, game trails or open country above timberline. Many such "off-the-beaten-path" areas await the hiker, each offering rewards of scenery, beachcombing, wildlife observation, camping, hunting or fishing. Most hiking areas are accessible only by boat or aircraft, a circumstance that virtually assures the crowds will be elsewhere. The following thumbnail descriptions, keyed by number to the accompanying map, give a sampling of the many hiking possibilities in Prince William Sound.

1. Portage Pass. From the community of Whittier, accessible via The Alaska Railroad from either Anchorage or Portage, hike west about 2 miles [*3.2 km*] toward the railroad tunnel, to a valley on the left side of the tunnel. For a spectacular overlook view of Portage Glacier, follow an old rock-strewn jeep road on the right edge of this valley, which leads to the top of the pass. Roundtrip distance is about 2 miles [*3.2 km*] from the tunnel entrance, with an elevation gain of about 700 feet [*213 m*]. Hiking time roundtrip from the tunnel is less than three hours. Because of deep snow, which often lingers through June, late summer is the best time for this trip.

2. Shrode Lake. Anchor in Long Bay off Culross Passage. Shallow-draft vessels may be able to proceed during high tide as far as a lagoon at the head of Long Bay, although numerous rock hazards are found in the channel. Follow a 0.5 mile [*0.8 km*] unmarked path that roughly parallels the southeast (left) side of Shrode Creek to Shrode Lake. A U.S. Forest Service public recreation A-frame cabin is situated on the edge of the lake (see Facilities chapter). The stream and lake afford good fishing for salmon and trout.

Photo opposite: This waterfall, near Long Bay in Culross Passage, is one of dozens throughout the sound. Short walks often feature an added bonus of great sportfishing.
© NANCY SIMMERMAN, 1973

*This view of Portage Glacier is the reward of an afternoon's walk
from Whittier to the top of Portage Pass.*
© NANCY SIMMERMAN, 1972

3. Esther Falls and Lake. From the middle of the northeast side of Lake Bay
on Esther Island, follow a 0.5 mile [*0.8 km*] long, unmarked path along
Esther Creek, which skirts a spectacular waterfall en route to Esther Lake.
This lake is about 3 miles [*4.8 km*] long and contains dolly varden char. The
roundtrip walk takes about one hour, with an elevation gain of about 100
feet [*30 m*].

4. Esther Passage. Edged by steep granite cliffs and pockets of moss-fes-
tooned spruce and hemlock trees, Esther Passage is one of the most
beautiful areas in the sound. Open alpine vegetation borders the shoreline
at the north end of Esther Passage, opening toward Port Wells. Easy walking
across open country, with little elevation gain, is found on a headland on the
north side of the north end of Esther Passage. Here one may take a 0.5 mile
[*0.8 km*] long walk north to the more unprotected waters of Port Wells.

5. Heather Island. Visitors traveling to Columbia Glacier by floatplane or small boat may stretch their legs on Heather Island. Although boggy in places, the 2 mile [*3.2 km*] long island is easily hiked and offers stunted subalpine vegetation reminiscent of a Japanese garden, as well as a solid-ground vantage point for spectacular views of the largest glacier in the sound (see Geology chapter).

6. Mineral Creek. To reach this historic mining area near Valdez, follow Mineral Creek Canyon Road for 5.5 miles [*8.9 km*]. Where the road becomes overgrown with vegetation, park and hike up the abandoned roadbed. The trail, which winds for about 1 mile [*1.6 km*] through alder and salmonberry bushes along the edges of Mineral Creek, ends at an old stamp mill that crushed gold ore for processing. Mineral Creek Canyon once contained hundreds of gold mining claims. Elevation gain is about 100 feet [*30 m*] with a roundtrip travel time of about one hour.

7. Milton Lake Trail. Located north of Cordova and reached by boat or floatplane, this 1 mile [*1.6 km*] long trail begins at a U.S. Forest Service public recreation cabin on the south shore of Simpson Bay and leads to Milton Lake, which contains silver salmon during September and a year-round population of cutthroat trout. Elevation gain on the trail is about 100 feet [*30 m*].

8. Canoe Passage Trail. Anchor in Canoe Passage on the north side of Hawkins Island. A 4.2 mile [*6.8 km*] long trail leads from a U.S. Forest Service public recreation cabin on the east side of the passage and crosses rolling terrain to the south shore of Hawkins Island. Activities along this route include berry picking, fishing for cutthroat trout, and deer hunting. Prior to the 1964 Good Friday earthquake, Canoe Passage could be navigated with small, shallow-draft boats. Because of land emergence during the quake, however, the southern part of the passage is now impassable.

9. Crater Lake – Mount Eyak Trail. From Cordova follow Eyak Lake Road to a sign marking the head of Crater Lake Trail. This 2.4 mile [*3.9 km*] long trail is steep, crossing a 1500 foot [*457 m*] pass before reaching Crater Lake. The trail is a favorite of Cordovans, as it offers panoramic views of the town and of the sound. Many people scale nearby 2506 foot [*763.8 m*] Mt. Eyak. Deep snows that often linger through July make late summer the best time for hiking.

10. Boswell Bay. Accessible by small boat if the skipper has local knowledge or by floatplane, Boswell Bay, about 12 miles [*20 km*] southwest of Cordova, and named for pioneer Billy Boswell, is the site of several privately owned cabins, remains of bootleg liquor stills that operated during

Prohibition, and a currently operating F.A.A. station on the north side of the bay. Hike south one mile [*1.6 km*] to reach sandy beaches on the seaward side of Strawberry Hill, named for the numerous berries to be found there in late summer. Thousands of sea birds nest on sea stacks at the mouth of Boswell Bay. Beachcombers may find shells, driftwood and glass fishing floats along several miles of sandy coastline from Point Bentinck to Point Steele. The proximity of these open sandy beaches to the anchorage in Boswell Bay makes this area easily accessible for beachcombing.

CHECKLIST OF MAMMALS OF PRINCE WILLIAM SOUND

Land Mammals

Masked shrew	*Sorex cinereus*
Pygmy shrew	*Microsorex hoyi*
Dusky shrew	*Sorex obscurus*
Northern water shrew	*Sorex palustris*
Black bear	*Ursus americanus*
Brown bear	*Ursus arctos*
Marten	*Martes americana*
Shorttail weasel	*Mustela erminea*
Least weasel	*Mustela rixosa*
Mink	*Mustela vison*
Wolverine	*Gulo luscus*
River otter	*Lutra canadensis*
Red fox	*Vulpes fulva*
Coyote	*Canis latrans*
Gray wolf	*Canis lupus*
Lynx	*Lynx canadensis*
Hoary marmot	*Marmota caliguta*
Red squirrel	*Tamiasciurus hudsonicus*
Beaver	*Castor canadensis*
Northern bog lemming	*Synaptomys borealis*
Tundra redback vole	*Cleithrionomys dawsoni*
Longtail vole	*Microtus longicaudus*
Meadow vole	*Microtus oeconomus*
Alaska vole	*Microtus miurus*
Muskrat	*Ondatra zibethica*
Porcupine	*Erethizon dorsatum*
Snowshoe hare	*Lepus americanus*
Sitka black-tailed deer	*Odocoileus hemionus (sitkensis)*
Moose	*Alces alces*
Mountain goat	*Oreamnos americanus*

Life exuberantly abounds in the skies, waters and on the islands. Here Pete Isleib feeds black-legged kittiwakes.
CHARLES D. EVANS

Marine Mammals

Gray whale	*Rhachianectes glaucus*
Sei (rorqual) whale	*Balaenoptera borealis*
Fin (finback) whale	*Balaenoptera physalus*
Minke (piked) whale	*Balaenoptera acutorostrata*
Humpback whale	*Megaptera novaeangliae*
Pacific killer whale	*Orcinus rectipinna*
Pacific harbor porpoise	*Phocaena vomerina*
Dall porpoise	*Phocoenoides dalli*
Sea otter	*Enhydra lutra*
Steller (northern) sea lion	*Eumetopias jubata*
Harbor seal	*Phoca vitulina*
*Fur seal	*Callorhinus ursinus*

*Irregularly observed

II
CHECKLIST OF BIRDS OF PRINCE WILLIAM SOUND

Common loon	*Gavia immer*
Yellow-billed loon	*Gavia adamsii*
Arctic loon	*Gavia arctica*
Red-throated loon	*Gavia stellata*
Red-necked grebe	*Podiceps grisegena*
Horned grebe	*Podiceps auritus*
*Northern fulmar	*Fulmarus glacialis*
*Sooty shearwater	*Puffinus griseus*
Fork-tailed storm petrel	*Oceanodroma furcata*
Double-crested cormorant	*Phalacrocorax auritus*
Brandt's cormorant	*Phalacrocorax penicillatus*
Pelagic cormorant	*Phalacrocorax pelagicus*
Red-faced cormorant	*Phalacrocorax urile*
Great blue heron	*Ardea herodias*
Whistling swan	*Olor columbianus*
*Trumpeter swan	*Olor buccinator*
Canada goose	*Branta canadensis*
Black brant	*Branta nigricans*
*Emperor goose	*Philacte canagica*
*White-fronted goose	*Anser albifrons*
*Snow goose	*Chen hyperborea*
Mallard	*Anas platyrhynchos*
Gadwall	*Anas strepera*

Pintail	*Anas acuta*
Green-winged teal	*Anas carolinensis*
Blue-winged teal	*Anas discors*
*European wigeon	*Mareca penelope*
American wigeon	*Mareca americana*
Shoveler	*Spatula clypeata*
Canvasback	*Aythya valisineria*
Greater scaup	*Aythya marila*
Common goldeneye	*Bucephala clangula*
Barrow's goldeneye	*Bucephala islandica*
Bufflehead	*Bucephala albeola*
Oldsquaw	*Clangula hyemalis*
Harlequin duck	*Histrionicus histrionicus*
*Steller's eider	*Polysticta stelleri*
*Common eider	*Somateria mollissima*
*King eider	*Somateria spectabilis*
White-winged scoter	*Melanitta deglandi*
Surf scoter	*Melanitta perspicillata*
Black (common) scoter	*Oidemia nigra*
*Hooded merganser	*Lophodytes cucullatus*
Common merganser	*Mergus merganser*
Red-breasted merganser	*Mergus serrator*
Goshawk	*Accipiter gentilis*
Sharp-shinned hawk	*Accipiter striatus*
*Rough-legged hawk	*Buteo lagopus*
*Golden eagle	*Aquila chrysaetos*
Bald eagle	*Haliaeetus leucocephalus*
*Marsh hawk	*Circus cyaneus*
*Osprey	*Pandion haliaetus*
*Gyrfalcon	*Falco rusticolus*
Peregrine falcon	*Falcon peregrinus*
*Merlin (pigeon) hawk	*Falco columbarius*
*American kestrel	*Falco sparverius*
Spruce grouse	*Canachites canadensis*
*Willow ptarmigan	*Lagopus lagopus*
Rock ptarmigan	*Lagopus mutus*
*White-tailed ptarmigan	*Lagopus leucurus*
*Sandhill crane	*Grus canadensis*
*American coot	*Fulica americana*
Black oystercatcher	*Haematopus bachmani*
Semipalmated plover	*Charadrius semipalmatus*
*Killdeer	*Charadrius vociferus*
American golden plover	*Pluvialis dominica*

Black-bellied plover	*Squatarola squatarola*
Surfbird	*Aphriza virgata*
Ruddy turnstone	*Arenaria interpres*
Black turnstone	*Arenaria melanocephala*
Common snipe	*Capella gallinago*
Whimbrel	*Numenius phaeopus*
*Bristle-thighed curlew	*Numenius tahitiensis*
Spotted sandpiper	*Actitis macularia*
*Solitary sandpiper	*Tringa solitaria*
Wandering tattler	*Heteroscelus incanum*
Greater yellowlegs	*Totanus melanoleucus*
*Lesser yellowlegs	*Totanus flavipes*
*Red knot	*Calidris canutus*
*Rock sandpiper	*Erolia ptilocnemis*
*Sharp-tailed sandpiper	*Erolis acuminata*
Pectoral sandpiper	*Erolia melanotos*
*Baird's sandpiper	*Erolia bairdii*
Least sandpiper	*Erolia minutilla*
Dunlin	*Erolia alpina*
Short-billed dowitcher	*Limnodromus griseus*
Long-billed dowitcher	*Limnodromus scolopaceus*
Semipalmated sandpiper	*Ereunetes pusillus*
Western sandpiper	*Ereunetes mauri*
*Bar-tailed godwit	*Limosa lapponica*
Hudsonian godwit	*Limosa haemastica*
Sanderling	*Crocethia alba*
*Red phalarope	*Phalaropus fulicarius*
Northern phalarope	*Lobipes lobatus*
Pomarine jaeger	*Stercorarius pomarinus*
Parasitic jaeger	*Stercorarius parasiticus*
*Long-tailed jaeger	*Stercorarius longicaudus*
*Skua	*Catharacta skua*
Glaucous gull	*Larus hyperboreus*
Glaucous-winged gull	*Larus glaucescens*
Herring gull	*Larus argentatus*
Mew gull	*Larus canus*
Bonaparte's gull	*Larus philadelphia*
Black-legged kittiwake	*Rissa tridactyla*
*Sabine's gull	*Xema sabini*
Arctic tern	*Sterna paradisaea*
*Aleutian tern	*Sterna aleutica*
Common murre	*Uria aalge*
*Thick-billed murre	*Uria lomvia*
Pigeon guillemot	*Cepphus columba*
Marbled murrelet	*Brachyramphus marmoratum*

Kittlitz's murrelet	*Brachyramphus brevirostre*
*Ancient murrelet	*Synthliboramphus antiquum*
Parakeet auklet	*Cyclorrhynchus psittacula*
*Crested auklet	*Aethia cristatella*
Rhinoceros auklet	*Cerorhinca monocerata*
Horned puffin	*Fratercula corniculata*
Tufted puffin	*Lunda cirrhata*
*Mourning dove	*Zenaidura macroura*
Great horned owl	*Bubo virginianus*
*Snowy owl	*Nyctea scandiaca*
Hawk owl	*Surnia ulula*
*Great gray owl	*Strix nebulosa*
*Short-eared owl	*Asio flammeus*
*Saw-whet owl	*Aegolius acadicus*
*Common nighthawk	*Chordeiles minor*
*Anna's hummingbird	*Calypte anna*
Rufous hummingbird	*Selasphorus rufus*
Belted kingfisher	*Megaceryle alcyon*
*Common (yellow-shafted) flicker	*Colaptes auratus*
*Hairy woodpecker	*Dencrocopos villosus*
Downy woodpecker	*Dendrocopos pubescens*
*Black-backed three-toed woodpecker	*Picoides arcticus*
*Northern three-toed woodpecker	*Picoides tridactylus*
*Alder (Traill's) flycatcher	*Empidonax traillii*
*Olive-sided flycatcher	*Nuttallornis borealis*
Violet-green swallow	*Eremophila alpestris*
Horned lark	*Tachycineta thalassina*
Tree swallow	*Iridoprocne bicolor*
*Bank swallow	*Riparia riparia*
Bar swallow	*Hirundo rustica*
Cliff swallow	*Petrochelidon pyrrhonota*
*Gray jay	*Perisoreus canadensis*
Steller's jay	*Cyanocitta stelleri*
Black-billed magpie	*Pica pica*
Common raven	*Corvus corax*
Northwestern crow	*Corvus caurinus*
*Black-capped chickadee	*Parus atricapillus*
Chestnut-backed chickadee	*Parus rufescens*
*Red-breasted nuthatch	*Sitta canadensis*
Brown creeper	*Certhia familiaris*
Dipper	*Cinclus mexicanus*
Winter wren	*Troglodytes troglodytes*
American robin	*Turdus migratorius*
Varied thrush	*Ixoreus naevius*

Hermit thrush	*Hylocichla guttata*
*Swainson's thrush	*Hylocichla ustulata*
*Gray-cheeked thrush	*Hylocichla minima*
Golden-crowned kinglet	*Regulus satrapa*
Ruby-crowned kinglet	*Regulus calendula*
Water pipit	*Anthus spinoletta*
*Bohemian waxwing	*Bombycilla garrulus*
*Northern shrike	*Lanius excubitor*
*Starling	*Sturnus vulgaris*
Orange-crowned warbler	*Vermivora celata*
Yellow warbler	*Dendroica petechia*
*Yellow-rumped (Myrtle's) warbler	*Dendroica coronata*
Townsend's warbler	*Dendroica townsendi*
*Northern waterthrush	*Seirus noveboreacensis*
*Common yellowthroat	*Geothlypis trichas*
Wilson's warbler	*Wilsonia pusilla*
*Rusty blackbird	*Euphagus carolinus*
Pine grosbeak	*Pinicola enucleator*
Gray-crowned rosy finch	*Leucosticte tephrocotis*
*Hoary redpoll	*Acanthis hornemanni*
Common redpoll	*Acanthis flammea*
Pine siskin	*Spinus pinus*
*Red crossbill	*Loxia curvirostra*
White-winged crossbill	*Loxia leucoptera*
Savannah sparrow	*Passerculus sandwichensis*
Dark-eyed junco	*Junco hyemalis*
*Tree sparrow	*Spizella arborea*
*White-crowned sparrow	*Zonotrichia leucophrys*
*White-throated sparrow	*Zonotrichia albicollis*
Golden-crowned sparrow	*Zonotrichia atricapilla*
Fox sparrow	*Passerella iliaca*
Lincoln's sparrow	*Melospiza lincolnii*
Song sparrow	*Melospiza melodia*
Lapland longspur	*Calcarius lapponicus*
Snow bunting	*Plectrophenax nivalis*

*Irregularly observed

History

The Chugach Eskimo, by Kaj Birket-Smith (Copenhagen, Natl. Museets: 1953). 262 pages.

Chugach Prehistory: the Archaeology of Prince William Sound, by Frederica de Laguna (Seattle, University of Washington Press: 1956). 289 pages.

Copper Tints: A Book of Cordova Sketches, by Katherine Wilson (published by the Cordova Centennial Committee, 1967, Copyright 1923: Cordova Daily Times Press).

The Diary of a Ninety-Eighter, by Basil Austin (Printed by John Cumming, Mt. Pleasant, Michigan: 1968). 191 pages.

Dimond of Alaska, Adventurer in the Far North, by Edward Albert Herron (New York, J. Messner: 1957). 190 pages.

The Eyak Indians of the Copper River Delta, by Kaj Birket-Smith and Frederica de Laguna (Copenhagen, Levin & Munksgaard, Ejnar Munksgaard: 1938).

Glacier Pilot: The Story of Bob Reeve and the Flyers Who Pushed Back Alaska's Air Frontiers, by Beth Day (New York, Holt: 1957). 348 pages.

Harriman Alaska Expedition, Alaska: Volume I: Narrative, Glaciers, Natives, by John Burroughs, John Muir and George Bird Grinnell (Copyright 1901 by Edward Harriman with the Cooperation of the Washington Academy of Sciences). 183 pages.

The Iron Trail: An Alaskan Romance, by Rex Beach (New York, Burt: 1913). 391 pages.

The Klondike Fever; The Life and Death of the Last Great Gold Rush, by Pierre Berton (New York, Knopf: 1958). 457 pages.

Lord of Alaska: Baranov and the Russian Adventure, by Hector Chevigny (London, Hale: 1946). 255 pages.

North to Danger, by Virgil Burford as told to Walt Morey (Caldwell, Idaho, Caxton Printers: 1969). 167 pages.

Where the Sea Breaks Its Back, by Corey Ford (Boston, Little, Brown: 1966). 206 pages.

Wilderness: A Journal of Quiet Adventure in Alaska, by Rockwell Kent (New York, Halcyon House: 1920). 217 pages.

The rickety, weather-bleached ruins of the old copper mining town of Latouche have been abandoned for decades.
NEIL AND ELIZABETH JOHANNSEN

Wildlife

Alaska's Wildlife and Habitat, by the Alaska Department of Fish and Game (January, 1973). 299 pages.

Between Pacific Tides, by Edward Rickets and Jack Calvin, Fourth Edition revised by Joel Hedgpeth (Stanford University Press, Stanford, California: 1968). 614 pages.

Birds of the Chugach National Forest of Alaska: A Checklist, as compiled by M. E. (Pete) Isleib (U.S. Forest Service, Department of Agriculture).

Birds of the North Gulf Coast, by M. E. (Pete) Isleib and Brina Kessel (Biological Paper No. 14, University of Alaska, Fairbanks, Alaska, November, 1973). 151 pages.

Rookery Island, by Gary Daetz (Rand McNally and Co.: 1967). 72 pages.

Plantlife

Alaska Trees and Shrubs, by Leslie A. Viereck and Elbert L. Little (Agriculture Handbook No. 410, Forest Service, U.S. Department of Agriculture, Washington, D.C.: 1972). 265 pages.

The Alaska-Yukon Wild Flowers Guide, Helen A. White, Editor (Alaska Northwest Publishing Company: 1974). 218 pages.

Wild, Edible and Poisonous Plants of Alaska, by Christine A. Heller (Cooperative Extension Service, University of Alaska, College, Alaska: 1953). 88 pages.

Wild Flowers of Alaska, by Christine Heller (Graphic Arts Center, Portland: 1966). 104 pages.

Boating

The Complete Book of Boating: An Owner's Guide to Design, Construction, Piloting, Operating and Maintenance, by Ernest A. Zadig (Englewood Cliffs, N.J., Prentice-Hall: 1972). 640 pages.

Tidal Current Tables (1974 Edition, U.S. Department of Commerce, National Oceanic and Atmospheric Administration). 254 pages.

Piloting, Seamanship and Small Boat Handling, by Charles F. Chapman (1972 Revision, Motor Boating and Sailing Book Division, The Hearst Corporation, New York, N.Y.).

United States Coast Pilot 9, Pacific and Arctic Coasts, Alaska, Cape Spencer to Beaufort Sea (1972 Edition, U.S. Department of Commerce, Coast and Geodetic Survey). 330 pages.

General Information

Dictionary of Alaska Place Names, by Donald J. Orth (Geological Survey Professional Paper 567, United States Government Printing Office, Washington D.C.: 1967). 1084 pages.

Chugach National Forest Land Use Plan, by the Staff of the Chugach National Forest (Anchorage, Alaska: July 1974). 300 pages.

55 Ways to the Wilderness in Southcentral Alaska, by Helen Nienhueser, Nancy Simmerman and Hans van der Laan (Mountaineering Club of Alaska and The Mountaineers: 1972). 161 pages.

The Great Alaska Earthquake of 1964, by the Committee on the Alaska Earthquake of the Division of Earth Sciences, National Research Council, National Academy of Sciences (Washington, D.C.: 1971). 834 pages.

Photo opposite: An immature mew gull searches for a meal from its perch on an iceberg. Birds, marine mammals and fish are particularly abundant near tidewater glaciers.

M. WOODBRIDGE WILLIAMS
NATIONAL PARK SERVICE TASK FORCE

243-245; tidal flats, 106; weather, 85-86; what to see and do, 174-175
Valdez Arm, 54, 98, 128, 152, 167, 243
Valdez Dock Company, 183
Valdez Formation, 71
Valdez, Fort, 66, 172
Valdez Glacier, 169, 174; plant succession, 135; Trail, 52-53, *53*, 56, 173
Valdez Motel, 30
Valdez Narrows, 68, 169, 225, 228
Valdez, Port, 54, 57, 68, 82, 152, 243; fishing, 121, 122; wind, 86
Valdez Village Motel, 30
Valhalla, Mt., 78
Vancouver, George, 50, 51, 79, 167, 172, 183, 188, 217, 233, 238, 255, 262
van Emple, Jan, 204
Van, Louie, 161
Vassar Glacier, 78, 238
Vegetation, 135-138; zones, 136-138
"Voskresenskaya Gavan," 201, 257

Warner, Clarence, 58
weather, 83-88, *84, 87, 226;* forecasts, 227; handling in rough weather, 227
Wellesley Glacier, 78
Wells Bay, 71, 126, 163, 242
Wells Passage, 225, 251
Wells, Port, 51, 98, 100, 152, 155-156; fishing, 116, 118, 121, 128, 129; logging, 67; mining, gold, 54; small-boat cruise, 237-238; wind, 86
Westours, 23, 24
West Twin Bay, 251
Whale Bay, 259

whales, hunting of, 47, 172; where to see, 181, 188, 206, 210, 263
whale, blue, *101;* fin (finback), 100, *101;* gray, 100, *102;* humpback, *99,* 99-100, *102,* 188, 210, 215; killer, 3, *98,* 99, *103,* 188, 210, 215, 255; minke, 100, *103;* sei, 100, *101,* 188; sperm, *101*
Whidbey Bay, 262
Whidbey, Joseph, 51, 207
White Pass and Yukon Railway, 61
Whitshed, Point, 48, 74
Whittier, 15, 16, 36, 148-151, *149,* 153; accommodations, 22, 30; boat charters, 25-26; campgrounds, 33; ferry access, 19; logging, 67; naming of, 149, 1964 Good Friday earthquake, 73-74, *74;* Port of, 204; railroad access, 145-148; small-boat harbor, 230, 231; weather, 85-87
Whittier-Anchorage Multiproduct Pipeline, 148
Whittier Boat Rentals, 25-26
Whittier Glacier, 153, 235
Whittier Railroad Shuttle, 16, 22-23
Wilderness: A Journal of Quiet Adventure in Alaska, 206
wilderness camps, 36
Wilderness Trek Guide Service, 36
Willamette Valley, 193
Willard Gibbs, Mt., 78
Willard Island, 155
williwaws, 86, 253, 257
Wilson, Katherine, 57
wind, 86, 155; Seward, 258
Wingham Island, 63
Witherspoon, Mt., 78
Wooded Islands, 97, 263
World War II, 191, *204,* 204-206, 235, 257, 265
worm, marine, 111

NEIL AND ELIZABETH JOHANNSEN